The Welcoming Door

The Welcoming Door

PARABLES OF THE
CARPENTER

Kenny Kemp

HarperSanFrancisco
A Division of HarperCollins*Publishers*

HarperCollins books may be purchased for educational, business, or sales promotional use. For information please write: Special Markets Department, HarperCollins Publishers, Inc., 10 East 53rd Street, New York, NY 10022.

HarperCollins Web site: http://www.harpercollins.com

HarperCollins®, 🏭 ®, and HarperSanFrancisco™ are trademarks of Harper-Collins Publishers, Inc.

FIRST EDITION

Interior Illustrations by Kenny Kemp

Library of Congress Cataloging-in-Publication Data
    Kemp, Kenny.
        The welcoming door : parables of the carpenter / Kenny Kemp. — 1st ed.
            p.   cm.
        ISBN 0–06–008264–X (cloth : alk. paper)
        1. Jesus Christ—Fiction.   2. Bible. N.T.—History of Biblical events—
    Fiction.   I. Title.
    PS3561.E39922 W45   2002
    813'.54—dc21   2002068716

02 03 04 05 06 RRD(H) 10 9 8 7 6 5 4 3 2 1

And with many such parables spake he the word unto them, as they were able to hear it.
—*Mark 4:33*

Contents

PROLOGUE

ix

Prologue

On the shore of the Middle Sea, at the far eastern reach of the Roman Empire, a small nation strains under the yoke of bondage. Its people, long of history and patience, look to the past for their future, prophecies of a day when God will raise up a man to liberate them from their oppressors. A *messiah*.

Most people of this small nation live within a day's ride of Jerusalem, the city created by the great warrior-king David. Jerusalem sits on a wedge-shaped plateau between two steep valleys, protected by watchtowers guarding the approach from the north. Hundreds of years ago, the Babylonians laid siege to the city, and from then until now, a succession of foreign armies has assaulted it. And when the great Roman general Pompey entered the Holy of Holies in the Temple, their freedom came to an end.

To the north, in the green hills that roll between the Middle Sea and the lake called Galilee, worlds collide more peacefully. Trade routes make distant peoples partners, travelers acquaintances, and strangers friends. The people of Galilee work fields of barley and wheat, harvest sweet figs and savory olives, fish in the clear waters of the Galilee, and live in harmony with Assyrian and Roman alike.

Rome, for the most part, grants its subjects religious freedom. Roman gods are plentiful, so there is no fear that they will be eclipsed by the Jewish god. But though they are benign in spiritual matters, the Romans are exacting in temporal ones. Heavy taxes are borne by all their subjects, and to the Jews in Jerusalem who watch the Roman legions circle the Temple on holy days, Rome is a brutal oppressor.

To the Galileans, Rome's presence is not so onerous. Yet still they yearn for freedom, and so their hearts often turn to the prophecies of the Messiah.

A few miles south of Sepphoris, the seat of Roman government in Galilee, lies Nazareth, a small village overlooking the fertile Jezreel Valley. Fewer than twenty families live here, working the trades and crafts, tilling the soil, and tending livestock.

In a small carpenter shop works a man named Joseph bar Jacob. When his eldest son was born in Bethlehem during a census journey, a marvelous star led shepherds and royalty alike to the manger where the child lay. And after, warned by an angel that King Herod was seeking the child's life, Joseph and Mary fled to Egypt and lived in the shadow of pyramids and strange gods. There Joseph worked in his trade, and the boy grew.

When news of Herod's death reached him, Joseph returned home. Now, many years later, the boy has grown into a man and works with Joseph, cutting and sanding and varnishing wood; building tables and chairs and houses; cutting and fitting stone; and digging culverts and wells.

Joseph watches Jeshua work and remembers the portentous words of the angel who foretold his birth: "He shall save the people from their sins." If the scribes and rabbis are right, those same gentle hands that work the wood so tenderly now will someday be required to take up the sword.

Jeshua looks up from the chair leg he is planing. He sees the dark look on Joseph's face and asks, "What is it?"

"Nothing," says Joseph. "Just worrying."

Jeshua looks at his father in that piercing way Joseph has never gotten used to. Jeshua holds the chair leg up for his father to see.

"Don't worry," he says, smiling. "I know what I'm doing."

Joseph sees the strength and kindness and wisdom in the young man's eyes. "Yes," he says, nodding. "I can see that you do."

Part One

—⚹—

THE
WELCOMING
DOOR

ONE

An Unexpected Visitor

Jeshua bar Joseph stopped at the gate and set his wooden toolbox on the low stone wall that surrounded the large dooryard. He straightened and stretched. His back ached. It was hot, even though it was early, and he was tired, having walked several miles this morning.

A servant boy came running out of the house, his sandals slapping on the hard dirt. He ran quickly, waving at Jeshua, excitement on his face. As he drew closer, he stopped abruptly, and the excitement disappeared. "Oh. I thought you were someone else," he said, and turned back to the house.

"Who was I supposed to be?" asked Jeshua. The boy didn't answer; he was already halfway across the dooryard.

Jeshua stepped through the gate, which was topped by a curved trellis upon which spring's first green grape leaves were sprouting. He surveyed the house. It was made of limestone, large and solid, with big windows draped in fine, colorful tapestries to keep out the heat. The walls were plastered with tan stucco; it was no doubt cool inside. The sloping roof was made of sturdy brown tiles. The well just inside the gate reminded him of his parched throat. He would like a drink, but it would be rude to help himself before being invited to do so.

The boy disappeared inside, and the heavy oak door thudded closed behind him. Jeshua walked across the dooryard and examined the door. It was thick and dark, the varnish long since worn off. The red leather hinges were worn and sagging, one nearly torn in two. The door handle was rusty black iron, worn smooth and bent with use.

Just then the door opened. Jeshua had to take a step back as it swung outward, creaking loudly. Before him stood an imposing old man with a full gray beard. He wore a gray knee-length tunic and a wide leather belt. His eyes were dark and his fists were clenched on his hips. "What are you doing inside the dooryard?" he boomed. He slammed the door shut behind him.

"Peace be unto you. I am Jeshua bar Joseph. Of Nazareth."

"Jeshua bar Joseph?"

"You asked me to come."

"I did?" asked the old man, his eyes scanning the horizon beyond Jeshua.

"To fix the door," said Jeshua, pointing at his toolbox.

"What door?" asked the man. Then suddenly his eyes opened wide. "Aah! You're the carpenter!"

Jeshua nodded.

The old man extended a huge hand, taking Jeshua's and pumping it vigorously. "Yes, yes! The door!" He gestured at the road beyond the stone wall. "I'm sorry. We were expecting someone else."

Jeshua nodded. "Who?"

The old man looked thoughtfully at Jeshua for a long moment, then: "You are a journeyman . . . ah . . . "

"Jeshua. Yes, I am."

"Jeshua. Of Nazareth. A journeyman," said the old man absently, as if cataloging the facts for later use. "I am Eli and this is my home. From now on, you will ask permission before entering the dooryard, is that clear?"

Jeshua nodded. "Yes. My apologies."

The old man studied Jeshua, sizing him up. "Well," he said, standing aside and gesturing at the door. "Here it is. In bad need of repair, don't you think?"

Jeshua took a step past the old man to get a closer look. He nodded. "Yes, it is old and nearly worn out."

Behind him, Eli harrumphed. "Like me."

Jeshua smiled to himself as he examined the door, running his hands over the wood. "But it is of fine quality and has aged well." He straightened and turned to Eli, who was again looking at the road, which disappeared over the green rolling hills of Galilee. "Like you," Jeshua said quietly.

Eli turned. His brow was furrowed. He pointed at the door. "Can it be saved?"

Jeshua nodded. "It must be taken apart, planed, refinished—"

"How much?" queried the old man crossly.

Jeshua was examining the leather hinges and felt the question like a hard jab in the ribs. He turned to face Eli. "As was agreed, sir. No more."

Eli frowned. "And certainly no less, I'm sure." He pushed past Jeshua, pulled the door open, and strode inside. "To work, then, young man," he said, and the door creaked shut behind him.

Master of the Universe

Jeshua turned to his donkey and began unloading his tools and saw-horses. The same young boy who thought he was someone else was drawing water from the well, watching him out of the corner of his eye. Jeshua smiled. "Peace be unto you," he said, leading the donkey over.

"And unto you, peace," said the boy tentatively.

"What is your name?"

"Arah," said the boy, his eyes suspicious but interested.

"I like that name," said Jeshua. "It means 'wayfarer.' Have you come far, Arah?"

The boy gave Jeshua a perplexed look. "Only from my house, over there." He pointed to a group of small buildings behind the main house. "What does *wayfarer* mean?"

"One who travels or wanders. Also a seeker of knowledge."

Arah smiled. "The only thing I seek is a full waterskin." He hauled the skin over the stone edge of the well and poured it into a large brown clay urn.

"When I'm thirsty, that's what I seek as well," hinted Jeshua, his tongue still dusty. "You have an important job, Arah."

"Tell that to the others," said the boy, tossing the waterskin back into the well.

"My name is Jeshua. I'm here to work on Master Eli's door."

"I know," said Arah, hauling the skin back up. "I saw you come."

"So you did," said Jeshua. "I'll bet you see everything here."

Arah nodded. "I do. I see everything."

"Hmm," said Jeshua, running his hand through his donkey's tangled mane.

Arah's face lit up. "Would you like to water your donkey?"

Jeshua nodded and smiled. "You are observant, Arah. That's exactly what I was going to ask."

Arah gestured to the side of the house. "There is a trough back there. Your donkey looks tired. And thirsty."

Jeshua patted the donkey on the withers. "Yes. Probably both. He is a hard worker. Like you, Arah."

The boy blushed.

"Hard work is a gift," said Jeshua as he led the donkey around the side of the house.

Arah followed Jeshua, lugging the water urn. He shook his head. "A gift?" He laughed.

Jeshua looked back over his shoulder. "Absolutely. From our Heavenly Father."

"Who?"

"The Master of the Universe. He is also our father."

"I never heard that," said Arah. "I know he created us, and is our Lord and we his subjects, but how is he our father?"

They stopped at the trough. Arah lifted the urn. The cool clear water splashed into the basin, and the donkey began to drink noisily. Jeshua turned to the boy. "Think about it. What kind of things does a father do for his children?"

They began to walk back toward the well. Arah carried the urn, thinking hard. His face lit up. "A father feeds his children and gives them shelter. He teaches them. And best of all . . . he gives them presents!"

Jeshua laughed. "Yes. A father gives his children gifts, even life itself. And this world," he said, motioning about, "is a gift from our Heavenly Father."

Arah put the empty urn down and picked up the waterskin, pondering. "So God is our father . . . and we're his children." He tossed the skin into the well. It hit the water with a loud *plop*. The boy hauled the heavy skin up. "I think I know what you mean," he said, pouring the water into the urn, lifting it to Jeshua. "And I'm sorry I didn't offer you this before." Jeshua cupped his hands and Arah poured the water into them. Jeshua buried his face in the cool, clear water and received another handful, drinking deeply. When he was finished, he straightened and nodded at Arah.

"You are just like your father," said Jeshua.

"You knew my father, Philip bar Joakim?" asked the boy, surprised.

Jeshua shook his head. "No. I never met him. Who was he?"

"He was a servant, like me. He died a long time ago. He used to take me into the fields. I would play in the barley while he worked." The boy looked wistful. "He was taller than you are."

"And he was a good father."

"Yes, he was," said Arah thoughtfully. "But if you never met him, why did you say I was just like him?"

Jeshua looked heavenward, and Arah did as well. "Oh," said Arah, smiling. "Like my Heavenly Father."

Jeshua nodded.

"How can that be? How can I be just like him?" asked the boy.

"Good fathers are the same, on earth or in heaven. Your father watched over and cared for you. Heavenly Father watches us as well, and when we need something he gives it to us."

Arah looked doubtful. "Always?"

"Yes. But sometimes what we think we need is not really what we need. But he knows the difference, and we always receive what is best for us."

Arah looked up, steeled. "Then why did he take my father away?"

Jeshua looked at the boy for a long moment, then said, "That's a good question, Arah." He put his hand on the boy's shoulder. "Why don't you ask him?"

Arah looked up. "Ask him? How?"

"Find a place where you can be alone and close your eyes and ask him."

"Will he answer?"

Jeshua smiled. "Yes. But, Arah . . . "

The boy looked up at him.

"His answers come in many forms. You will have to be patient and listen. Don't be discouraged if the answer doesn't come immediately. Your Heavenly Father will answer you, but remember your own father: he didn't always give you what you wanted the instant you asked for it."

"That's true," said Arah. "When I was little, I asked him if I could work in the fields with him, but he said no, I was too young. I was angry at him."

"Do you think that meant he didn't love you, just because the answer he gave you didn't please you?"

"No," said Arah, shaking his head. "I've worked plenty since then. Maybe it just wasn't time."

"All things have their season, Arah."

"Jeshua, are you a rabbi?"

Jeshua was putting on his leather apron. "No, Arah. I'm a carpenter." He withdrew a worn chisel and examined a nick in the cutting edge.

"So how do you know what you say about Heavenly Father is true?" asked the boy.

"I just do, Arah. And so do you."

Arah looked quizzically at the carpenter, his lips pursed. After a moment of thinking, he nodded. "I guess I do. I just never knew I did."

Jeshua laughed. "So you're getting answers already?"

Arah looked surprised. "Was that an answer? That feeling I just had?"

Jeshua nodded. "Life is funny, isn't it? The answers are there, if we just listen."

Just then Eli stormed out of the house, the door banging hard against a large urn by the entrance, almost knocking it over. He strode past Jeshua and Arah, stabbing his staff into the ground as he walked, his eyes fixed on the fields beyond the dooryard. He ducked under the grape trellis and continued on across the road toward the green fields, his shoulders hunched and his face red with anger.

Arah looked concerned as he watched Eli pick his way between the rows of low green shoots. He turned back to the well and lowered the waterskin. "But fathers also punish children," he said quietly, his voice echoing in the well. The skin splashed in the water far below. He began raising the rope.

Jeshua looked at Arah, noting his changed mood. "They also forgive."

Arah pulled the skin over the well edge and poured it into the clay urn. He shook his head. "Not all of them."

THREE

Simeon bar Eli

By midmorning, Jeshua had unhooked the door from its tired leather hinges and removed the handle and lock. Between trips to the fields with the water jar, Arah kept an eye on him. Something about Jeshua was different. Even though he was busy working, when people said hello, he always stopped and asked them questions—questions that went beyond mere courtesy. Once, when Arah was hauling a load of firewood, he overheard Jeshua's exchange with Hannah, Master Eli's cook, who was drawing water for the kitchen.

"I knew your father," said Hannah, as she tucked a wisp of gray hair back under her scarf. She extended a ladle of water to him. "And your mother. She is well?"

Jeshua drank deeply and handed the ladle back. "Yes. Thank you. And I remember you, Hannah. You lived in Nazareth many years ago. How is your husband, Enan?"

Hannah looked down. "Passed on," she said simply.

"I'm sorry," said Jeshua. "My father always said Enan was a fine man."

Hannah looked up at him, her eyes bright. "He said that? Your father?"

Jeshua nodded.

Hannah straightened and held her head high. "He was a fine man, my Enan." And with that she went back to drawing water, but Arah noticed a smile on her face. Everyone Jeshua talked to was happier after their conversation, even old Hannah, who was hardly ever happy.

Arah carried the heavy water jar into the fields, filling the large bucket kept there so the workers could have water when they needed it. What Jeshua had said about asking God about his father stayed on his mind. Arah was raised as a practicing Jew; his mother had seen to that. He and his two sisters went to synagogue each Sabbath, and at their yearly Passover seder, two chairs remained empty: his father's and the prophet Elijah's. Arah had come to think of his father as a kind of prophet as well: severe, pious, and serving God in heaven.

But his mother, Muriel, had not taught Arah to pray beyond the short, memorized prayers offered at meals and at bedtime. They had never traveled to Jerusalem for the holy days, not even the Feast of the Tabernacles, because it came during the harvest, and Master Eli would not permit it. They were servants, after all, a shekel or two above slaves. Master Eli was not cruel; he was simply indifferent.

Maybe that's why Jeshua had made such an impact on him. He'd never had an adult speak to him so directly about anything. He treated Arah like a real person, not just a lowly servant boy. And he listened to him, something no adult had ever done.

And what he'd said about talking with God—Heavenly Father—that was something to ponder. When Arah thought about God, he imagined him with Master Eli's stern, bearded face, and so it was hard to imagine God even listening to the prayers of little boys, much less answering them.

Jeshua examined the doorjamb carefully. It was in acceptable condition. A little sanding, filling, and repainting and it might serve a long while yet. He turned to the door, which lay on two sawhorses nearby. He closed his eyes and ran his hands slowly over the old wood to find its weaknesses and strengths, considering by feel how much planing and sanding it would require.

"What are you praying for? More money?"

Jeshua straightened and turned. In the doorway stood a man with dark, curly hair, a little younger than he, dressed in a dirty work tunic, wiping his hands on a rag. Jeshua nodded. "I was praying for the skill to fix this door, sir," he said.

"Don't call me 'sir,' carpenter," said the man, walking brusquely past him. "I'm a servant here, like her." He pointed to Hannah, who was pouring water into a brown cooking pot. He took the pot from her, lifted it to his mouth, and nearly drained it before handing it brusquely back to Hannah, whose eyes were carefully lowered. He ran a sleeve across his mouth and turned to Jeshua.

"Peace be unto you. I'm Jeshua bar Joseph," said Jeshua, bowing his head deferentially.

"From Nazareth. That's a small town."

Jeshua smiled. "Yes. Barely larger than Cana—your nearest town."

The man ignored the rejoinder. "It's hard to find a good carpenter around here."

"That's true. My father is the finest carpenter I know, but he and my brothers are working in Sepphoris, rebuilding after the big fire." He pulled out his hammer and bent over the door.

"Yes," said the young man, watching him with a frown on his face. "That fire has inconvenienced everyone."

Jeshua pulled a bent nail from the door and held it up. "I suppose we'll all have to make do with what we have." He straightened it with two swift blows of his hammer and placed it in his leather apron. "Besides, the more skilled a craftsman is, the more he charges."

"And you're a skilled craftsman, I suppose."

Jeshua shrugged. "My rates are fair."

"Fair to whom?" barked the young man. "Certainly not to me!" Without waiting for an answer, he turned and strode toward the fields.

The skin splashed in the water below, and Jeshua turned. Hannah nodded toward the fields as she pulled the rope up. "That was Simeon, Eli's son."

"Ah," said Jeshua. "His son."

"His elder son," she added.

Jeshua cocked his head at her.

"Master Eli has another son—a younger son—but he has left. Gone into the world."

"I see," said Jeshua. "And Simeon is angry about it."

Hannah nodded and poured the water into the cooking pot. She picked it up and set it on her hip, tossing her green scarf back across her shoulder. She walked toward the house. "Master Simeon is angry about everything."

FOUR

Out in the World

Such a city! Reuben had never seen the like, and he'd been to Jerusalem many times. But while Jerusalem had one glorious structure—the Temple—Damascus had scores of them: the huge, colonnaded porticos of the palace and government buildings, the largest marketplace he'd ever seen, and the incredible, many-storied homes of the wealthy and powerful.

It was a feast for the eyes, which, unfortunately, did not quell the rumblings of his stomach, now empty for most of the day. He'd left home almost a week before, early in the morning, wanting to get away before anyone tried to talk him out of it. Eli pleaded with him to stay, but once Reuben felt the money in his hands, it was as if he was already gone. Nothing anyone could say could make him stay. The only one who hadn't begged him to reconsider was Simeon, who stood behind his father, arms folded, his mouth set in a straight line, still as a stone.

Reuben might have stayed if Simeon had asked him to. He loved his older brother, even though he had never expressed it. It was quite impossible to tell Simeon anything, much less things of the heart. He was absolutely certain he was right about everything. An admission of love would be seen as proof that Simeon was indeed superior to his younger brother. Why, if Reuben ever told his brother how much he respected him, Simeon would hold it over him forever. So Reuben had never said any such thing, and now he was hundreds of miles away, proof that he didn't need anything from Simeon anymore.

This was as it should be. After all, Simeon was the firstborn and by law would receive Eli's entire estate as his inheritance. Reuben felt the money pouch under his tunic, proud of his wisdom in leaving when he did. If he had waited for Eli to die, he would have had to beg his inheritance from Simeon, who would have found an excuse for denying it. Even if he'd acquiesced, he might be fair, but he would never be generous. He never was, not even with himself.

Simeon lived like a miser, and why? He had everything: the love of the beautiful Rachel, the respect of the servants, and the honor of his father. Compared to Simeon, Reuben was almost a servant. Father had been preparing Simeon from birth, teaching him how to run the estate, when to plant and harvest, how to discipline the workers, and when to indulge them. And Reuben, only three years younger, was left to watch and try to learn by overhearing snippets of their conversations.

Things became very clear to Reuben last year, when Simeon and Rachel were married. Everyone was pleased, but Reuben knew that now that Simeon was married, Eli would soon turn the holdings over to him and Reuben would then have to serve his brother—and there was no way that was going to happen.

So Reuben asked for his inheritance. He implored, harangued, and begged, and when he threatened to leave without it, Eli finally gave in. He told Reuben his time was coming and he would not be forgotten, and though Reuben wanted to believe him, Simeon made him doubt.

When Eli withdrew Rueben's inheritance from his strongbox, Reuben was amazed at the size of it. A score of large, golden talents— enough to sustain him for the rest of his life—poured out into his hands, and he stood there, looking up into his father's weathered face, astonished, but feeling Simeon's angry eyes on him. Father wasn't smiling, but he wasn't angry, either. He was disappointed, and Reuben understood. He loved his father; knew his father loved him, but he couldn't stay. Not to serve a taskmaster like Simeon.

All through the night, Reuben loaded his train. When he set off at first light, Father stood in the doorway, waving good-bye. Simeon stood behind him, pouting. *He'll be a rich man*, thought Reuben, spurring his camel out of the dooryard, *but he won't rule over me.*

The trip to Damascus had taken a week, and now that he was here, he released the two servants who had accompanied him and bade them farewell. Then he stood in the marketplace in the largest city he'd ever seen and contemplated his future. A man of means in a cultured, exotic city, full of tempting delights to charm the senses. He felt like an ascetic who has spent his life in the wilderness, seeking wisdom among the rocks and sand, but who finally gives up his quest for God and finds his home in Babylon. His long fast was coming to an end. He would indulge himself. He had earned the right.

Reuben urged his camel into the busy marketplace. It wasn't long before a man approached him and asked if he could be of service, admiring Reuben's heavily laden caravan.

"You most certainly can," said Reuben expansively, feeling his stomach rumble again. "Do you know where might I get a good meal?"

FIVE

The Carpenter's Apprentice

The next morning Jeshua arrived early and stood for fifteen minutes outside the dooryard, waiting to be invited in. Several servants came and went, but no one extended an invitation to enter. Jeshua's donkey was impatient, though, and entered without delay. Jeshua felt peculiar waiting while the donkey headed for the trough.

Then a dusty tapestry hung across the doorway was pulled aside and Arah's brown face appeared. His teeth flashed as he yelled, "It's Jeshua! Come in, Jeshua!"

Jeshua walked under the grape trellis. Arah ran to the well and began drawing water. He nodded at the donkey standing at the trough. "It's empty," he said, pulling the waterskin up and running to pour it into the basin. The donkey set to work, slaking his thirst. Arah patted the animal on the haunches. "He's really thirsty," said the boy. He ran back to the well and tossed the skin back down. "I'll get you a drink, too, Jeshua."

Jeshua sat down on the stone well surround. Arah pulled the waterskin up, dipped the ladle in, and handed it to Jeshua, who shook his head. "You first, Arah."

Arah quickly drained the ladle and dipped it again, handing it to Jeshua, who drank the cool water down. Jeshua wiped his mouth and said, "Thanks for the drink." He withdrew something from his cloak and motioned for Arah to extend his hand. "Take this," he said, placing a small nugget of hard candy in Arah's palm.

"For me?" asked Arah, his eyes wide.

Jeshua shook his head. "For him," he said, gesturing at the donkey.

Arah was disappointed but walked over and gave the sweet to the donkey anyway. The donkey crunched the candy quickly and went back to drinking. Arah slowly trudged back to the well. Jeshua watched him, smiling at his fallen countenance. "I have something for you, too, Arah," said Jeshua, reaching into his cloak again.

Arah looked up, his eyes bright. "What is it?"

Jeshua withdrew his hand. It held an old metal scraper with a worn wooden handle. He extended the tool to Arah, who took it reluctantly. "What's this?"

"An opportunity."

The boy looked at him suspiciously. "What kind of opportunity?"

"To be my apprentice."

Arah's mouth dropped open. He blinked, twice. "Really?"

Jeshua nodded. "It's just while I'm working for Master Eli. You can learn a lot if—"

"When do I start?" asked Arah, looking at the scraper like it had suddenly changed into gold.

Jeshua said, "First, ask Master Eli for permission. If he approves, and you have time between your other chores, you may help me."

"I'm sure he will," exulted Arah.

"There is more," said Jeshua, standing. He placed his hands on his hips and regarded the boy evenly.

Arah looked up at him, his eyes bright with hope. "What?"

"As my apprentice, you must watch and listen carefully and do exactly as I say."

"Of course," said Arah, nodding furiously. "I will. Like you were my own father."

Jeshua smiled. "Now you've given me a challenge, Arah, asking me to be like your father. I'll do my best not to disappoint you." He reached into his cloak again. "This is for you," he said, withdrawing a sweet and giving it to the boy.

"What's it for?" asked Arah, popping the hard candy into his mouth.

"A reminder," said Jeshua. "Of the gifts our fathers give us."

SIX

Playing the Part

"This will do just fine," said Reuben, looking around the large room. "Just fine."

The landlord nodded and pocketed the coins. "If there is anything else you need, please let me know." He left quietly.

Reuben looked out the window at the large house across the square. Two stories of white marble, a flat roof, and green rolling hills beyond. Wide granite steps led up to two huge oak doors. Planters bursting with red and white irises lined the veranda fronting the magnificent, colonnaded building.

"Just like mine," said Reuben proudly. He turned and examined himself in the looking glass. New tunic and cloak of the finest linen, bright blue (not those muted Jewish earth tones), a dashing red leather belt, and a new pair of sandals. His old clothing lay on the floor by the bed, a plush, cushioned affair fit for a king, festooned from the ceiling with hanging drapes and mosquito netting. He smiled. He would soon share that bed with a lovely woman, perhaps the one he met last night at the tavern, the one with raven black hair and flecks of gold on her eyelids. Golden eyelids! Reuben had never imagined such a thing. After dinner they all went out—Reuben and his new friends and the beautiful woman—to attend a Greek theatrical farce with singing and dancing. Imagine! Singing and dancing, and not at a wedding, either. He laughed louder than anyone, told the funniest jokes, and drank more than his share of sweet plum wine. And when he saw the woman admiring his expensive clothes, he knew she would soon be his.

After all, he had to play the part to get the part—he heard a character in the play say that. So he intended to perfect the role of the wealthy young man. Tonight would be a repeat performance of last night; his companions already awaited him downstairs, drinking wine served by Reuben's new servants.

He lifted his chin and looked in the mirror. Tonight he would eat the meat of rare game birds, drink the finest wines of Assyria, marvel at the fascinating exploits of well-traveled adventurers, and finally, after midnight, take the golden-eyed woman by the hand and escort her upstairs, where he would complete his transformation from country boy to worldly man.

SEVEN

Doomsayer

Arah meant to ask Master Eli for permission to help Jeshua, but when Eli walked past him, he was too afraid to speak. After lunch, out in the fields, the men were weeding the rows of barley sprouts. Arah dumped the water into the barrel and walked over to where Micah knelt, pulling weeds.

"Hello, Micah," said Arah, handing him a ladle of water.

"Praise Him," said Micah, as he always did, before saying anything else. "I was dying of thirst."

"You'll never die of anything," said Arah, laughing. The old man was always talking about ways he might die, ways other people had died, and what kind of funeral they'd have for him when he was gone—and, on his gloomiest days, what kind of funeral they *wouldn't* have for him when he was gone.

"I'll die," said Micah flatly, looking up at the blazing sun. He was bald but refused to wear a hat. As a result, he was cooked brown like a walnut, and his pale blue eyes and long gray beard made him look like the prophet of doom he was. "I won't be around to harvest this crop, I can tell you that much," he said, frowning.

"You'll eat the bread we make from it," said Arah, smiling. "Even though you don't have any teeth."

"I have teeth," said Micah. "See?" He opened his mouth, and sure enough, there were two teeth on either side of his lower jaw. They were the only two teeth he had, but they were sufficient for gumming bar-leymeal. "Won't need 'em where I'm going."

"Micah," said Arah. "Can I ask you a question?"

"I might not live long enough to answer it, Arah," said Micah morosely.

"Is God really our father?"

Micah squinted up at the boy. "We are his subjects; he is our king. The two are different. Fathers are fallible; they grow old and die. God is infallible and cannot die, so he cannot be our father." Secure in his solid logic, he went back to weeding, moving along the row on his hands and knees, his bony elbows moving rhythmically in his oversized tunic. "Now pitch in or go," he said.

"I have another question," said Arah, following Micah down the row. "Jeshua said we could ask God anything and he'd answer us. Is that true?"

"God well knows what we need even before we ask. Our duty is to obey his commandments. If we do, we need not worry for ourselves."

"But does he answer prayers?" pressed Arah.

Micah let out a long sigh. "Obviously not. I'm still here, aren't I?" He turned away, closing the subject.

"Micah?" asked Arah.

"Go away, boy," said Micah.

"Would you ask Master Eli if I could work with the carpenter? He asked me to be his apprentice."

Micah turned around, frowning. "You want to leave us?"

"Oh, no," said Arah, shaking his head. "It's just for while he's here. I thought I might learn something besides filling buckets with water." Micah smiled. It suddenly occurred to Arah that the old man would genuinely miss him if he left. "Master Eli listens to you," he said.

Micah laughed. "No one listens to me." He shook his head, his long gray beard ticking back and forth.

"I listen," said Arah quietly.

Micah pointed a finger. "Then listen now: don't believe everything that carpenter says, boy. He has some strange ideas."

"He's nice," said Arah.

"Well, nice or not, you mind yourself. Learn what you can about carpentering, and stick to the old ways when it comes to religion. Never steer you wrong. Now, get back to work. I'll square it with Master Eli, if I live long enough to ask him."

Micah didn't die that day, and Arah was given permission to work with Jeshua after his other chores were done. So all afternoon, between trips to the well for the field workers and the women in the house, Arah helped Jeshua, who put him to work scraping the old varnish off the door planks. The boy worked hard following instructions. Jeshua complimented him regularly, and they ate their lunch together under the old olive tree shading the well. Arah found a length of twine, threaded it through the hole in the scraper handle, and hung it around his neck, proudly showing it to the other children who played in the dooryard. It was obvious that Arah had achieved a certain status through Jeshua's recognition, and the other children, who had been shy to approach Jeshua before, now came over to see what he was doing. He took a moment with each one, asking their names and a little about their families. Jeshua noticed that Arah's step was livelier and he hurried with his watering chores so he could return to help with the door.

EIGHT

News from a Distant Land

A couple of days later, Jeshua finished dismantling the door. It was a long process and required the utmost care and patience. He would gently pour water on the joints and wait for the wood to swell, loosening the glue. Then he would place the door in the hot sun, allowing the timbers to dry and shrink back to their original size. After repeating the process several times, the joints released. The door parts lay in a neat pile near his sawhorses.

Jeshua was examining one of the timbers when someone yelled. He turned and saw Arah running across the green fields toward the house, waving his cloak in the air. In a moment Eli emerged from the house. Arah leaped over the low rock fence and ground to a stop before Eli, panting. "It's Azariah! He returns from Damascus!"

The old man stared at Arah, then leaned heavily against the door frame, his hand on his forehead, muttering, "Damascus. Reuben."

Arah nodded, trying to catch his breath.

Jeshua looked at the road. Clearing a stand of trees at the edge of the property, a caravan of mules and camels appeared, loaded down with a merchant's wares.

"My staff," shouted Eli. Arah ducked inside and reappeared with the old man's walking staff. Eli took it and draped his other arm over Arah's shoulders, and together they walked slowly toward the advancing caravan. Jeshua noted Eli's eyes were bright as he passed. By the time he had reached the wooden gate at the low stone wall, the caravan had arrived. A small, well-fed man jumped down from his camel and walked briskly toward Eli. They met in the gateway and hugged each other fiercely, kissing each other on the cheeks.

The rotund merchant pulled away and looked up at Eli. "Peace be unto you, Eli, my old friend!"

"And unto you, peace, Azariah," said Eli "You have news? Of Reuben?"

Azariah frowned. "Slake my thirst and I will tell you all I know."

Eli motioned at Arah, who came running with the waterskin. "One must always bargain with you, Azariah," he said heartily. Azariah took the ladle and drained it. Then he took another and did likewise. His entourage was large, with ten camels, fifteen horses, and several mules. They looked tired. He waved the riders down and pointed to the well, raising his eyebrows at Eli.

"Of course!" said Eli, waving them in. "Come in. Water your stock. Azariah, come inside, I want to hear everything!"

They advanced a few paces into the dooryard when Azariah stopped, his face serious. He looked up at Eli. "It's been a hard journey, and a long one."

"Yes, I'm sure," said Eli, motioning for him to continue inside.

Azariah stood his ground. "As fits such a journey, I have hard news, Eli."

The old man seemed to sag. He bent his head toward Azariah. "Of Reuben?"

Azariah nodded. And waited.

"Please," said Eli quietly.

"Reuben is yet alive—thanks to the Master of the Universe. But he is not well."

"My boy is sick?" asked Eli, shocked. "What sickness?"

"Sickness of the soul, Eli. He is living riotously, drunk much of the time, consorting with harlots. And . . ." he paused and lowered his eyes, "blaspheming the Lord. God forgive him."

Eli's hand went to the neck of his tunic, pulling it down, straining the fabric. His eyes were wild. He ran a hand through his shaggy gray hair in dismay. "You've seen him?" he finally asked, as if from a great distance, his voice small and thin.

"I've seen him," affirmed Azariah.

Eli shook his head in disbelief. "So he is in Damascus. Among the Assyrians?"

Azariah nodded his head sadly. "I asked him if he had a message for you."

"And what did he say?"

Azariah shook his head. "He laughed at me." Azariah put his hand on Eli's shoulder. "I'm sorry, Eli."

Eli shook his hand off and straightened, his eyes looking heavenward. He grabbed at the neck of his tunic with both hands and split his shirt to his belt. The servants took a step backward, familiar with Eli's rare but terrible fury.

"What will you do?" asked Azariah carefully.

Eli turned, his head bowed with grief. Azariah made to follow him, but Eli waved him away. "There is nothing I can do. He has chosen his path," he said as he trudged toward the house. As he passed Jeshua, Eli said to himself, "God's punishment must fall."

After Eli disappeared indoors, all eyes turned to Azariah, who looked heavenward. "Forgive me, Lord, for bearing these bad tidings. Send your angels to lighten Eli's heart."

From inside, Jeshua heard Eli's voice. He could not make out what he was saying, but he was in conversation with someone. Azariah's company came into the dooryard to water their stock, but Eli's servants stood frozen, not knowing what to do. They looked apprehensively at the house, as if it might say something. The talking inside continued. Then, after several minutes, Simeon appeared in the doorway, shaking his head. He said, to no one in particular, "I knew it," and walked into the dooryard. Seeing Azariah, his eyes lit up, but there was still darkness in him.

"Azariah!" he shouted, slapping the little merchant on the back and steering him toward the camels. "What have you brought us?"

Jeshua turned back to his work. He steadied a door plank across a sawhorse, adjusted his plane's cutting edge, and worked steadily, planing in long, even strokes. Shortly, he heard a noise behind him. There was Eli in the doorway, his features a thundercloud of anger. At his appearance, the servants sprang into action and went about their business. Eli squinted at the crowd at the well, then turned his gaze toward Azariah's camel beyond the wall, which was being unloaded. A rug had been thrown over the low stone wall, and wares were being arranged upon it. Examining the merchandise, Simeon stood, his arms folded and his brow furrowed. To his side stood Azariah, who kept glancing over his shoulder at Eli. Simeon looked at Eli, then fixed his interest on the goods.

Jeshua turned toward Eli. "Master Eli?" Eli's torn shirt revealed his gray chest hair, wet with tears. "Master Eli, I have a question."

Eli frowned at Jeshua. "It's none of your business, carpenter."

Jeshua nodded. "It's about the door. There's a problem."

Eli smiled bitterly. "There always is," he said.

Jeshua gestured at the plank he'd been planing. "See this?" A rough brown oval lay inside the smooth, newly planed section. "Wood rot. And here," he said, picking up a torn leather hinge. "The hinges are beyond repair. And finally," he said as he picked up the diagonal cross member, "This: it's so warped I cannot plane it straight without destroying its strength."

Eli glanced at the door but then looked back at Simeon and Azariah. He waved Jeshua away. "It looks fine to me, carpenter. Just fix it as best you can."

Jeshua moved into Eli's field of vision, between the old man and Simeon beyond the wall. "It cannot be fixed, sir," he said quietly. "It's too old and worn out."

"Nonsense. You haven't the experience to—"

Jeshua snapped the cross member over his knee and dropped the two pieces on the ground with a clatter. Eli, his attention now fully Jeshua's, raised his chin, but the hardness quickly went out of his eyes. "What do you propose?" he said tiredly.

Jeshua walked toward the doorway. Eli followed him. Jeshua turned and said quietly, "A new door, Master Eli, but made of the finest wood. . . . Mahogany, I believe, would serve best. It will be thicker and stronger than the old oak door, yet lighter and easier to open."

Eli looked over at Simeon and Azariah. Simeon stood with his arms folded, nodding at Azariah. Even from this distance, Jeshua could see the haughtiness in Simeon's stance. Eli turned back to Jeshua, then looked at the broken cross member on the ground.

"All right, carpenter. A new door. Just be quick about it."

And with that he turned and walked inside.

NINE

A Righteous Man

Three days later, Jeshua arrived with a load of new wood on the back of his donkey. He was unloading it, thinking about the drawing of the door that he had sketched the night before on a piece of parchment. It was a simple design, and though he was no architect, he thought it would serve nicely. He felt the folded plan in his pocket as he pulled the timber off the donkey, eager to discuss it with Eli, who needed something to take his mind off his two disappointing sons. He was giving the donkey a handful of grain when someone said, "Ho, now, what's this?"

He turned and saw Simeon standing next to the pile of new timber. He was pointing at the wood but looking at Jeshua. Jeshua walked over to Simeon. "Peace be unto you, Master Simeon. Is Master Eli around this morning?" he asked.

"He's gone to Cana. And I asked you a question, carpenter."

"It's wood for the new door, it's mahogany—"

"New door?" barked Simeon. "What new door?"

Jeshua nodded toward the door frame, now draped by the tapestry. "The old door was beyond repair," he said.

Simeon laughed sharply and shook his head. "Carpenter, are you a righteous man?"

Jeshua was taken aback. "The Lord will decide if I am."

Simeon laughed bitterly. "Well, you must be, because your prayers have been answered: you've managed to wheedle even more money out of my father."

Jeshua crossed his arms across his chest and looked evenly at Simeon. "Isn't that right?" taunted Simeon.

Jeshua said quietly, "Simeon, what have I done to anger you?"

Simeon turned on his heel. "You are here, carpenter. And by the time you and others like you are gone, there will be nothing left to inherit."

Jeshua watched him march across the dooryard and jump the low stone wall, heading for the fields.

TEN

The Life of the Party

"Do you ever think about your home?" asked Rahab, sipping her wine.

"Yes, Reuben," said Ahmad. "Won't you tell us about Galilee?"

Reuben shook his head. "The answer to both questions is no."

There was a great shout as the people around the table leaned forward, eager for what Reuben wouldn't say. But he was drunk and afraid he'd say something to reveal his low origins. He'd learned the hard way, weeks before when he had arrived in Damascus, to be careful of his tongue. "You learn by listening," old Eli had always said, and in this case he was right.

There was nothing he wanted to tell them about Galilee, but much he wanted to know about it. When Azariah approached him in the tavern two weeks ago, he wanted to ask his old friend how Eli and Simeon were doing, but he was too drunk. Azariah stood there while Reuben's friends ridiculed his clothing, speech, and weight—all in good fun, of course. But Azariah was not amused, and the hurt on his face shamed Reuben. All through Reuben's youth Azariah had brought him a gift every time the caravan passed Eli's estate: a large, pink shell from the Middle Sea, a stone from the Temple mount, glass beads from Greece. He had always been kind to Reuben, yet there he stood, suffering the insults, while Reuben's tongue proved too thick with wine to defend him. And when Azariah finally asked if he had a message for his father, Reuben had laughed, mostly out of embarrassment. Azariah bent his head and left. The rowdy crowd cheered, but Reuben felt sand filling his heart. He drank so much that night he couldn't remember how he got home.

Rahab leaned in, her perfume making Reuben's head spin even more than the wine. She batted her golden eyelids. "Tell *me* about Galilee, then. I can keep a secret."

"That's true, Reuben," said Ahmad. "She kept her true vocation a secret from you for almost two weeks!" Everyone laughed. Reuben blushed. It was true. He thought Rahab was just a beautiful woman who was interested in him. And while she was beautiful, she was never interested in him, only in his money. By now she had managed to get hold of quite a bit of it. Reuben had no doubt that her questions about Galilee were just another way to find out if he had more money there.

"Come, Reuben," said Rahab. "We have better things to do."

Everyone laughed as she tugged on Reuben's arm. But tonight he would not give in. Many nights she had taken him back to his house, and the next morning, when he woke up alone, he noticed things were different: vases shifted, clothing in drawers rumpled, doors open that were closed the night before. Things missing.

And yet, the next day, when he went out and stopped by her house, Rahab would be there, smiling prettily at him as always. She would take his hand and walk with him through the marketplace to buy clothing or jewelry or hand mirrors—with Reuben's money, of course.

Reuben looked around at the gathering. His entourage had grown to more than twenty people—some of whose names he didn't even know—and their nightly forays into Damascus were becoming more of an event than the theaters and taverns and inns they frequented. Reuben noticed how people whispered when they passed, shaking their heads, some frowning, but all willing to take the gold coins he offered. Yes, they might think he and his friends were ill behaved, drunken, and loud, but they lined up to be paid for what little they did to earn the money he gave them.

"I have to talk to Ahmad," said Reuben, shaking Rahab's hand off his arm and standing unsteadily. He pointed at the tall, sandy-haired man sitting across from them. Out of the corner of his eye he saw Rahab scowl and turned to face her, but she was smiling sweetly at him again. "I'll be back," he said, furrowing his brow at her, daring her to disagree.

"I'll be here," she said, winking.

Reuben motioned Ahmad aside. They stood near the door of the crowded tavern. "I am concerned about the investment," said Reuben, taking care that his words did not slur.

Ahmad placed his hand on Reuben's shoulder. "It is going fine, don't worry."

"I *am* worried," emphasized Reuben. "It's been too long. You said the merchandise would be here a week ago."

Ahmad shrugged. "It's here when it's here. Patience, Reuben."

Reuben shook Ahmad's hand from his shoulder. "I've been patient enough. I want results."

Ahmad looked Reuben square in the eye. "Reuben," he said quietly, bending toward the shorter man, "it will be here. Don't pester me any more about this." He turned and walked back toward the crowd at the tables. Reuben watched him walk away, scowling.

"Sir?" came a voice.

Reuben turned. "What is it?"

The innkeeper, a short, thin man with wisps of brown hair plastered across his bald head, stood before him. "If you please."

Reuben waved him away. "I'll settle with you when we leave."

"Perhaps you forget," said the small man uncomfortably. "You left last night without paying."

Reuben frowned at him. "That's not true. I always pay my bills."

"I'm sure that's true. But you were rather . . . uh . . . inebriated when you left. Perhaps you forgot."

Reuben shook his head. "I'm never so drunk that I forget whose hand is in my pocket, innkeeper," he hissed. "You're lying."

The man's face went bright red. "Please, sir, I beg of you. I am not lying. I am simply telling you you're behind in your account. It's the truth."

"Reuben!" called Rahab. "Come back. Nidab has a story about Babylon you must hear!"

Reuben turned back to the innkeeper. "I don't have the money now."

"What?"

"I don't carry that kind of money on me," whispered Reuben. "What kind of fool do you think I am?"

The innkeeper frowned at Reuben. "Perhaps you are the kind of fool who doesn't carry enough money to pay his bills." His eyes bored into Reuben's.

"I'll pay you when I pay you," snapped Reuben, echoing Ahmad. "Tomorrow."

"Sir, I must object—"

"I said tomorrow. Now I'm done with you. Send someone to my house in the morning. And don't mention this in front of my friends."

"Your friends," said the innkeeper sarcastically, "could help you pay your bill."

"My friends are my business," said Reuben.

"Your business, it appears, is spending money you don't have. I will send a boy around tomorrow, before your business suffers any more . . . losses." He turned on his heel and walked away.

Reuben watched him go. "Reuben! Come back!" pleaded Rahab, patting the pillow next to her.

"Yes, Reuben, come back," shouted Ahmad. "We're thirsty!"

Everyone laughed.

ELEVEN

Pointed Questions

Eli dismounted slowly from his black horse and shook the dust from his cloak. He glanced around the deserted street and sighed. Looking up, he saw the upper window where Benjamin worked. A sheer curtain shifted in the morning breeze, and for some reason Eli was not surprised at all when he saw Benjamin's white whiskered face suddenly appear in the window.

"Eli, my friend, what brings you to Cana?" asked Benjamin, leaning out of the window.

Eli looked around, glad the street was empty. "Peace be unto you, Rabbi. I need your counsel."

Benjamin shook his head. "And unto you, peace. No, Eli, it is your counsel that is needed. Come up."

Eli made his way up the narrow outside stairs cut into the stone wall. The door at the top opened and Benjamin appeared. He was a tall man, taller even than Eli, but his shoulders were narrow and he walked bent forward, his large hands hanging from his thin arms like oversized gloves.

Benjamin's tailor shop was, as usual, a complete disaster. Mounds of material lay about; a dozen half-completed tunics and robes hung on hooks by the door. Another tailor hunched over his work, his eyes mere inches from the fabric as he meticulously sewed stitch after stitch. Benjamin motioned Eli in and returned to his own stool by the window, which was surrounded by piles of colorful material. Eli looked around. There was no place to sit, so he stood uncomfortably in the center of the room.

Benjamin picked up a striped fabric of at least ten radiant colors, a veritable rainbow. "Like Joseph's coat, no, Eli? Colors and colors and more colors. I bought it on a whim because of its beauty. So, now that you're here, tell me: what shall I make of it?"

Eli shrugged, shifting his weight to his other leg.

Benjamin reached up into his head covering and withdrew a needle, deftly threading it, all the while looking at Eli, a question on his face but none on his lips. Again, Eli shifted his weight and looked over at the other tailor, who was busy sewing.

Finally, Benjamin said loudly, "Goodness, Daniel, leave us in peace. Eli is here to talk to me. Alone."

Daniel raised his head and squinted at Eli. "Oh, Eli, I didn't hear you come in. My apologies." He stood and quickly exited the room. Eli reached for Daniel's stool and pulled it over toward Benjamin. Now only the large mounds of fabric separated them.

"Daniel," sighed Benjamin, shaking his head. "Deaf and blind, but what hands. He can thread a needle behind his back, under water, in the dark." He laughed, but when he saw Eli sitting there so stiffly on the small stool, he raised his chin toward the old man. "Eli, my friend."

"Rabbi," said Eli, and his voice trailed off. He looked at his sandals and laced his fingers together, shaking his head. "I . . . I . . . don't know how to—"

"Reuben," said Benjamin quietly.

Eli looked up, surprised.

"The trade route passes Cana before it reaches your home."

Eli's face drained of color. "Then you know."

Benjamin took a stitch and looked out the window.

Eli buried his head in his hands and shook it slowly. "So everyone knows."

Benjamin looked at Eli, who finally raised his head to meet his gaze. "Yes, including the Lord."

"That is what I wanted to talk to you about, Rabbi. You know what Reuben has done."

Benjamin nodded gravely. Eli continued, "He has broken the commandments and violated the Law. And I know the Lord's justice must fall upon him."

Benjamin put his work aside and leaned forward, pointing at Eli with the needle. "But you are wondering about your justice—what *you* should do."

Eli nodded miserably.

Benjamin looked past Eli and quoted scripture, "'The wicked shall be cut off from the earth, and the transgressors shall be rooted out of it.'"

Eli groaned.

Benjamin continued, "'To do justice and judgment is more acceptable to the Lord than sacrifice.'"

Eli shook his head. "Does it really say that?"

Benjamin continued, "You know the Law as well as I do, Eli. And so you know the Law must be obeyed: the sinner must be punished."

Eli nodded again, looking at the floor.

"It has always been that way," said Benjamin quietly. "From the beginning of time. Justice must prevail. The wicked must be punished so the name of the Lord will be glorified."

"But ... he's my son," said Eli simply, his eyes pleading with Benjamin.

Benjamin sighed. "Eli, my friend. Every wicked man is someone's son. But that cannot shield them from the Lord's justice."

"But what about mercy?" pleaded Eli. "Has mercy no place?"

Again Benjamin focused on the wall behind Eli. "When the Lord gave the Law to Moses, he said he would show mercy unto those who kept his commandments. Only those who kept his commandments. All others must suffer the sword of his justice."

Eli shook his head but said nothing for a long time. Even Benjamin seemed out of words. He scanned the piles of colorful fabric, searching his mind for consolation for his friend, a man he loved with all his heart and a man who deserved better than he was getting, both from his son and from his rabbi. A particular pattern of colors caught his eye. They formed a rainbow, and Benjamin remembered another of the Lord's promises.

"But there is hope," he said slowly. Eli looked up and nodded at Benjamin to continue. Benjamin took a deep breath and leaned forward. "The prophet Isaiah foretold the day when the Messiah would come. All things will change, like winter changes to spring. Our enemies will be vanquished, and the Messiah will teach us a new law, some say a *higher* law."

"What is this *higher* law?" asked Eli.

"I do not know. I only know that on that day the Messiah will come and save his people."

"Even my Reuben?" asked Eli.

Benjamin picked up the fabric and carefully made a stitch. He shrugged. "As I said, I do not know. But when the Messiah comes, the Law of Moses will be fulfilled. Everything will change." He looked heavenward and closed his eyes. "May the Messiah come quickly."

Eli nodded and closed his eyes as well, a prayer on his lips. "Yes. May the Messiah come quickly."

TWELVE

An Obedient Son

Eli returned home late that afternoon. Jeshua had been hoping to see him all day to show him the door design, but when Eli came into the dooryard, he waved Jeshua off and walked inside, tired from his trip. Jeshua busied himself working on the doorjamb, sanding smooth the wood inserts he had fashioned.

Inside, Eli's feet were being washed by a servant girl. Simeon stood by, impatient at the slowness of the ritual. When she finally finished, Simeon sat on a large cushion opposite his father.

From the doorway Jeshua saw that Eli took some time to notice Simeon, instead studying a census tally of his flocks. Jeshua felt the tension in the air and wished he were somewhere else. But until Eli approved the door design, he had to work on the jamb; there was nothing else to do.

Finally, Eli looked at Simeon and said, "You may speak."

Simeon leaned forward. "Thank you, Father. I have something to say about Reuben, if I may."

"You may not," said Eli with finality.

Simeon shook his head slowly, anger building in his dark eyes, and moved to get up. When he was at the doorway, Eli spoke. "You've always been an obedient son, Simeon."

Simeon turned back. His father sat amid the cushions, his dinner on a tray next to him, uneaten. Eli looked very old tonight, and Simeon felt bad for him. "I've always tried to be," he said quietly, returning to his cushion and seating himself. He waited, looking at Eli, who was lost in thought.

"You are my firstborn," said Eli.

Jeshua sanded the doorjamb. He wished his sanding stone were silent, but neither Eli nor Simeon seemed to notice him working just a few paces away.

"You have been faithful and obedient to me."

Simeon nodded. "I will always be obedient to you, Father."

Eli took a deep breath. "I know. Speak your heart, then, Simeon. Even if it is hard, I will hear you."

Simeon once again leaned forward. "Reuben has been gone for some time," he began slowly. "The reports we've received reveal his disrespect for the Lord."

"The Lord loves your brother, Simeon, as do I. And whom the Lord loves, he chastens."

Simeon laughed. "Chastens? Azariah says Reuben is drunk all the time, spending money on expensive clothing, gambling, and consorting with harlots and blasphemers!" The last word came out like a curse. He looked away and just managed to catch Jeshua's eye. He frowned at the carpenter, then turned back to Eli, nodding toward Jeshua.

Eli ignored the hint. "What is it, Simeon? Can you not see the pain this causes me?"

"I'm sorry, but I don't see any chastening, by the Lord or by anyone else. But let's suppose the Lord does punish Reuben. Then whatever he suffers is God's justice. Certainly you must see that. He takes his inheritance before his rightful time, squanders it, and dirties our family name in a distant land. The roads are full of talk of his wickedness, and we are laughed to scorn!" He sat back, his chest heaving with righteous indignation.

Eli's head was bowed. After a long time, he asked slowly, "What do you want, Simeon?"

Simeon gritted his teeth. "Cut him off, Father. Let everyone know he is no longer your son—as he is no longer my brother, and—"

"Enough!" yelled Eli, the rafters shaking with his anger. "Enough, I tell you!" He looked at Simeon with slit eyes, full of fire. "You tell me things I already know. I know the commandments better than you. I know the Lord's punishment will fall upon Reuben; must mine fall also?"

"He has disrespected you, Father," said Simeon flatly.

"Yes. He has," said Eli, his eyes smoldering still.

"The Law and the prophets are clear: he must be cut off. You know this is true."

Eli groaned, so loud and so sad that Jeshua had to leave. He stood outside in the darkness, the rectangle of yellow light spilling across the stoop behind him. His heart ached for Eli, but it ached even more for Simeon's bitterness. From inside, he heard nothing, just Simeon's breathing. After a moment, footsteps passed across the flagstones. A door closed.

For a long time Jeshua stood, looking west. A tiny sliver of purple lined the horizon, the remnant of a colorful sunset. He listened for movement inside but heard nothing. Perhaps Eli had left the room as well. He felt the parchment in his apron. He went to the doorway and looked in.

Eli sat, staring into the distance, alone in the room. Jeshua gingerly knocked on the door frame. Eli's great head slowly turned toward him, his gray eyes glazed and red. Jeshua noted that the tears the old man had been shedding hung to the gray strands of his beard. He seemed entirely gray, his clothing, his hair, his beard. Even his skin seemed gray.

"What is it, carpenter?" the old man asked weakly.

Jeshua stepped inside. "I'm sorry, Master Eli, but I need you to look over the design for the new door."

"Will it ever be done?" asked Eli wearily.

"Building a door takes time, but yes, it will soon be done."

Eli waved Jeshua over and took the parchment. He examined it for a long time, tracing the lines with his finger but saying nothing. He handed the parchment back. "Fine, carpenter. Now, go . . . I care not for doors or anything else. I have lost a son."

Jeshua walked toward the doorway, then stopped. He turned slowly to see the old man sobbing quietly into his robe. Jeshua said, "Master Eli, one more thing."

The old man continued crying.

"The new door. It should open inward." He waited.

Eli looked up and wiped his eyes. "Inward? Doors don't open inward, carpenter. An apprentice knows that."

"I know," said Jeshua, nodding. "They never have, for many reasons: protection—a door that opens out cannot be battered in—simplicity, tradition, and so on. But this door, this fine, beautiful mahogany door we are building, should open inward, to welcome travelers, friends, and family. A door that opens inward invites all to share the love and bounty of the household."

Eli shook his head and laughed bitterly. He mouthed the words *love* and *bounty*, but no sound escaped his lips. He blinked at Jeshua. "While all else in my life lies in ruins around me, here you are, talking to me about a door. A door. As if it mattered." He shook his head again. "I was about to terminate this project, but you have piqued my curiosity and I long to think about something besides my two disappointing sons. A door that opens inward. That I must see."

Jeshua folded the parchment and placed it in his tunic, bowed, and walked outside. As he led his donkey homeward along the silver path in the cool darkness, he looked up at the bright band of stars crossing the black sky and thought of his own father.

THIRTEEN

Micah's Prediction

For several days Jeshua worked steadily on the new door. The days were hot and there was no shade, except for the large olive tree that guarded the well. Jeshua thought of setting his workbench up under the old tree but reconsidered. The sawdust he was raising might sift down and dirty the well water. Instead he settled for the shade offered by the house in the morning; by afternoon he worked in the full, hot sun.

The mahogany he'd purchased for the door was from Antioch. It was expensive, and he had haggled long and hard with the timber merchant, but in the end both of them got a bargain. The wood was aromatic as he sawed it, a sweet, dark smell that pleased him. From the time he was a boy, he had always loved the smell of newly cut wood and hated to varnish over it. But wood soon darkened and rotted without protective coating, so Jeshua enjoyed the brisk, lively odor while he could. In the evenings, after a long day at work, when he bathed before prayers and dinner, he often regretted washing away that sweet smell, even as the water sluiced off the dirt and grime. Often, when he toweled dry after his bath, he would consider how lucky he was to enjoy the pungent smell of worked wood, even though he was getting dirty in the process. But refreshed from his bath, dressed in clean clothes, his hair oiled and combed, he would bend his head over the evening meal and thank God for the privilege of working at something he loved, even as his muscles ached from a long day's labor. Later, in the stillness of night, sleep came swiftly to the carpenter, a deep, untroubled sleep he knew he would not always enjoy.

One day at lunch, Jeshua sat with the servants under the olive tree, enjoying a story Hannah was telling about a young calf that several of the small children had been trying in vain to catch. The calf bawled loudly, she said, enclosed in a ring of children, who were covered with mud from scrambling after it, yet the calf's smooth tan coat remained perfectly clean, untouched by any of them.

"Did they catch it?" asked Arah, caught up in the story.

Hannah picked up a skewer resting over the fire. She pulled off a piece of meat and popped it into her mouth. "What do you think?" she asked, grinning broadly.

Arah was shocked. "We're eating it—right now?" He looked at Hannah in dismay.

Hannah laughed and shook her head. "No . . . but we will!" She winked at the boy.

Everyone laughed as she pointed to the small stock pen near the side of the house. There, the same small brown calf stood, looking curiously at them as if it knew they were talking about it.

Micah didn't laugh but shook his head. "We won't be eating that calf. Ever."

"Why not?" asked a servant. "It's fat. It would make a tasty meal."

"That it would," added Hannah, still chewing the piece of meat.

Micah stood, finished with his lunch. "Master Eli is saving that calf for young Reuben's return." He shook his head and slowly walked from the circle.

Everyone sat in silence for a moment, then Hannah nodded and said, "I'm afraid Micah is right. That calf will outlive us all."

FOURTEEN

A Distant Star

For several days Arah considered Micah's words of warning about the carpenter. He'd known Micah all his life. He knew the old man to be kind and sincere, if a bit gloomy. He'd known Jeshua only a few days but already felt Jeshua loved him like his own father. He wanted to believe what the carpenter said. Jeshua had stated that "the truth always tastes good, if we're hungry for it." Arah was hungry for answers, and the things Jeshua said about God and answers to prayers not only tasted good, they echoed in his soul, making him think about life in new ways.

Until Jeshua arrived, Arah felt that he'd spent his whole life looking at the ground, lugging heavy water buckets to and from the fields, or staring into the blackness of the well, hauling the wet, slimy rope up, to empty the waterskin and drop it again. Repetition was the nature of his life, day in and day out, and he was just a boy. He wondered if he would still be hauling water when he was as old as Micah, who crawled along the rows of barley, his eyes also focused on the ground.

But something about Jeshua made him look up at the heavens with new eyes. He began to see faces in the fluffy white clouds, feel the miracle of the sun on his face, and imagine his father walking the streets of heaven with God. The thought made Arah's eyes mist, and he had to turn away so Jeshua wouldn't see him. But the image tasted so good that he wanted to hug Jeshua and thank him for taking away the image of his father dying on his low, hard bed, eyes sunken and skin yellow and his hair falling out. "Consumption," they called it; Mother said it was the "wasting disease," and when Father died, he weighed no more than Arah.

Jeshua talked about Arah's father as if he was alive and well; that he was still Arah's father and still concerned about him. What kind of boy would he grow up to be? Honest? Kind? Generous? Or would he be angry, sullen, and bitter, like so many people? Jeshua said everyone's life was hard—he showed Arah a number of white, ridged scars on his own hands—but a hard life didn't have to make us hard as well.

And when Arah protested, saying he was a water boy and that would never change, Jeshua handed him his hammer and asked, "Are you a carpenter yet?"

"No," said Arah, hefting the heavy hammer.

"So you're still a water boy?"

Arah nodded. "That's what I mean."

Jeshua held out a piece of wood and handed Arah a small nail. "Hammer it in."

Arah did so. The nail, miraculously, went straight in. He looked up and smiled.

"Now you're a carpenter, Arah," said Jeshua. "Things are changing already."

Arah was standing in Eli's orchard now, hidden among the fig trees. It was well after dinner, and he'd sneaked out, his head full of conflict and heart full of hope. He had queried Jeshua all day, as subtly as he could, about the mechanics of prayer and how answers came. Jeshua told him little, except to say that faith was important.

Arah knelt, wondering if he had faith. Jeshua said faith was believing in something that was true, even though you couldn't see it. Arah knew his father existed once, but he wasn't sure if he still did. If it was true, and he believed it, then he supposed he had this faith Jeshua was talking about. But the belief felt like a small smooth stone in his hand—comforting and warm, but of no real use.

He sat down on a rock and looked up at the sky between the trees. The stars twinkled in the darkness. Jeshua said they were suns, like our sun. Micah had laughed when Arah told him that, shaking his head. "Foolishness," he'd said. "They're not suns. Look how small they are," and he'd gone back to his weeding.

"But they're far away, that's what Jeshua says," the boy had countered.

Micah had pointed a gnarled finger at the boy. "Watch yourself, Arah," he'd said.

Arah, like all boys, knew about the wheel of the night sky, how it spun around the north star. He imagined God and his own father living on that star, or else why would everything revolve around it? So he focused on the star, perched above the horizon, and closed his eyes.

"Heavenly Father," he said, trying to picture God, but only Micah's grizzled face came into his mind's eye. He shook his head and tried again, but this time Jeshua's face came into focus. He had white hair and a long white beard, but it was still Jeshua, and Arah wondered at the image, which persisted, so he went on: "Jeshua says my father is with you. Is it true?"

He listened to the wind sighing through the trees and the crickets chirping. The night was warm, but he shivered, knees pulled up, arms around them. Nothing came.

He opened his eyes and looked at the star. "Why did you take him away?" The star twinkled distantly, and Arah was distracted by movement in the orchard. He turned. A dog, maybe, or a squirrel. He turned back to the star. "Why?" he asked, his lips barely moving, holding his breath.

He sat there for a long time, listening. But no voice came, no inner voice, either, the kind Jeshua had said to listen for. The star twinkled but said nothing. Finally, he gave up.

As he walked back to the family quarters, he wondered how long he'd been out there. The oil lamp still burned inside. The moon had not yet risen. *There is more to being a carpenter than swinging a hammer,* he thought. *And there is more to prayer than asking and listening.*

FIFTEEN

Rachel and Simeon

S imeon hated the fields. The work was dirty, and the sun beat down on his back like a slaver's lash. He straightened from weeding the seedlings and put his hands on the small of his back, grimacing. He looked around. The other laborers were congregated together, laughing as they worked, enjoying a private joke. He noted that they never worked near him. They worked hard enough; the rows were weeded and watered, but they made him feel like an outsider, even though he was their master.

Of course they're happy, he thought, gathering up a bunch of weeds and tossing them into a large woven basket. *They have no hope of anything more. They've come to accept their lot. But I cannot.*

He straightened again and looked around for the servant boy. He was nowhere in sight. "Where's that boy?" he called out to no one in particular.

"He's helping the carpenter, Master Simeon," said old Micah, whose back was too stiff to bend over anymore. Instead, he worked the rows on his hands and knees. It embarrassed Simeon to see Micah working this way, but when he'd suggested the old man help the women around the house, Micah had shaken his head furiously. "I will work like a man until I die," he'd said with finality. But watching him work on his hands and knees made Simeon uncomfortable, and he tried whenever he could to give Micah work that was less strenuous. Micah did as he was told, but it soon became clear to Simeon that he preferred working with the other men, so Simeon threw up his hands and let things be. It seemed he had no impact at all on the servants. He was just another worker, and though they called him "master," he knew they had no love for him. They respected him, perhaps because he was the hardest worker of all, starting in the fields at the break of day and continuing until nightfall. Yet no one ever complimented him or expressed gratitude for the work he did. It was simply expected of him.

Simeon grabbed a bunch of weeds and pulled them from the ground. Sweat ran into his eyes. He could feel it trickling down his spine. And he was thirsty. Where was that boy?

Oh, yes, helping the carpenter. The carpenter who had managed to turn a two-day job into a three-week stay. And the way the children flocked around him, listening to him and running errands for him, galled Simeon. Why did this carpenter deserve all the attention? Would he be here in a month, laboring with the servants in the hot sun, worrying about their families and what would happen to them if the harvest was poor or nonexistent? No, he would be gone, off to another job, caring nothing about these people. And yet they would speak glowingly of him, even within earshot of Simeon, not understanding that Simeon cared more deeply for all of them, and without pay or gratitude, than this carpenter ever would.

His anger was making him even thirstier. "Where is that boy?" he yelled loudly, even as he pulled another clump of grass.

"Simeon, don't shout," said a gentle voice.

Simeon looked up. It was Rachel. She stood behind him, holding a water urn, the overflowing ladle held out in front of her, smiling.

"Rachel!" he said, jumping up, taking the ladle and draining it. "How did you know I was thirsty?"

Rachel laughed, a clear, sparkling laugh that made Simeon forget his anger. "A man craves water as a woman craves a kind word." She dipped the ladle into the urn and gave it to him again.

Simeon drank it, the water running down his beard and onto his tunic. He ran a brown hand across his mouth and smiled. "You've satisfied my thirst, so now I will satisfy yours. You are more beautiful every day."

Rachel motioned old Micah over. He came as quickly as his old bones would allow and took the water urn to the other workers. She turned back to Simeon.

"Thank you, husband," said Rachel, her green eyes bright with pleasure. She put both hands on her large stomach, and smiled at Simeon. "We both thank you."

Simeon smiled. "How do you—both of you—feel today?"

"I am tired and he is restless." She patted her stomach. "We keep different hours. I fear he will outrun you when he is a year old."

Simeon nodded. "I can't wait for that race."

Rachel grew serious. "I cannot wait, either, Simeon. We cannot wait. Have you spoken to your father?"

Simeon put his arm around Rachel and led her a few steps away, out of earshot of the others. He whispered, "I've pled with him a number of times that our time has come."

"But he is not persuaded," said Rachel flatly.

"No," answered Simeon, his eyes downcast. "He is not persuaded."

"Then you must no longer plead—you must demand," she said.

Simeon looked at his lovely wife. Her dark hair was pulled back, framing her flawless skin. Her eyes were searching him for answers.

"What can I demand?" he said. "He is my father. All that I have— all that we have—he has given us. He knows our needs. We live in his house."

"Yes," said Rachel. "We live in his house. You and I, two grown adults, living in your father's house—like two children. And soon we will have our own child. It is time for us to be on our own, Simeon. Beyond time."

Simeon nodded. "He loves us, you know that."

"But he loves Reuben more," said Rachel.

"That's not true," said Simeon weakly.

"Isn't it? Then let him prove it. You are the elder son. By rights, you should have had your inheritance before Reuben. You would never have done what Reuben has. Why hasn't your faithfulness been rewarded?" Her face was red now with frustration, and Simeon could only nod his agreement.

Rachel looked at Simeon, sweaty and dirty from working in the hot sun, and her anger ebbed. Here he was, the most honest, hardworking man she had ever known, standing there with his head down, convicted of being faithful. Of being obedient. Of loving his father. Her heart softened, but the truth remained hard. "When does our life begin, Simeon?" she asked gently.

Simeon shook his head, at a loss. Rachel reached out and took his hand, raising it to her cheek, her anger gone. Simeon was aware that his hands were dirty and would mar her beauty, but her warm skin felt good on his palm. Rachel closed her eyes and murmured, "We have been patient, my love. Our time has come. Do not ask Eli anymore—tell him." She opened her eyes.

He nodded sadly. "You are right, Rachel. It is time."

SIXTEEN

Storm Clouds

Reuben clenched his fists as he stomped down the street. "That damned Ahmad!" he hissed to himself. "I should have known!"

He had gone by Ahmad's home. The servant said he was gone. When Reuben said he hadn't seen Ahmad in several days, the servant simply shrugged. "When is he returning?" asked Reuben, trying to remain calm.

"He didn't say," said the servant, frowning. "He left the city."

"What?" howled Reuben. "Why?"

"He didn't say," repeated the servant coolly.

Reuben had acted on impulse then, barging past the servant. He found himself in the great room of the house. It was empty of furnishings, except for a few pillows and tapestries. He gestured about. "What does this mean?"

"Master Ahmad is gone. I don't know where. Before he left two days ago, he dismissed us and told us to sell the remaining furnishings."

Reuben snatched up an embroidered pillow. The servant grabbed at it, and they stood there, each tugging on a corner. "I want my money," said Reuben, hauling the pillow in.

The servant, a half-head taller than Reuben, pulled the pillow back. "It is mine."

"He owes me money," yelled Reuben, pulling the pillow.

The servant laughed. "He owes everybody money. Have you ever seen him work?"

Reuben clutched the pillow harder. "I figured he was a wealthy man, like me."

"Like you?" sneered the servant. "Well, one of you is wealthy, now." He released the pillow and Reuben fell down, the pillow held tightly in his arms. He hit the marble floor hard, cracking his head.

"Now get out," said the servant, looming over Reuben. "Or I will call the Centurion."

Reuben went to Rahab's house. She, too, was gone, but he found her in the marketplace, discussing the price of walnuts with a merchant. "Rahab," he yelled. She turned, and as he approached, he saw her face change from pleasure to steeled emptiness.

"Ahmad is gone," moaned Reuben, pulling her aside.

"So?" asked Rahab, still holding a handful of walnuts.

"So? He took all my money!" lamented Reuben.

"What do you mean, all your money?"

Reuben shook his head. "An investment. In precious stones. He took my money."

Rahab shrugged. "He'll be back."

"His house is empty. All I got was this." He held up the embroidered pillow.

Rahab laughed. "Then even as a poor man, you'll sleep comfortably." She turned back to the merchant.

Reuben grabbed her arm. "I have no money," he repeated.

Rahab pulled her arm away. "Neither do I."

"But I've given you a thousand drachmas if I've given you one."

Rahab held up a coin. "And here is the one," she said, handing the coin to the merchant and putting the walnuts in her bag. "Now I'm as destitute as you," she said, batting her golden eyelids and reaching into the bag. "Here. Have a walnut."

All day, Reuben went from friend's house to friend's house but was turned away each time. When word got out he was penniless, they even quit answering the doors. He returned to his house and sat on the steps. When the head servant returned, he found Reuben on the granite steps, holding his head in his hands, weeping. "Master Reuben, what is it?"

"I'm lost, Gershom. Lost."

"What have you lost, sir?"

Reuben looked up at the old man. "My money. All of it."

Gershom took a step back. "But you haven't paid us this month!"

Reuben shook his head, waving Gershom away.

"But we must be paid," insisted Gershom. Reuben wouldn't meet his eyes. After a long time the old man walked inside and shut the door. The bar was dropped with a loud *clang*, and Reuben shuddered. A few minutes later, a cloak wafted down from the upper story and landed beside him on the step. He looked up. Gershom's face appeared in the window above.

"The rest we will sell for our wages, sir," he said emphatically.

Reuben looked up. He picked up the fine blue linen cloak, dusting it off. "Is this all you're letting me take?"

"Well," snorted Gershom, "we are not barbarians!" The shutters slammed closed.

Reuben sat down on the embroidered pillow. He folded the cloak in his lap and stared across the square. A score of people had witnessed the event, and they stood stock-still, watching Reuben, an actor in a tragic play. He buried his head in his hands.

SEVENTEEN

Patience

Jeshua finally finished the slow work of cutting and planing the timbers. He laid them out across the sawhorses and was scribing them for the dadoes he would cut for the diagonal cross member so it would fit flush in the door. Dadoes of this sort were rarely used in Galilee; many considered them a fancy affectation, but Jeshua thought them a good idea, and he hoped Eli would agree. He wanted to build a beautiful, unique door for the old man.

Simeon was speaking with Eli at the dooryard gate. He'd been in the fields all day and was nearly the same color as the ground on which he stood. Eli was sitting on the stone wall, his head bowed, listening. Occasionally he would look up as Simeon pointed to the horizon, where their fields stretched. The crops were coming in full now, new green shoots of barley where just a few weeks ago there were only dark furrows in the dirt.

"We cannot wait any longer, Father," said Simeon loudly enough to make Jeshua turn. "Rachel and I have been patient. The crops are coming up and you have enough help. Please."

"Simeon," said Eli wearily, "now is not the time." He stood and moved slowly through the gateway. Simeon followed him.

"Father! When Reuben took his inheritance before his rightful time, I said nothing."

"That was wisdom. Be wise now," said Eli, stopping at the well, motioning for Arah to draw him water.

"But he took my inheritance!" pleaded Simeon, his hands splayed outward, his voice reedy and tight.

Eli drained the ladle and waved Arah away. He turned to Simeon. "He did nothing of the kind, Simeon. Your inheritance remains."

Simeon looked around, shaking his head. "You're spending it!" He shot Jeshua an angry look. Jeshua was facing the other direction and didn't see the look, but he knew who Simeon was talking about. "Rachel is nearing her time," stated Simeon flatly. "When does *our* life begin?"

Eli drew himself up to his full height. He was still taller than Simeon. "You would start a household at the very moment your wife is about to bear your first child? Foolishness. Besides, you are needed here. The lull after the planting lasts only a few weeks and then the work begins again in earnest. The weeding, watering, and thinning. The spring has been hot and summer will be like an oven. The crops that look promising now will wither and most will die. Without your help, our harvest will be lean, Simeon."

Simeon started to talk but Eli cut him off. "Don't argue with me. It's true, your brother's selfishness has cost our family dearly. It has been a hard season without his labor, and it will get worse. I have your best interests at heart—you and your family's. Your time will come, and when it does," he said, putting his hand on Simeon's shoulder, "you will receive all you deserve and more."

Simeon shook the old man's hand off and stalked toward the house, glaring at Jeshua as he passed. Eli watched Simeon go, shaking his head. "Patience, my son," he said quietly.

EIGHTEEN

A Shadow of a Doubt

Arah got up early and walked east to Reoboam's Hill, the highest promontory in the area. Before going, he'd filled all the water jars in the house and even those in the fields so he would not be missed for several hours. Jeshua said he would be late because he had business to attend to in Nazareth this morning.

That gave Arah the whole morning to attend to his own business. As he reached the summit, the sun was just peeking over the mountains, many leagues to the east. In their shadow, the Galilee Sea shone like a dark, wet stone. Arah sat down under a large sycamore tree, scanning the horizon. He'd never been out of Galilee, but he'd heard people say it was paradise compared to the rest of the world. He ached to see Jerusalem. Perhaps his prayers would be more effective if he offered them in the Temple. He could save and buy a pair of turtledoves and make a sacrifice. He would stand at the foot of the marble steps while the priest burned his offering in the bronze brazier, and he would pray, asking God about his father. Maybe God would hear a prayer offered in his own house, if he couldn't hear it out here in Galilee.

The rolling hills to the east were a lush green, dotted with forests and cut by roads, sloping down toward the Galilee Sea. A couple of years ago, Reuben had taken Arah and his friend Libni fishing on the lake. It was the biggest adventure of Arah's young life. They'd hired a boat and ventured out into the water. They had a small net, which they cast over the side. Reuben was an expert fisherman, and when he lofted the net into the air, for an instant it was a perfect circle hanging in the sky. Then it landed flatly on the water with a loud *smack* and sank quickly. Reuben yelled, "Pull!" and the three of them hauled the net in. Arah was astonished to see they had caught five silver fishes, but Reuben tossed them all back into the water.

"Too small," he laughed.

"You mean there are bigger fish out there?" asked Arah, looking furtively across the water.

Reuben stretched his arms out as far as they would go.

"I don't believe you," said Libni, frowning. "You're a liar."

Arah was surprised at Libni's bold statement, but Reuben just laughed. "You're right," he said. "I am a liar. But I'm not lying about this."

For the rest of the day Arah listened to Reuben, wondering which things he said were true and which were lies. Reuben was handsome, smart, and funny. But his frank admission that he was a liar troubled Arah throughout the rest of the trip. Arah had once lied to his mother about doing his chores, but when he'd been caught his father would not speak to him for a week. His father's absence in Arah's life was so painful that Arah had vowed to never lie again. But here was Reuben actually boasting about lying. The idea that someone could be proud about lying was simply beyond Arah. So since that day, Arah had been wary of Reuben, even though he couldn't help but like the young man, who was always full of fun and energy.

Arah closed his eyes, remembering the haul of fish they'd taken back to Master Eli's estate and what a feast they'd had—even the servants. And he remembered Reuben smiling at him, winking, as he picked his teeth with a fish bone. Arah was still confused, but months later, when Reuben left for Damascus, he found himself crying in the stable. He still thought about Reuben every day, wondering where he was and if he was all right. And wondering if he was still telling lies and getting away with it.

He closed his eyes. "Heavenly Father, how is Reuben? Can you see him from where you are?"

And, as Jeshua had counseled, he listened. In a nearby tree, a bird sang a short melodic phrase and the wind lifted Arah's hair off his forehead. He felt a shiver down his spine, but it was probably just the cool wind, not God's breath.

"I'm sorry to ask so many questions. Micah says I know too many. But if you'll just tell me about my father, I won't ask you any more."

Again he listened, feeling the sunshine on his face, remembering his father's sharp features and curly hair. Arah imagined his father with him in the little boat out on the Galilee Sea, watching as Arah threw the net far out into the water. His father nodded at him.

"What is it?" asked Arah, hauling the net in.

His father just smiled.

On the hillside, under the sycamore tree, Arah opened his eyes. He looked at the lake, now bright in the full sun. The hills beyond it rose dramatically, split by rocky outcrops and topped by groves of trees. You could probably see the entire Galilee from there. Maybe even the entire world.

"I'm trying to have faith," he said quietly, eyes not leaving the hills. "But it's hard."

The bird sang in the tree again. Arah stood and brushed off his tunic. He turned toward home and saw his shadow moving in front of him. He stretched his arms out like a bird, watching his shadow do the same. *Faith must be like my shadow*, he thought as he walked down the hill, his shadow slowly disappearing as he entered the hill's shadow. *Some days I have it, and some days I don't.*

NINETEEN

Mercy, the Robber

A week later, the door was near completion. The mahogany planks were sawed even, planed smooth, and joined together by top, bottom, and diagonal cross members dadoed into the red wood, flush with the planks. Jeshua had spent many hours sanding the wood to make it smooth. He had carefully drilled the holes for the new black iron lock, which was sturdy as well as beautiful. Tomorrow he would apply the finish with a fine horsehair brush he had bought from Azariah, a brush unlike any he had ever seen before, which came from distant Alexandria. Jeshua held the brush, feeling its balance, marveling at the smoothness of the bristles. Surely a brush like this would leave no trace of itself in the varnish. Eli would be pleased at such a luster.

He heard voices and turned to see Eli arriving on his fine black horse. Micah appeared and helped Eli down. Eli then watched as Micah led the horse to the stable. Jeshua reached back into the toolbox for the brush. He wanted to show it to Eli, who would certainly recognize its value. The old man stood by the gate, looking to the horizon.

Jeshua approached him, the brush in his hand. "Master Eli?" he said.

The old man didn't turn. "What is it, carpenter?" His voice was deep and sorrowful.

Jeshua immediately forgot about the brush. "What is it, Master?"

Eli sat on the wall. He still looked to the west, where the orange sun was perched on the horizon. He sighed heavily. "How is the door coming?" It was question without interest.

Jeshua asked, "Master Eli, what troubles you?"

The old man sighed and said, "My friend Azariah has sent a message. He is far to the north and was in Damascus, where he again saw my Reuben." The old man's head wagged from side to side to dispel the unpleasant thought. "My Reuben," he repeated.

Jeshua put his hand on the old man's shoulder, but if Eli felt it, he gave no indication. Eli continued, "He has lost all his money and his friends. Reduced to poverty, he is gleaning the fields for husks they feed to swine. My boy—eating what the swine eat!" He looked heavenward. Jeshua expected to see tears in the old man's eyes, but they were dry.

"Perhaps you should go to him," suggested Jeshua.

Eli ground his teeth. Jeshua almost moved away from the old man, whose fierce temper he had seen before, but he kept his hand lightly on Eli's arm, waiting.

Finally Eli said, "I cannot go to him." He glanced at Jeshua for a moment, then away. "Simeon is right. Reuben is no longer my son. He must be cut off. So says the Law."

"But mercy—"

"Mercy cannot rob justice," said Eli, pulling away.

"Yet you love him."

"Yes," sighed Eli. "I do."

Both men sat quietly, Eli pondering the sunset and Jeshua looking at the brush in his hand. Finally, Jeshua drew a breath. The old man stiffened, prepared for an argument.

"Master Eli?" asked Jeshua. After a long moment passed and Eli didn't respond, he stood. "Nothing," he said, and started to go.

Eli's large gray head turned toward him. His jaw was set, but his eyes were pleading. "What is it, Jeshua?"

Jeshua stopped, his back to Eli. "It can wait."

Eli shook his head. "You were going to say something, young man. Say what's on your mind," he said plaintively.

Jeshua turned and faced Eli. "I have a question."

"Go ahead," said Eli, his eyes fixed on Jeshua hopefully.

"All right," said Jeshua, taking a deep breath. "I was wondering if you'd given any thought to the hinges." Eli furrowed his brow, but Jeshua continued. "Leather hinges won't support the weight of the new door. The hinges must be strong, so they should be made of iron, which can be oiled so they open easily. Above all, the door must open freely, don't you agree?"

Eli stared up at the carpenter and blinked.

"New hinges," coaxed Jeshua. "So the door opens freely . . . "

"New hinges."

"There comes a time," said Jeshua quietly, "when we must put away old things and embrace new ones."

"So I have heard," said Eli, shaking his head at his own foolishness. He should have known better than to think an uneducated carpenter would know a way out of his dilemma. He nodded and patted Jeshua's arm. "Whatever you wish, carpenter." Then he turned back toward the horizon and awaited the sunset.

TWENTY

The Welcoming Door

"Hold it steady, Arah," said Jeshua. "I've almost got it."

Arah struggled, pushing the door upward with all his might. Jeshua looked at the boy and smiled. "You don't have to hold it up, Arah, just hold it steady. We're almost there."

"But it's heavy," grunted Arah.

"And you're strong," said Jeshua around the pin he held between his teeth. "Now, just a little higher . . . higher . . . and . . ." He placed the pin in the slot and drove it home with a blow of the hammer. "There," he said, jumping off the footstool, grabbing Arah around the waist, pulling him deeper into the room so they could get a better view. "It's done."

The door hung motionless for a moment, then slowly began to close. "Look," said Arah. "It closes by itself." He beamed up at Jeshua.

"That's because the top hinge is set slightly toward the outside."

"Listen. It doesn't make a sound!" said the dark-haired boy in awe.

"That reminds me." Jeshua bent on one knee before the boy. "I have a task for you."

"Anything!" said Arah.

Jeshua shook his head, barely concealing a smile. "It's nothing grand, but it is important. Very important."

"What is it?" asked the boy, remembering the sweets the carpenter occasionally gave him.

Jeshua produced a small clay jar from his apron. It had a cork stopper in the top. He gave it to Arah. "This is oil for the hinges."

The boy's countenance fell. Jeshua wagged a finger at him. "You said 'anything,' didn't you?"

Arah nodded.

Jeshua looked up at the hinge. "The hinges and the lock are made of iron, and they are very expensive." He toggled the lock handle up and down. It moved smoothly and silently. "But to remain strong, they must be cleaned and oiled regularly. The first of every month."

The boy was looking at the vial of oil, his brow furrowed. "Every month," he repeated, committing it to memory.

Jeshua smiled at the boy's concentration. "Without fail. The door you and I built depends upon it." He took another step back, examining their work. The door, fully closed, fit snugly into the frame, not a bit of sunlight peeking through on any side.

Arah smiled. "We built a fine door, didn't we, Jeshua?"

Jeshua nodded. "Now, let's oil the hinges together. Next month, you will do it by yourself." He lifted Arah up, and the boy carefully unstopped the clay vial and deposited a few drops of oil on the door pin. Jeshua set him down and reached for the handle. "After you oil it, open the door a few times to work the oil in." He opened the door.

Eli and Simeon were standing on the stoop. Their faces showed surprise as the door opened. Eli nudged Simeon. "What did I tell you? It opens inward!"

Simeon looked doubtful as he stepped inside. Eli followed him as Simeon continued his inspection. Jeshua shut the door and stood aside as the two men considered his work.

"It opens inward," repeated Simeon, still perplexed. "A very strange idea."

Eli nodded at Jeshua, who said, "It opens inward to welcome friends and family—an invitation to share the comfort and hospitality of a fine home."

Eli ran his hands over the door. "I have never felt such a smooth finish," he said. "That brush you bought from Azariah really is amazing. This finish is flawless."

Jeshua winked at Arah, who grinned back.

"It ought to be," said Simeon, irritated. "It took him long enough. I thought he was building a ship out there."

"The finish protects the wood," said Jeshua, "against the elements."

They admired the door's deep red color. The planks and cross members fit snugly together. Eli ran his hands over the joints. "I can barely feel the seams."

"To last a long time, a door must be heavy," said Jeshua. "And because of its weight, it needs strong, yet flexible, hinges. And the lock must be secure, now that the door opens inward."

Eli looked at Jeshua and shook his head. "Why, carpenter, that's more than you've said the entire time you've been here."

Jeshua smiled. Eli clapped him on the back. "It's good to see a man take pride in his work. And even better to see that his pride is well placed."

"And what's this?" queried Simeon, pointing to a small rectangle in the door at eye height, a thin piece of mahogany that slid upward in two wooden tracks. "A window of some sort?"

Jeshua nodded. "Yes. A window." He grasped the small knob on the tiny shutter and raised it, letting in a narrow shaft of sunlight, which fell directly on Eli's chest.

Eli placed his hand on his chest, where the light fell. "It warms my heart, carpenter, to see such work," he said, unable to take his eyes off the small circle of light on his chest. When he looked up, there was brightness in his eyes as well, and he shook his finger good-naturedly at Jeshua, smiling. "You are quite a surprise, young man." He pulled out a coin pouch and withdrew several coins, giving them to Jeshua. "You have earned this."

Jeshua nodded his thanks, then turned to the door. "Arah can tell you about the hinges."

The men turned and the boy gulped, surprised and shy. "Go ahead," said Jeshua. "Tell Master Eli about the hinges."

Arah held up the clay vial and said, "Iron hinges are strong, but they must be oiled. The first of every month." He looked at the ground, embarrassed.

Eli bent down before the boy. "And you have been given this important task?"

Arah nodded.

Eli nodded. "So be it. Do not fail in your duties, Arah. We are depending upon you."

The boy looked up, surprised to be the center of attention. "Yes, sir," he said, nodding furiously. "Yes, sir!"

"All right," said Simeon, unmoved by the boy's enthusiasm. "Let's see these amazing hinges everyone keeps talking about." He grasped the handle, which slipped easily from the catches, and pulled on the heavy door, which opened without a sound. Simeon bent toward the lock, intrigued. "This is a unique mechanism, Jeshua—"

"Master of the Universe!" exclaimed Eli, clutching at Simeon's shoulder.

Simeon looked up, then followed Eli's gaze out the door. He straightened and squinted into the bright day.

Far down the dusty road trudged a lonely figure. His head hung down, and he was dressed in rags. Eli took one step and grasped the doorjamb, holding his breath. In an instant, Arah was out the door, running toward the traveler. "Reuben!" he yelled.

Hannah, who was drawing water, looked up as the boy rushed by, causing her to drop her water jar, which shattered into pieces. But her surprise turned to joy when she looked toward the road. She grabbed her long skirt around her and ran toward the servants' quarters, shouting, "Master Reuben has returned! He's returned!"

Eli leaned against the doorjamb, afraid to move for fear Reuben would disappear. Simeon squeezed by him and stepped out into the dooryard. A number of servants straightened from their weeding, hearing Arah's yells. Micah got off his knees and began hobbling toward Reuben. Shouts of recognition carried toward the house.

Eli turned to Jeshua, a question in eyes bright with tears.

"There is no justice, there is no mercy," said Jeshua quietly. "There is only love."

Eli grasped Jeshua with both hands. "Jeshua bar Joseph," he said, tears splashing off his cheeks and onto his tunic, "now I see what you have really been building here. Thank you."

Jeshua smiled. "Go to him."

Eli nodded and stepped into the dooryard. Jeshua had never seen the old man move so quickly. He strode by Simeon, clapping him on the shoulder as he passed. Eli made the distance to the low stone wall and easily jumped right over it.

Reuben, surrounded by servants, saw Eli coming. He broke free and ran. "Father!" he shouted. They met in the middle of the road, embracing and exchanging kisses. Eli shouted, "Reuben! Reuben! My son! My son!" over and over. In an instant they were again in the midst of a crowd. From both sides of the house, more people ran toward the joyful reunion.

Only Simeon stood his ground, his hands on his hips as if he were made of stone. Jeshua walked over to him. Simeon glanced at him out of the corner of his eye. His lips were set in a straight line, and his eyes squinted into the bright sun.

"Someday you too may be lost and hoping to be found," said Jeshua gently.

"Never," spat Simeon. "I would never disrespect Father like he did." He scowled at the knot of people on the road, several of whom were dancing with joy. Eli, the tallest of all, turned toward the house and beckoned Simeon to join them. Simeon turned away, disgusted.

"Simeon, are you a righteous man?" asked Jeshua, a smile on his lips, remembering their exchange that morning so long ago.

Simeon shot Jeshua a hard look. He, too, remembered, and he quoted Jeshua: "The Lord will decide if I am."

"Well, I believe you are, Simeon."

"How would you know?"

"A righteous man respects his father."

Simeon crossed his arms across his chest. "So?"

In the distance, Eli still beckoned Simeon, who looked down and moved a foot, stirring dust.

"You have always respected your father. And you will respect him now," said Jeshua.

Simeon looked up at the reunion. By now there were twenty people in the road, but Eli's head towered above them all. While everyone moved buoyantly, Eli remained still, one arm around Reuben, but his face turned toward Simeon, his eyes hopeful. His other hand remained aloft.

Simeon drew a breath, steeling himself. "For my father, then," he said, and started toward the road.

Eli's hand jumped up another six inches. "My son!" Eli exclaimed. "Simeon! My son!"

As Simeon walked slowly toward across the dooryard toward the road, Jeshua whispered, "It is a beginning."

He turned back to the house. The new mahogany door hung majestically on its sturdy black hinges. He took the handle and pulled the door toward him. It closed with a satisfying thud. He took off his apron, picked up his toolbox, and started toward the gate.

From behind him he heard a soft mewl and turned to see the little tan calf in its pen. He walked over to it, withdrawing a sweet from his pocket and holding it out. The calf came forward gingerly, took the sweet, and munched it with relish.

"Some reunions are good-byes," said Jeshua, scratching the calf behind the ear.

Then Jeshua bar Joseph led his donkey through the gate in the low stone wall surrounding Eli's grand house and stepped into the road, turning west toward the Nazareth hills and home.

THE CARPENTER TEACHES

A few years later, Jeshua was conversing with a number of tax collectors and sinners, and his followers were dismayed that he would associate with such wicked people. But Jeshua, knowing the thoughts of their hearts, looked about at the people and opened his mouth.

And he said, "A certain man had two sons. And the younger son said, 'Father, give me my inheritance.' And his father did so. And shortly after, the younger son took his journey into a far country and there wasted his inheritance with riotous living. And when he had spent all of his money, there arose a mighty famine. And because he had no more money, he hired himself out to feed swine in the fields of a rich man. And because no one would feed him, he ate the husks that the swine ate.

"And when he came to himself, he thought, *Even my father's servants have more than enough bread to eat, and yet I perish with hunger! I will go to my father and I will say, Father, I have sinned against both heaven and you. I am not worthy to be called your son; instead, make me one of your hired servants.*

"And he arose and came to his father. But when he was still a great way off, his father saw him and had compassion, and ran and took him in his arms and kissed him. And the son said, 'Father, I have sinned and I am no more worthy to be called your son.'

"But the father shook his head and said to his servants, 'Bring the best robe and put it on him. Put a ring on his hand and shoes on his feet. Kill our fattest calf, and we will eat and celebrate! For my son was dead and is alive again; he was lost and is found.' And they began to prepare for the feast to celebrate the arrival.

"Now, during this reunion, the elder son was working in the fields, and when he came back to the house at the end of the day, he heard music and dancing. He asked one of the servants what these things meant, and the servant said to him, 'Your brother has come home, and your father has ordered a feast because he has returned safe and sound.'

"Now the older son was angry and would not go inside and join the feast. One of the servants told the father, and he came out and asked the son to join them. And the older son said, 'For many years I have served you, and I have never disobeyed any of your commands. Yet you never gave me a feast that I might make merry with my friends. But as soon as your younger son returns—the son who spent your money on harlots—you make this great feast for him!'

"And his father said to him, 'Son, you are always with me. All that I have is yours. But it is right that we should celebrate and be glad, for your brother was dead and is alive again; he was lost, and now is found.'"

Part Two

—∿—

LIVING
WATERS

ONE

Two Brothers

"It is going to be hot," James said, scanning the morning sky. "Too hot for digging."

Jeshua looked to the east, where the sun perched on the rolling hills. James was right; there would be no clouds to shield them from the heat today. "But not too hot for swimming, I'll bet," he said, patting his donkey on the haunches. "And if we dig deep enough, there will be plenty of water for that."

Jeshua looked at his little brother, who was just turning thirteen. He was tall for his age, with dark eyes and hair, a good-looking young man. And he would soon be taller than Jeshua. Today was James's first time working away from his father, and he was eager to prove himself. He had spent an hour last night organizing and reorganizing his tools for today's job.

When Jeshua and Joseph had walked out the door to discuss the coming week's work, James had made a grand display of putting on his canvas apron and standing, arms folded, considering his tool collection. He didn't acknowledge his father and brother standing behind him in the doorway, but Joseph smiled at Jeshua and nodded toward James. "Don't wear him out," he said as he went back inside.

James wheeled around, fire in his eyes. He pointed at Jeshua and said, loud enough for Joseph to hear, "He won't wear me out, I'll wear him out!" From inside the house he heard his sisters laughing and Mary shushing them.

Jeshua walked over to the tools strewn on the ground. "You have everything you need?"

James nodded. "It's only a well, so we just need the digging and stonecutting tools, right?" He looked up at Jeshua so sincerely that Jeshua couldn't suppress a smile.

"True. But we'll be building a well surround, too, so bring the carpentry tools. We'll be gone at least two weeks."

He turned to go inside, but James stopped him. "Jeshua?"

Jeshua turned.

James slowly took off his apron, his face now lowered in thought. "I was wondering . . . "

Jeshua waited. Finally, the boy looked up and, seeing Jeshua's sincere concern, broke into a grin. "I was wondering how much I'll be paid. I'm almost a man, you know."

Jeshua smiled. "Then you'll receive almost a man's wages."

"And how much is that?" James started placing the tools into his wooden box.

Jeshua picked up a maul and handed it to James. "Less than you want, more than you're worth."

James looked up sharply. "I'll show you what I'm worth!" he shouted, tackling Jeshua, throwing him to the ground. Jeshua pushed the boy off easily and got up. James attacked again, and soon they were rolling in the dooryard, covered with dust, laughing.

"Jeshua! James!"

There, in the lighted doorway, stood Mary, drying her hands on a towel, glaring at them. "If you two have so much energy this late, perhaps you'd like to go to the well and draw the water for tomorrow."

Jeshua jumped up, embarrassed. James stood up, joyously defiant. He made a mock swing at Jeshua, who sidestepped it easily, holding the boy off with one arm. "I mean it. Now!" said Mary sternly.

They started off toward the well. Jeshua looked over his shoulder to see Joseph appear in the doorway and put his arm around Mary. Joseph said, "This will give you two journeymen one last chance to examine a real well before you dig your first one."

James nudged Jeshua in the ribs. "Hear that? We're both journeymen. Ha!" He scooped up the clay water jar and dashed off into the darkness. "And journeymen get full shares!"

Jeshua smiled, picked up the other jar, and followed James into the darkness.

One Orchard

Jacob's immense orchard spread out before them, occupying almost the entire shallow valley. In the clearing below, a giant granite house sat, shadowed by tall trees. Servants were busy with chores. James let out a whistle. "He's rich, isn't he?"

Jeshua led his donkey down the path, which curved between ancient olive trees. "Jacob inherited the land from his father, Eleazar. His family has worked here for more than a hundred years. Look." He pointed at the house. A short, thin man appeared, scanning the horizon. He saw them and waved.

"Is that him?" asked James.

"No, that's his overseer, Esau."

"Is he the one who hired us?"

"He is," said Jeshua. "We've never met, but Father worked for him once. So now you know why we must do a good job here."

James rolled his eyes. "I know. To make Father proud."

Jeshua looked at his brother. "No. Because he expects us to do the same quality work as Father does. He trusts us because he trusts Father. The person we need to please is Esau."

"But it will also please Father if we do it right," said James.

"I'm sure that's true," said Jeshua.

Several workers passed them, carrying clay jars of water up the hill. The path wound down through the trees. Jacob's orchard was varied. There were orange, lemon, and other citrus trees, along with a vineyard of considerable size, the low-slung vines resting on wooden T supports. Summer was full, and the tree boughs were heavy with fruit, though not as heavy as should be expected. Many trees were shriveled and brown. Obviously Esau had to choose which trees to water, as he didn't have enough for all of them.

"Jeshua bar Joseph! Peace be unto you!" came a high, piping voice. As they rounded a large tree, Esau was striding toward them, hands held out, a broad smile on his face. Before Jeshua could speak, the little man reached up and kissed him on both cheeks, then released him and clapped his hands. "And you must be James," he said, pulling James off the donkey and hugging him fiercely. James looked at Jeshua with surprise.

"And unto you, peace, Esau," said Jeshua. "This is James. Forgive him, for he is slow of speech."

Esau considered James, who was indeed dumbstruck. "Is he . . . ?" Esau pointed to his head and nodded sadly at James.

Jeshua smiled. "Yes. I'm afraid he is—"

"I am not!" barked James, finding his voice. "My tongue—and my head—are just fine, thank you." He bowed before Esau, but his face was still red. When he straightened, he looked daggers at Jeshua.

"He has these fits . . ." said Jeshua, winking at Esau.

"I do not!" scowled James, taking a step toward him.

"You see?" said Jeshua, shaking his head sadly.

Esau smiled at Jeshua and then at James. "Yes, indeed. I do see."

"See what?" asked James angrily.

Esau put one hand on Jeshua's arm and the other on James's shoulder. "I see you two are brothers. Come!"

"Here it is," said Esau, pointing at the well. They looked into the rough-hewn hole. Esau tossed the goatskin bladder into the darkness.

They heard it hit the ground far below with a loud, muddy *plop.* Esau grimaced. "Dry as Idumea."

"I see," said Jeshua. "But it served a long time, didn't it?"

"Yes. It was dug by Master Jacob's grandfather. All these trees were watered by it," he said, gesturing around proudly. "Including all these little trees." He pointed at a bunch of children who were playing just outside the house's main door. "The master's children."

"Have you found a new water source?" asked Jeshua.

Esau started walking, heading into the grove. "Yes. We noticed a certain section was doing well, even though we hadn't watered it in several weeks."

By now they were deep inside the orchard, where the trees were planted in evenly spaced rows about five meters apart. Esau was right. All around, the trees were brown and shriveled. But here were a dozen or so still hanging on, still a pale, fading green.

"We did a dowsing," said Esau. "The dowser believes there's water here." They were standing in a small clearing.

"That's obvious," muttered James.

Jeshua gestured at James to be quiet and turned to Esau. "The valley drains through this area. In fact, you can see where a spring is shallow enough to water the trees. Look."

He pointed down the valley and traced a crooked line of trees with his finger. Esau's face brightened. "Ahh! I never noticed it before. The healthy trees *do* form a line of sorts. All I was seeing were the dying trees." He smiled. "I think I have hired the right man for this job."

Jeshua turned his head slightly toward James, still looking at the small man. Esau nodded, comprehending. "Ahh! The right *men*," he said, nodding at James, who brightened. Esau passed Jeshua and held out his hand to James. "James bar Joseph, I am proud to have you working for me. I know you will find water for us."

"I'll try," said James, taken aback.

"Good. That is all we can ask," said Esau. "Best of luck, gentlemen."

James watched him go. "He's awfully large for such a small man," he said thoughtfully.

Jeshua smiled. "Now, Master Carpenter James bar Joseph, what do you think we should do?"

James hitched up his leather belt and squinted into the sun. "I say we get to work."

Three Servants

Ishmael looked around the darkened room, a scowl on his face. Before him stood Hanock, the chief servant; Zerah, Hanock's assistant; and Naaman, the stable master. They all quavered as he glared at them, their eyes downcast and shoulders hunched. Ishmael reconsidered his journey. Was it wise to leave his household in their charge?

"Hanock!"

Hanock dropped to his knees before his master. "Yes, sire, what is thy bidding?"

"Oh, stop it. Grovel on your own time. Get off your knees, straighten your spine, and look me in the eye."

Hanock gave his assistant, Zerah, a look of anguish, then stood, meeting Ishmael's angry visage. He tried hard to stand tall. It wasn't easy, for though Hanock was the tallest of the three servants, Ishmael stood a full head above even him.

For a long moment Ishmael considered Hanock, his mouth a straight line, his brow furrowed. Then, with a flourish, he reached into a chest held by another servant—*what was this one's name? Oh, never mind, they're all useless anyway*—and withdrew five large silver coins, each as big around as a man's palm, and held them aloft before Hanock's startled face.

From his kneeling position, Zerah saw the coins and his mouth dropped open. He stole a look at Naaman, whose nose was still pressed to the tile. Zerah nudged him, and Naaman looked up to see the shiny coins held just inches in front of Hanock's nose.

"You know what these are, don't you?" asked Ishmael.

"Yes, sire," answered Hanock, wondering if this was some sort of test. He had to force himself not to move. Ishmael's breath was hot on his face, his eyes hard.

"As you know, I am leaving for Jerusalem. I will be gone several weeks. I have never left my household for such a long time before. I am very concerned about its care in my absence."

"Yes, sire," answered Hanock, wishing he could say something more. "I understand."

"Do you?" asked Ishmael, scowling. "Hold out your hand."

Hanock noticed Ishmael's left hand, which always held his crop, a long, stiff willow branch wrapped tightly with leather strips. It was tapping a slow rhythm against Ishmael's leg, as it always did before it lashed out at a servant who was too slow to move. Hanock extended his hand, certain he had failed whatever test Ishmael was administering, and steeled himself for the sudden, painful *whack!* across the palm that always signified the beginning of punishment in Master Ishmael's household.

But Ishmael simply placed five silver talents in Hanock's hand. Hanock looked up, dumbfounded.

"Surprised?" asked Ishmael slyly.

"Yes, sire."

"I have given this great thought. These are for you, Hanock, as chief steward. Since I am a businessman, a very successful businessman"— and with this he gestured around at the two-storied room, rich with tapestries and rugs and floored with fine mosaic tile from Greece—"I am always looking for a way to increase my holdings, as well as to teach others of the value of money. Therefore, I give you these five silver talents, and with them a charge."

"What is that, sire?" stuttered Hanock.

"The charge is this: while I am gone, I expect you to multiply this money."

"How, sire?"

"In whatever way you wish. They represent the five years you have been chief steward. You have served me well during that time."

Hanock brightened. He had never received a direct compliment from the master before. He stared at the coins, enraptured with their brilliance.

Suddenly, Ishmael's crop whacked Hanock's forearm. "Are you listening, Hanock?"

"Yes, sire," said Hanock, wincing.

"I was saying that as a reward for your service, I am giving you an opportunity: to use this money wisely in my absence, and upon my return you and I will reckon together and you will be rewarded accordingly. Understood?"

"A reward?" asked Hanock, stuck on the important part.

"Yes. But remember, there are rewards and then there are punishments. I am trusting you with my goods. And you know how interested I am in my goods."

Hanock stared at the coins, which were heavy in his palm. He'd never held so much money before. It was making him lightheaded.

"Well?" boomed Ishmael.

"Yes, sire."

"Excellent. I can tell you have the right attitude about this." He turned to Zerah and barked, "Zerah! Get up, for goodness' sakes!"

Zerah scrambled to his feet but kept his eyes on the floor. Ishmael loomed over him. Zerah rarely talked to the master, as most of his orders came through Hanock.

"You heard what I said to Hanock?"

"Yes, I did, Master Ishmael. Your generosity is legendary."

Hanock stole a jealous look at Zerah, whose tongue never ceased wagging. Ishmael grunted, reached into the chest, and removed two talents. He held them in front of Zerah's face. "These represent the two years you have worked as assistant steward." He placed them in Zerah's hand. "The same goes for you: your charge is to multiply these. You will be rewarded accordingly. Do you understand?"

Zerah grasped the two coins tightly in his fist. He looked up at Ishmael and nodded fiercely. "Yes, sire," he said.

Ishmael moved to Naaman, who was still bent on the ground. Zerah nudged him and Naaman looked up. Ishmael crooked his finger, silently commanding him to stand. Naaman stood, trembling, lips quivering. Ishmael leaned forward. "I forget your name. What is it?"

Naaman opened his mouth, but nothing came out. Zerah elbowed him, but his tongue would not work. Ishmael gave Zerah a withering look and Zerah stepped back. The crop beat rhythmically against Ishmael's leg, its cadence speeding. Ishmael stared at Naaman, who looked up at him with bulging eyes, mouth working but no sounds emerging.

"His name is Naaman, Master," said Hanock gingerly.

"Hmm. Naaman," said Ishmael. Naaman nodded vigorously. "You *can* speak?"

Naaman nodded furiously.

"Just not right now?"

Naaman shook his head furiously.

Ishmael laughed. He looked at Hanock and Zerah and said, "I prefer no words at all to dull or flattering speech." Then he focused on Naaman. "But your ears work, don't they?"

Naaman nodded.

Ishmael produced a single silver talent and held it out to him. "You have been stable master for one year. My horses are shod, well fed, and groomed. The tack is in repair."

Naaman beamed.

"I charge you as I have the others. Take this, invest it wisely, and I will return for an accounting. Do you understand?"

Naaman nodded. Ishmael handed him the coin. Naaman thought he would faint. He had never held a whole talent before. He wanted to say something, but his mouth was still disconnected from his brain. He simply smiled up at Ishmael, who frowned back.

Then Ishmael boomed, "Make haste! I am leaving!"

He strode out of the house, followed by the three and a dozen lesser household servants. In the courtyard, his black Arabian pranced proudly, draped in its purple coverlet with the braided gold reins. A caravan of twenty horses and mules waited behind. The servants assembled themselves in two neat rows, prepared for his review.

Ishmael mounted the horse and looked at the huge expanse of his property: the large house, the verdant vineyards, the pastures full of fat sheep and cattle, and the prosperous groves of citrus, fig, and date trees. Then he focused on Hanock, Zerah, and Naaman and pointed his crop at each of them in turn. "Remember," he said simply.

As one, each of the three gulped and nodded.

Ishmael spurred his horse and was gone.

FOUR

Two Destinies

James and Jeshua spent an hour walking around the orchard. James couldn't understand why they didn't just start digging. But Jeshua wouldn't even answer questions. He walked in ever-increasing circles, eyes on the ground, pausing occasionally to examine a wilting leaf. It was frustrating for James, who wanted to learn, but Jeshua wasn't teaching. He was just standing there, looking thoughtfully at a palm full of dirt. James was about to say something when Jeshua cast the dirt skyward and the hot wind lifted it away. He turned to James.

"I know the place," he said, clapping James on the shoulder. But then he walked right past the dowser's stake and went thirty steps farther into the trees. "This is it."

James followed his brother. "Didn't the dowser say it was over there?" he asked, pointing at the clearing behind them.

"The water isn't there."

"How do you know?"

Jeshua put his hand on the trunk of an orange tree, feeling the smoothness of its bark. "Can't explain how. I just believe there will be water here."

"But how can you be sure?"

Jeshua looked at him. "A better question is: why don't you trust me?"

James looked at his brother. There was something special about Jeshua, but whatever it was, it wasn't on the outside. There was talk among his older siblings that Jeshua had a marvelous destiny, but James couldn't help but feel that he, too, had important things to accomplish.

"What kind of destiny do you think I have?" James had asked Jeshua one day, months ago.

"Nothing like you imagine," answered Jeshua, who then cut off other questions by placing his finger to his lips.

The answer upset him because he had a very good imagination, and not always for good things. He dreamed of bloody battles and ways he might die. But he never told anyone about his dreams. Only Jeshua seemed to know when he was pondering a particularly chilling image that remained with him into the daylight hours. At such times, he would sneak up on James and steal his head kerchief or grab him around the waist and toss him high in the air until he laughed, in spite of the dread the dream had wrapped him in. Jeshua even threw him into a cold stream one day, for no apparent reason. When James came up sputtering, Jeshua laughed and danced on the shore, which made James so angry he forgot all about the bad dream that had plagued him all morning.

It suddenly occurred to James that maybe Jeshua had known about his nightmare and how much it had scared him. He looked up at Jeshua, wondering if Jeshua knew about finding water the way he knew about James's bad dreams.

"I trust you," said James.

Jeshua squeezed James's shoulder. "That means a lot, James. Let's get to work, then."

They corralled their donkeys and unloaded the tools. Jeshua handed James a spade, and both began digging. Before long they were soaked with sweat. The ground was hard from the drought, and there were roots from the trees that had to be cut away.

"Good thing I remembered to bring my woodcutting tools," said James, arming sweat away as he sawed through a thick black root.

Jeshua nodded, tossing a shovelful of dirt aside. "Yes, we are fortunate to have both your brains and your brawn. I had only counted on one of them."

James put the saw down and proudly flexed his muscles. Jeshua recoiled in mock amazement, then took a long swallow of water from the goatskin bladder.

James stripped off his shirt, exposing his skinny chest. He crowed, "I am the Great Well Digger! I divide asunder roots and branches! Watch me tunnel through rock and stone! Stand back and be amazed!" He held his arms high.

Jeshua tipped the water bladder over his brother's head. James shuddered at the sudden cold, wheeled around, and scrambled out of the hole. Jeshua cowered. "I am so sorry, O Great Well-Digger. I thought you must be thirsty, with all that boasting."

James grabbed the bladder, which was still half full. Water sloshed over the lip as he moved closer to Jeshua, who backed away. "Are you thirsty, too?" He drew the waterskin back, preparing to hurl its contents on Jeshua.

"Don't waste my water!"

They turned to see Esau making his way between the trees. James set the bladder down and turned back to the hole, grabbing his tunic and pulling it over his head. Esau looked around, first at the hole, then at the clearing where the dowser's stake was.

"Why are you digging here?" asked Esau. "And not over there?"

Jeshua picked up his spade and said quietly, "I felt it was a better place, Master Esau."

"Why didn't you consult with me before digging?"

"I'm sorry."

"You said you hired the right men," said James, and both Esau and Jeshua turned to him. Esau's face went red with anger, and James immediately regretted the comment. Jeshua's eyes told James to be quiet. "Sorry," said James.

"I should hope so!" stormed Esau, walking to the excavation. "But sorry won't cover the time lost if you're wrong." He wheeled on Jeshua. "You're sure about this?"

Jeshua nodded. "We want to find water as badly as you do."

"I doubt that," said Esau, his eyes wandering over to the dowser's stake.

"If we are wrong, we will dig until we find water."

Esau frowned. "Yes. Of *that* there is no doubt, young man. But we need water now, and there is no time for antics and horseplay."

Jeshua nodded and stepped back into the hole, which was only three feet deep, even after a long morning of digging. He set to work, leaving Esau to stare at his back, then at James, who was looking up at Esau, his spade held limply in his hand.

"Well?" barked Esau.

James jumped in the hole and went to work.

FIVE

Multiplication Tables

The rocky hill overlooked Sepphoris. They admired the city's glistening beauty in the morning light. Hanock turned to Zerah. "The rebuilding is going well, isn't it?"

"Yes, it is," agreed Zerah. "Much has been done, and quickly."

Naaman sat on his horse behind the other two. His eyes scanned the city. Sepphoris was indeed impressive, the seat of Rome's Galilee government. But he had never been here before and wouldn't know if the scaffolding and number of workmen were unusual or not.

Zerah patted his horse's withers and smiled. "Today's the day. We will make the old man proud."

Hanock nodded. "I know just the place where we can parlay our riches. A certain man I know, a scribe of sorts, knows how to make money." He pointed. "That is his house over there, beyond the tall stand of cypress trees."

"It didn't burn down, I see," said Zerah.

"No," replied Hanock. "He foresaw a fire someday and prepared long before by building a large cistern under the house. There was ample water to fight the fire when the rest of the city was cooking like fried meat."

Naaman ventured a question. "How much of the town burned down?"

Zerah spoke. "Everything built of wood. The granite and marble structures survived, including the governor's home."

"It is a big place," admitted Naaman.

"Just stick with us," said Hanock, spurring his horse. "We'll watch out for you." Zerah gave Naaman a condescending smile and followed Hanock down the wide, rutted path toward the town. Naaman reached into his tunic and felt the coin in the pouch he wore around his neck. A whole talent! And the chance to turn it into more. But how would they do that? His knowledge of money was limited. He knew a great deal about barter, but that was trading one object for another. Hanock's talk of lending the coins to a usurer, who would in turn lend them to others, who would pay him for the loan, seemed too complex. Where would the money come from to pay the "interest" they were talking about? He felt a rising fear in his stomach and wondered if Hanock and Zerah were as worldly as they claimed. Both of them held onto the talents they were given like they, too, had never touched money before. Something just wasn't right.

"Naaman! Laggard!" Naaman looked up. Zerah was waving him forward, and he could see Hanock shaking his head. Then he heard them laugh. The bad feeling got stronger. Nothing good would come of this. Lambs in a lion's den. He would have to be careful with the silver coin Ishmael had given him. Unlike the others, he couldn't afford to lose his money.

He waved back at Zerah. "Coming!"

The streets of Sepphoris were narrow, the houses jumbled close together. He could see remnants of the fire of three years ago. Much had been rebuilt in that time, but many people were living in what looked like burned-down houses. Dirty-faced children ran alongside his horse, begging for alms, but he ignored them. Ahead, Hanock and Zerah rode silently, surveying the people as if they were rich merchants like their master. Naaman noticed Hanock's imperious frown and adopted a similar one. It felt better, looking down his nose at the beggars, who reached for the brocaded edges of the saddle blanket. He goaded his horse to avoid their filthy touch.

They emerged in the main square. Ahead of them, atop twenty broad stone steps, rose the fluted marble columns of the governor's palace. Word had it that he was in Tyre, on the sea, and his brother-in-law handled the day-to-day business of the territory. Besides, it was well known that the Romans had no fondness for Jews. They tolerated their religion but considered the One God to be about ten too few. The Romans, like the Greeks, worshiped a whole family of deities, powerful beings who behaved like spoiled children, plotting and scheming behind each other's backs. Naaman wasn't sure he believed in any god, especially the Roman gods. But maybe it was just because they were Roman gods. You had to respect the Romans, though. They ruled the world, and how could they do that unless their gods were powerful?

Hanock threaded his horse between the marketplace stalls. Zerah followed, but Naaman stopped. He was surrounded by vendors shoving clay pots and trinkets and bolts of cloth in his face, trying to engage him in a barter. His hand went instinctively to his pouch. For a long second, Naaman couldn't feel the coin and his heart jumped, but then he got it between his thumb and forefinger and heaved a sigh of relief. He snapped the reins, and the horse nearly trampled an old woman holding up a prayer shawl. He caught up with Hanock and Zerah.

"Are you having trouble with your mount, stableboy?" Hanock laughed.

Naaman never talked back to Hanock, whose rebukes were consistently nasty. He just shook his head and looked at the ground. Hanock dismounted and handed Naaman his reins. Zerah did the same. It seemed when his two masters were together, Zerah became a copy of Hanock. Naaman had learned to lower his eyes at such times and take his rebuke. Afterward, he wouldn't feel better until he had whipped one of the stableboys for some infraction, it didn't matter which one or for what. Only then would his own humiliation subside and he could once again look Zerah and Hanock in the eye.

"The money dealers are inside," said Hanock, gesturing at the broad palace steps.

"You've dealt with them before?" Zerah asked tentatively.

"Of course," said Hanock, but Naaman knew Hanock had never dealt with these men with his own money. This was a far cry from being sent on an errand for Master Ishmael. The money men knew not to abuse Ishmael, but would they hesitate to take advantage of a mere servant? Of that Naaman was not so sure. He stood still while Zerah scaled the steps, not knowing what to do. Should he stay with the horses? Or should he join the others inside?

"Naaman!" yelled Zerah from the top step. "Come on!"

"What about the horses?" asked Naaman, well aware that they were his charge, not Zerah's.

"Leave them. No one would dare bother a horse with Ishmael's braid."

Naaman fingered the rein with the gold strand laced into the intricate leather weaving. He motioned to an old man sitting nearby. The old man hobbled over and Naaman gave him the reins. "Hold these. And don't let go. And don't move." The old man nodded. Naaman wondered if he understood. "Can you hear?" he asked loudly. The old man nodded again. Naaman rolled his eyes and withdrew his money pouch from his tunic, pointing at the bulging leather purse, then at the horses, then at the old man. "Understand?" The man just nodded again stupidly.

Exasperated, Naaman looked at the steps. Hanock and Zerah were already inside. He hurried up, shaking his head, full of doubt.

Inside the palace, Naaman felt the coolness of the marble on his bare feet. The interior was lit by skylights far above. Shafts of golden sunlight angled down, striking the marble columns and lending everything a warm, muted light. The entry was crowded with well-dressed people conversing quietly. Naaman pulled his worn cloak tighter around him, feeling conspicuous. He knew he looked like a servant and smelled like a stable. Standing on tiptoes, he scanned the room for Hanock or Zerah. They were conferring with a man in a far corner. Naaman worked his way through the crowd, one hand on his money pouch. He trusted these finely dressed men less than the beggars outside.

When he joined them, Zerah turned and whispered, "This is Ocran. He knows how we can double our money. Can you imagine?"

"How can he do that?"

Zerah shrugged, obviously knowing little more than he just said. They both looked in wonder at Ocran, who was tall and dark and had large, soft hands with which he punctuated his speech.

"Take a look around you!" Ocran said emphatically. "The town is rebuilding and money is scarce. If you have what you say you have," he said, winking at Hanock, "then I can promise you a grand return. People are desperate for capital. You have come at the right time."

Zerah nudged Naaman, who didn't like the looks of this Ocran. He was too smooth, to begin with. Naaman could smell him above his own stable smell, and he didn't like it. He smelled like a woman.

But Hanock was warming to the idea. "We have been saving for some time, my friends and I," he said. "And we feel the time is right to become more aggressive. But how can we be certain of what you say? About the return, I mean?"

Ocran laughed and clapped Hanock on the shoulder. He looked around and spotted another well-dressed man talking with a group a few paces away. "Gera! Gera!"

The man turned and, seeing Ocran, smiled. "That is a fine cloak you're wearing, Gera," called Ocran loudly. "Who made it possible for you to purchase such wonderful clothing?"

Gera made a low, sweeping bow, straightened, and pointed directly at Ocran. He then turned back to his conversation. Ocran turned to Hanock. "He was as poor as you, my friend, just a few months ago. He too had a small sum to invest, and now look at him—one of the wealthiest men in the city."

"Is it legal, what you do?" blurted out Naaman.

The three men looked at him in shocked silence. Ocran stepped toward Naaman, towering over him. He sniffed the air and retreated a half step. "Are you questioning my honesty?"

Naaman slowly raised his eyes toward the man. *Yes,* said his look, and Ocran understood. He turned away, disgusted. Zerah caught his cloak and implored him, "Master Ocran, he means no harm. He's unacquainted with the ways of the world. It was a simple question asked by a simple man. He knows"—he cast a sidelong look at Naaman—"that a businessman who is dishonest is not long in business, am I right?"

Ocran nodded and folded his arms across his chest. Hanock said quietly, "We very much want to multiply our holdings. You come highly recommended. We do not question your knowledge or your honesty, do we, friends?" He was looking directly at Naaman.

Ocran smiled, but his eyes remained stern. He looked at Naaman. "What I do is as valuable to people as what you do, even if it isn't as noble." He picked a piece of hay off Naaman's tunic, then took Hanock by the arm and led him away. Zerah followed them. Naaman remained amid the swirl of merchants, feeling uneasy. He knew none of these people and didn't trust them. He trusted only himself.

From a few feet away, Naaman watched as Hanock and Zerah opened their pouches and gave Ocran their precious silver talents. When Zerah motioned for him to come over and do the same, he shook his head and turned away.

Hanock was exuberant as they descended the palace steps. "Now that our money has gone to work, so must we!" He grabbed the reins out of the hand of the old man, who was standing right where Naaman had left him twenty minutes before.

The old man gave Zerah his reins and held the horse steady as Zerah mounted. Zerah ignored the old man's outstretched hand and pointed at Naaman. "You made a mistake, not coming in with us. It will cost you."

Naaman looked at the ground. Zerah wheeled his horse and followed Hanock through the marketplace.

The old man handed Naaman his reins and smiled toothlessly, holding out his hand. Naaman jumped up on the horse. "I never said I would pay you," he barked. "Now get out of my way!"

The old man had to jump back to avoid being trampled. Naaman galloped at full speed through the marketplace, upsetting stalls and causing people to flee before him. He passed Hanock and Zerah at a full run.

"What's his hurry?" Hanock asked as Naaman disappeared down a narrow side street.

"Perhaps he knows of an investment that won't wait!" chortled Zerah.

SIX

Someday Soon

James and Jeshua labored all day in the hot sun. Only by late after-noon did the shade from one of the trees fall on the hole, which, despite all their work, was still only six feet deep. James crouched on the edge as Jeshua lifted up a large rock, handing it to him. James dropped the rock onto the rock pile, then picked up the waterskin and sloshed it. It was nearly empty. He looked at Jeshua, who was digging again, his back to him. James took a drink from the skin, draining it. He set it down and went back to the hole. "This is going to take for-ever, Jeshua."

Jeshua leaned on his shovel. Sweat ran down his face, making dirty tracks. He was too tired to talk but ventured, "We're doing fine, con-sidering." He turned back to his work.

"Considering what?"

"Considering it's only our first day."

James shook his head. "I wish Father were here. And Simon and Juda and Joses and—"

"There isn't room in this hole but for one of us at a time. What would they do here?"

"Help us."

"They're working in Sepphoris. Just don't think about how hard it is."

"It's hard not to think about it when sweat is stinging my eyes," said James, wiping his face with his tunic sleeve.

"I have an idea," said Jeshua, climbing up out of the hole and reaching for the waterskin. "You dig for a while. That will improve things." He slung the empty skin over his shoulder and started off toward the house.

"How will that improve things?" demanded James as he slid into the hole.

"Then at least one of us will be happy." He started whistling as he walked away.

"Jeshua!" yelled James, angrily grabbing the shovel. "That's not what I meant!"

Jeshua approached the house and skirted the old well. The flagstones around it were dry; no water had been taken from it in quite some time. He looked around. A small girl ran by, then stopped, watching him. Jeshua motioned her forward. She shook her head.

"What's your name?" asked Jeshua.

"R-R-Rebecca," stuttered the girl.

"Rebecca, is Master Esau around? Have you seen him?"

She shook her head.

"Don't be afraid," said Jeshua.

"I'm n-not afraid," said Rebecca.

"Rebecca!" Jeshua turned to see a tall woman in the doorway, her brown long hair loose around her shoulders, wiping her hands on her apron. "Leave him alone!"

As Rebecca ran off, Jeshua straightened. "Your daughter?"

"Master Jacob's youngest. I'm Elisabeth, the cook. You're digging the well, right?"

Jeshua nodded. "Trying to, at least. The ground is hard."

"I understand you're not digging it where Esau instructed you to."

Jeshua considered how to answer. The truth was not that simple. Finally, he just nodded. Elisabeth pointed a long finger at him. "A word of advice, young man. Always do what Esau says, how he says, and when he says. You'll avoid a lot of grief if you do."

Jeshua nodded. "I imagine that also includes where he says."

Elisabeth laughed. "I guess we'll find out. Now, is that empty?"

She took the skin from Jeshua and led him around the side of the house, where a stone basin stood, half full of water. She dipped the bladder in and filled it, handing it back to Jeshua. "I'm sorry. I didn't ask your name."

"Jeshua bar Joseph, of Nazareth. Peace be unto you."

"And unto you, peace. Well, I suppose it won't do for me to harangue you about the well. As Esau always points out, my job is to cook, not manage the estate." She laughed. "Even though I could easily do it better than he does. But then, I'm a woman, after all, with limited possibilities."

Jeshua nodded. "We're all limited on the outside, Elisabeth. But inside, we're all the same."

Elisabeth looked at Jeshua the way one looks a cripple. "That's something only men believe."

Jeshua shrugged. "I hope it's something we will all believe, someday."

Elisabeth laughed. "Someday may be one day, but it's never today." She turned and disappeared around the side of the house. Jeshua turned and saw Rebecca standing there.

"N-Never t-today," repeated Rebecca.

Jeshua knelt and took her hand. He sat her on his raised knee and rocked her gently. She put her thumb in her mouth and leaned against him, closing her eyes. He smoothed her hair and looked up at the sky. "Someday, Rebecca."

SEVEN

Buried Treasure

The fingernail moon rose above the horizon. The absence of clouds made for a short and colorless sunset. Naaman walked through the master's orchards, holding onto the coin pouch around his neck. He had listened as long as he could to Hanock's and Zerah's bragging about their adventure in Sepphoris and how much money they were going to make. The other servants listened intently, secretly jealous at the others' having that much money, and many offered their opinions on how best to multiply it. A great discussion arose about the money, but everyone agreed on one thing: it was imperative that they multiply it. When Hanock proudly boasted that Ishmael gave him five whole talents, the room fell silent, except for old Lazarus, who cackled that he had never heard a more inventive way to get rid of a servant.

"How is that?" asked Hanock imperiously.

"Well, Hanock, it seems clear," said Lazarus, gnawing on a piece of bread. "Master Ishmael knows you'll never be able to make much of that money, and he'll use that as an excuse to get rid of you. Or didn't you think of that?"

"That's nonsense," said Zerah, but he said nothing more.

Hanock reasoned, "I doubt the master would give me five talents—more than we all make in several years!—and risk me losing them, just to get rid of me. He could just fire me and that would be that, and he'd still have his money."

Lazarus pointed his crust of bread at Hanock. "That's what he wants you to think. He knows you are a smart man, Hanock. You won't make any foolish choices when it comes to the master's money. No gambling it away for you. He knew you would do exactly as you have: give the money to the lenders. But mark it! No matter how much return you obtain, it will not be enough for Master Ishmael. Think about it. When was he ever satisfied with anything we've ever done?"

He looked around at the silent crowd of servants, each thinking about the stripes they'd received at the master's hand. One by one, they nodded, until only Zerah and Hanock were not in agreement. And when Zerah looked at Naaman, he saw that Naaman, too, was nodding, thinking about his own scars from Ishmael's crop.

Naaman could sit still no longer. He bolted outside, into the darkness. As he walked along the ridge overlooking the olive orchard, he finally found space to think. *Old Lazarus is right,* he thought bitterly. *He may be blind in one eye, but he is not blind to the facts. There is no way to please Ishmael.*

Naaman sat down on a large rock and looked back at the household. The tapestries were pulled aside because of the heat, and the oil lamps cast their yellow light onto the dooryard. He heard singing from the servants' quarters but turned away. There would be no merrymaking tonight, even if Master Ishmael was gone to Jerusalem. He had thinking to do. Too much depended upon the right decision, and he couldn't be muddleheaded with wine and still make the right one.

He looked up at the moon, wondering why it changed during the month. Another example of his own ignorance. Was the earth round as some maintained, like a marble, with the sun and moon rotating around it the way the oxen circle the post at threshing time? Were the sun and the moon also round, like the earth? But why was one hot and one cold? And how far away were they?

He knew none of the answers to these questions. He was afraid to ask, fearing the others would laugh at his lack of education. But it wasn't his fault. He was an orphan and had never received any schooling. He was lucky to land a job here at Master Ishmael's, for whom he had no hatred, even when the old man was leaning into it, whacking him with his leather crop. He knew he deserved the beatings he got. He didn't hate Hanock or Zerah, either, when they blamed him for their mistakes. That was just how the world was. He wondered, though, if the boys under his supervision hated him for punishing them whether they deserved it or not. He felt bad about it, but that was the way of the world, too. He wondered if there was something more, some way of knowing how things really should work. Yet all he knew was the terrifying world of his youth in Jotapata, scrounging for meals, stealing whatever he could, and trying to avoid getting caught. Life had made him sly and sneaky, but it didn't teach him about why things were as they were. They just were.

He reached inside his tunic and withdrew the pouch, opening it. He pulled out the talent and held it up. Even in the pale moonlight, it glistened vividly. He looked around, suddenly afraid, wondering if anyone had followed him. He was sure that at least one of the other servants would gladly slit his throat to obtain his treasure. He held the coin so tightly in his hand that he could feel the impression of the emperor on the one side, the eagle on the other. He had to get rid of this thing one way or another, or it would mean his life.

But how can I multiply this thing? he wondered. *What if I get robbed? Ishmael won't care how I lost it, only that I lost it.*

He put the talent in the pouch and started walking again, hearing Lazarus's words in his mind: *When has he ever been satisfied with anything we've ever done?*

Naaman stumbled down the hillside. It was well after midnight, too late to be wandering around alone, but his mind wouldn't rest. He had turned it over and over a thousand times, and the same answer still came back: someone would steal the talent from him before he could find a way to multiply it. In fact, he remembered one of the stable hands, a large, strapping boy named Jonah, watching him during dinner. He watched Naaman even while the others talked, and Naaman looked up, not once, but twice, to see Jonah looking at him. Jonah had complained to Naaman not a week before about getting more money, and when Naaman told him that Zerah said no, Jonah muttered something to himself as he walked away. Was it a curse? A threat?

The thought made Naaman shiver. Jonah was bigger than he, and when they handled the animals, Jonah could easily startle a horse so it would crush Naaman against the stone barn wall, killing him. And no one would know it wasn't an accident.

Naaman heard something and froze, squinting into the darkness. Only a few trees populated the rocky ridge. His murderer could easily hide behind one and not be seen. Naaman ran down the far side of the hill.

He ran for long time, maybe a couple of miles, when he saw light ahead, a single oil lamp burning in a window of a house nestled in a small valley. Another estate, he gathered, although he didn't know the owner. He rarely left Master Ishmael's, and he wasn't from around here. He tried to quiet his labored breathing, to listen for the footsteps of his pursuer, but he couldn't hear a thing except his own pounding heart.

The oil lamp burned steadily, trimmed low, the traditional traveler's welcome. *I'm a traveler,* Naaman thought. *But the only hospitality I want is a place to hide this cursed money.*

He trotted into the safety of the orchard. The night was dark, even though the moon was directly above now. He had to watch his step. It wouldn't do to sprain an ankle here, who knows how far from home. He counted the trees since entering the orchard but lost track when a sound made him whirl around. "Jonah?" he asked, feeling stupid. As if

Jonah—or whoever it was—would answer. No, they would just keep quiet and then crack his head open with a rock and take the money.

Naaman stooped and picked up a large, flat stone, testing its weight as a weapon. He felt a little better with the stone in his hand. He looked back over his shoulder. The hot wind stirred the dry leaves, sounding like crones talking low together. Shadows shifted and moved. He didn't dare go back the way he had come. So he struck forward, his heart dark with fear and his mind full of doubt.

He hid behind a tree and wondered what to do. He would be discovered any moment—he had to get rid of the talent. He stooped and began digging with the flat stone at the base of the tree, pausing only to wipe sweat away and look around every few seconds for signs of his stalker.

I wish I had a shovel, he thought, remembering one he'd seen leaning against the house. But there was no time to return to get it. His fingernails tore, and blood soon wet his palms as he dug steadily, not looking at the hole but constantly watching the trees for signs of movement.

He was surprised when his stone hit a root with a dull *thunk*. He looked down. The hole was nearly two feet deep. He must have been digging for an hour.

He pulled the pouch from his tunic, feeling the roundness of the coin inside. He tore a piece of his undergarment away, wrapped the coin pouch in the white muslin, and placed the bundle in the hole. He quickly filled the hole back in, then stood, pressing his back against the tree. He tamped the earth flat with his feet as he looked around fearfully. He started away but stopped when a terrible thought grasped him: how would he find this place again?

Naaman looked around. Every tree was the same, all planted in neat, straight rows, all the same age, all with the same branches and wilted leaves. He sank down and sat on the mound of dirt, weary and out of ideas. Sweat trickled down his back, and his hands throbbed from digging. He sucked a forefinger, tasting blood where he had torn a nail loose. He put his head in his hands. He didn't dare leave this place to go back and count the trees because he'd never find it again in the darkness.

He sat there for a long time, feeling miserable. He felt something hard under him, and reached and pulled out the flat stone he had been digging with. He held it out before him, looking blankly at it.

Then an idea came to him. He reached for a sharp stone lying nearby. He turned the large stone over and scratched a big **X** on the underside. He brushed his hand across the stone. The ridges of the **X** were deep, deep enough to last. Satisfied, he turned the stone over and nestled it into the ground over the buried talent. Then he placed other, smaller stones around it, and tossed an armful of dried leaves on top. He stood back. It was hard to tell, but he thought it looked much like the base of every other tree in the orchard. Only the top of the flat stone stuck out. He nodded to himself, certain he could find that stone again and, with it, his money.

Naaman backed up, afraid to take his eyes off the stone. He looked away, then back. There it was. He took another three steps and looked back again. The stone was still there, guarding his treasure. Naaman wiped his hands on his tunic, feeling better. *I'll think of something to do with that money,* he thought. *But until I do, it will be safer here than hanging around my neck!*

He slowly walked away, looking back regularly, trying to memorize the area. If he could find the stone here, under a mere slice of moon, then he could easily find it again under the full moon, a few days from now, when he'd return again.

EIGHT

Family Matters

Jeshua looked up at the sky, where big, fluffy clouds soared eastward. They were moving at a fast clip, and that wasn't good. Plus, they weren't gray with the promise of rain. He bent over his shovel again.

James knew how to read the sky as well. He lowered the wooden bucket down the hole, and Jeshua shoveled three scoops of dirt into it.

"Go ahead," said Jeshua wearily. James tugged on the rope, and the bucket slowly made its way up. The well was now deep enough that the top was three feet over Jeshua's head. Esau had provided them with a ladder, but it would only serve another day or so.

"Jeshua, do you think deep dirt is heavier than shallow dirt?" James asked as he tugged the bucket up. It hit a root snag on the wall, tipped, and spilled onto Jeshua's head. "Sorry," said James as Jeshua spat out the dirt and shook it from his hair.

"That's just about enough!" said Jeshua in frustration.

James pulled the bucket up and leaned over the edge. "I said I was sorry."

"Give me the ladder, James."

James extended the ladder into the hole. Jeshua scaled it quickly. When he emerged, he was black with dirt, sweaty, and angry. James backed away. He wanted to apologize again, but he felt it would only make things worse.

Jeshua was looking around, still shaking dirt from his hair. He went to his toolbox and pulled out a hammer, then looked at James, fire in his eyes. "I'm tired of getting dirt in my hair." He started toward James, who jumped back.

"Jeshua!"

Jeshua stopped. "What?"

"I said I was sorry."

"I heard you," said Jeshua, walking past James. "Now, are you going to help me or not?"

"Help you do what?" asked James tentatively.

"We need to build a scaffold so the bucket won't empty itself on me every time."

"Oh," said James, relaxing.

Jeshua looked hard at James. "Did you think I was angry at *you*?"

James shrugged sheepishly.

Jeshua put his arm around James. "I'm not angry at you."

"I'm not much help, am I, Jeshua?" His voice broke.

Jeshua tousled James's hair. "I couldn't do it without you."

"That's not true."

"Have I ever lied to you, James?"

"No."

"Then believe me when I tell you that you are a great help. And I guess it wouldn't be work if we didn't get dirty and tired and irritable." He went back to the excavation and sat down on the edge. James sat next to him, and they looked into the hole for a long time.

Finally James ventured a comment. "When will we strike water?"

Jeshua shook his head. "I don't know. Maybe the dowser was right." He nodded toward the stake in the clearing.

James looked back at Jeshua. "But the water's here, not over there, right?"

Jeshua exhaled deeply. "I thought so, but I might be wrong."

James's jaw dropped. He never imagined Jeshua might harbor doubts about the well. And that meant he might have doubts about other things, too. The thought shook James, and he put both hands on the ground to steady himself.

Jeshua saw James's reaction. "James," he said quietly, "don't worry. It's just a well. If we don't hit water, it's not the end of the world. We just dig somewhere else."

"I'm too worn out to start another well."

Jeshua punched his brother lightly on the arm. "I cannot believe that the Great Well Digger, who divides asunder roots and branches, who tunnels with ease through rock and stone, is discouraged!"

James shook his head wearily. "More than that. The Great Well Digger is pooped."

Jeshua jumped up. "Well, I have just the cure." He went over and picked up his hammer and tossed it to James, who caught it neatly.

"What's that?" asked the boy.

"Success! Once we strike water, we'll forget how hard this was. Come on!"

They started off toward the house to scrounge some wood for a scaffold.

Esau stepped from the shade of the veranda and squinted at the road curving down the hillside. A man was walking briskly, his bare feet stirring dust, a large bag slung over his shoulder. He marched up to Esau and bowed deeply. "Master Esau?"

Esau nodded, chewing a piece of lamb. "Yes?"

"Peace be unto you. I am Joses bar Joseph. My brothers are working for you, I believe."

Esau nodded. "And unto you, peace. Yes. They're up in the orchard." He pointed.

"Thank you," said Joses, and started toward the orchard.

Esau called after him, "Are you here to help?"

Joses stopped and turned. "I came to retrieve James. He's needed at home."

Esau joined Joses as he walked toward the excavation. "Is it serious?"

Joses nodded. "Our sister Miriam is very sick. Mother needs James's help."

Esau considered the news. "So you're taking the boy, but you can't stay yourself?"

Joses shook his head. "I'm sorry."

They arrived at the well. A large, wooden three-legged tripod stood over the opening. A block and tackle was suspended from a metal hook, and a rope extended down into the hole. James was pulling on the rope, his back bent with the strain.

"James!"

James turned. "Joses!" He let go of the rope and ran to his brother. Before he reached him, however, a *thunk!* was heard and Jeshua's voice came from the well.

"Ouch! James!"

James, horrified, ran back to the well. "I'm sorry, Jeshua!"

Down in the hole, Jeshua rubbed his shoulder, looking up, scowling. He was covered with dirt, but his expression changed when Joses peered over the edge.

"Having fun?" asked Joses.

"Joses!" exclaimed Jeshua. "What are you doing here? James, get the ladder!"

James already had the ladder in hand, and in another moment it was in the well. Jeshua climbed up, and Joses reached and helped him the last three feet the ladder could not reach. They embraced tightly.

Joses pulled back, dusting himself off. "Now look, I'm as dirty as you are!"

"What are you doing here?"

Joses frowned. "Miriam is ill and Mother is worried. She needs James."

"Take him," said Jeshua immediately.

"Hey!" said James, pushing between them. "I don't want to go."

"An hour ago you wanted to quit," said Jeshua.

"I was joking," said James.

"What's this about Miriam?" asked Jeshua.

Joses said, "We don't know what it is. High fever. With all of us gone, Mother needs more help around the house."

"Why can't the girls help?" asked James.

"They *are* helping, James," said Joses. "But Mother asked me to fetch you home."

James looked up at Jeshua, questioning.

"Of course you must go, James. You know that."

James kicked the dirt with his sandal. "But Jeshua needs me here."

"It's okay," said Jeshua. "Joses can help me."

Joses looked at Esau, who was examining the well, trying to be inconspicuous. "Father says he can't spare me."

"Oh," said Jeshua.

"I'd rather be working with you, but Father . . ." He shrugged.

"I'll figure something out. But now," Jeshua said, wiping his hands on his tunic, "you have to get James home. James?"

James had turned away. "Don't I have a say in this?"

"Come on, James," said Joses, starting forward, but Jeshua waved him off.

"Of course you do," said Jeshua.

"Then I don't want to go," said James flatly, his back still to them.

"Fine," said Jeshua, "but consider this: of all the men in the family, Mother asked for you. Why do you think that was?"

"Because I'm the youngest."

"No. Because she knows how much Miriam loves you. And when someone is sick, they want those they love close to them. You see that, don't you?"

James shrugged. Miriam was two years younger than he was, and they got along pretty well, considering she was a girl. But, considering how much he teased her, he was surprised she'd asked for him.

"James," whispered Jeshua, "she looks up to you the way you look up to me. Even though I tease you."

James was surprised. Had he said those thoughts out loud?

Jeshua put his hand on his shoulder. "I'll be all right here. What you can do at home is more important."

Finally, James turned around, his mind made up. "Then I guess we'd better be going." He began collecting his tools, throwing them into his wooden toolbox. James turned to Jeshua. "I'm sorry."

"Something will work out. Give Miriam a kiss for me."

"Yuck! No!"

"Then just tell her I'm praying for her. Will you?"

"I'll pray for her, too. Even if she is my little sister."

Joses opened his bag and brought out a wrapped parcel. "From Mother. Bread, honey, and some oranges." He looked around the orchard and laughed. "But maybe you don't need another orange. Maybe I'll just take these back with me."

Jeshua snatched the parcel away from him. "I'll take whatever she sends me," he said, pushing Joses away. "Give my blessings to Miriam."

"I'll ask Father if he can spare one of the boys. You can't dig a well single-handed."

Jeshua nodded.

"You must do your best," said James, puffing his chest out. "For the

Great Well Digger can no longer help you. But I leave with you my power to hew all roots and to crumble all stones into pieces."

Jeshua bowed deeply. "Thank you, Great Well Digger. Now, on your way."

"Get to work!" said James. Joses cuffed him on the back of the head, and they walked toward the house.

Jeshua smiled and turned back to the well.

"Pity about your sister," said Esau from behind him.

Jeshua turned around. "Yes. I hope the Master of the Universe will answer our prayers."

Esau nodded, then changed the subject. "But you will continue working, won't you?"

"Of course," said Jeshua. "We will find water."

"But there is only you, son," said Esau.

"For now," responded Jeshua. "But perhaps the Lord will provide a ram."

"A ram?"

"Abraham? Isaac?"

"I know the story, young man," said Esau. "I just don't think God considers digging wells as important as the future of nations."

"Ah," said Jeshua, climbing down into the hole. "But I do."

NINE

The Stable Master

Zerah entered the stable, squinting into the darkness. "Naaman? Where are you?"

Naaman, who was sleeping in a cool corner on a pile of green hay, bolted upright. "Back here," he said, jumping up and lunging for a rake.

Zerah rounded the corner. "Did you hear?"

"Hear what?" asked Naaman, raking vigorously.

Zerah collapsed onto the hay and clasped his hands behind his head, closing his eyes and smiling. Naaman waited as long as he could, then blurted out, "What happened?"

"Our investment is up twenty-five percent." Zerah opened one eye to see the effect of the news.

Naaman put on his most casual face. "That's good." He had no idea what a percent was, but he wasn't going to let Zerah know that.

"It means," said Zerah, sitting up, "that it has increased by one-quarter."

"So you said," answered Naaman flatly. He turned and walked out of the stall, dragging the rake after him.

Zerah got up and followed him. "Hanock is some kind of genius. When we went to Sepphoris yesterday, he said he had heard about a new winery being built. The builder has run out of money, and the grapes are ready for pressing, so we went to him directly and talked him into borrowing money from us. Now *we're* money brokers, like Ocran! What do you think of that?"

Naaman picked up the brush and coaxed the cockles out of the mane of Master Ishmael's white gelding. "Good for you, Zerah. Now I have work to do."

Zerah frowned. "Are we feeling a little sorry for ourselves? Those of us who didn't invest our money?"

"I don't want to talk about it."

"I can see why. By the way, what are you going to do with your money?"

"I've taken care of it," said Naaman.

"I know you've done something with it because you're not walking around clutching your money pouch like you're ringing a chicken neck anymore. What did you do with it?"

"None of your business."

"No," quipped Zerah, "the truth is, it's none of *your* business, because you haven't done a thing with it. You probably just hid it."

Naaman pulled the comb through the horse's mane so hard the horse shied and kicked, narrowly missing Zerah's shin. Zerah stepped back, anger flaring in his eyes, but then regained his composure and smiled. "Come on, Naaman, admit it. You have no idea what to do with the talent Master Ishmael gave you."

"I have plenty of ideas," Naaman said through gritted teeth.

"Just no good ones." Zerah patted the horse on the haunches. "Well, just let me know if you change your mind. Maybe we'll share some of our good fortune with you." Naaman didn't look up but continued brushing the horse.

"You know, money is a lot like people," said Zerah, picking a piece of straw off Naaman's shoulder. "It accomplishes nothing just lying around." He turned and left.

Naaman stared after him, furious. Only a few seconds passed before he yelled, "Jesse! Jesse!"

A skinny, big-eyed boy appeared in the stable doorway. "Yes, sire?"

Naaman grabbed a riding crop off its hook. He whipped it through the air angrily.

"Come here! Now!"

TEN

The Laborer

E arly the next morning, Jeshua walked into the orchard. He leaned against the tripod and looked into the well. Bone dry. He looked over at the dowser's stake in the clearing. It was definitely a better location for a well, out in the open, plenty of room around it, and few tree roots to hack through. But that didn't mean there was water there. He still believed he would strike water here, but when?

He heard voices and turned. A group of workers walked toward him, each with a spade or hoe, and each carrying a full water bladder. Esau had seen his predicament and sent help! Jeshua felt a surge of gratitude toward the overseer.

But the workers passed him and soon disappeared in the trees. He heard someone say, "Start here."

He followed them and saw what they were doing. They worked in pairs, one digging around the base of a tree, turning the soil over, while the other poured a small amount of water onto the newly turned earth.

Deflated, Jeshua walked back to the well. It would be another scorching day. He hung the bucket on the hook and lowered it into the hole, then tossed his spade down after it. He crawled over the edge, his toes finding the topmost ladder rung. Reaching the bottom, he looked up. The walls above were rocky and uneven. They had had to work around several stones too big to move. He prayed silently, *Please, let it be today.*

He had to laugh. It was easier to be cheerful with James around. But down here, alone, it was difficult to be positive. Still, though, the work was simple, if hard: one shovel at a time, one bucket at a time, and eventually something would happen.

He heard noise above, the sound of stones clattering together. He hooked the bucket on the rope and climbed up the ladder.

Pulling himself over the edge, he hauled the bucket up while he looked around. A servant was walking away, carrying an empty woven basket. Another was lugging a basket full of stones toward the pile of stones Jeshua and James had made. He dumped the basket and looked briefly at Jeshua, then walked away.

"Thanks," called Jeshua.

"Anytime," said the worker.

Jeshua wondered if they would haul his stones away when they took theirs. Or if it would be the other way around. He knew the workers were laughing, thinking they'd put one over on him. Then an idea came. Perhaps he could turn their work into his own by using the rocks as flagstones for a plaza around the well. He smiled, and for the rest of the morning, as he climbed up and down the ladder, he visualized the impressive flagstone plaza he would build with the stones they so generously provided him.

ELEVEN

Paradise Lost

Naaman made an excuse to leave the fireside early, claiming he was tired. Zerah watched him go, and Naaman heard him say as he stepped outside, "It must be hard work, snoring!" Everyone laughed.

Naaman kicked the dirt. He had to accept defeat. The only way to silence Zerah was to give his talent to Ocran, the money lender. He was worried about it anyway. Jonah had been observing him closely since Naaman buried the talent, four nights ago. Of course, all the stableboys watched him; they wanted to get on his good side. So he had particularly enjoyed beating Jonah today when the boy didn't move quickly enough. He really laid into it, raising large red welts on Jonah's back, but the boy didn't cry out. When it was over, he just pulled his shirt down and said, "Thank you, sire." Then he left, leaving Naaman angrier than before.

Now, as he walked toward the other estate, Naaman shook away the thought of Jonah and comforted himself by remembering that tomorrow his money would go to work, and not a moment too soon. Ishmael was returning in two weeks.

He arrived at the orchard well after midnight. The moon shone brightly overhead, and he would have no problem finding his treasure. The only problem would be avoiding being seen. He stepped into the trees that paralleled the road, just to be sure.

Centered in the bowl-shaped valley was the granite house, a single unlit candle in the window. He crept to the house. There, leaning against the wall, were a half dozen spades. He reached for one, then heard a low growl and turned around slowly.

A large black dog faced him, its teeth bared, growling. He knew he didn't have much time before the dog started barking, or worse.

He slowly reached into his travel pouch and withdrew a strip of dried meat he had saved for his walk home. He held it out to the dog. "Here. For you."

The dog looked around guiltily, then came a step closer. Naaman felt along the wall with his other hand, never taking his eyes off the dog. His hand brushed against a handle. The dog sniffed at the meat warily.

"I won't hurt you," said Naaman as the dog took the meat, gobbling it down. Naaman grasped the spade handle and smiled. "Yet."

He whipped the spade around in a smooth arc, but the dog was too fast. It ducked away and scrambled for the trees. The force of the swing whirled Naaman around, and the spade struck the other shovels, causing them to fall with a loud clatter.

Naaman dropped the spade and bolted across the dooryard. He didn't look back until he was deep inside the orchard. Then he stopped, his heart racing. "Close one," he whispered, and his voice seemed like a shout in his ears. He looked toward the house, straining to hear footsteps coming. But his heart still beat too loud, and so he ran farther into the orchard.

A loud noise awakened Jeshua, who was sleeping in the barn. When he stepped out into the dooryard, he saw the shovels lying in a pile by the house. A gray cat walked along a windowsill. He stood the spades up again, then went back to bed.

Naaman peeked out from behind a tree. He'd waited twenty minutes for someone to appear out of the darkness, but no one came. He knew he'd been lucky. He had to retrieve his money and get out of here. No telling if the dog would show up again, this time hungry for Naaman's shank.

He crept through the orchard, keeping his eyes peeled for the stone marker. He would find his treasure and take it directly to Ocran in Sepphoris. He cursed himself for the time he'd lost. He'd been busy the last few days, toadying to Zerah and avoiding Hanock. But yesterday, when Zerah boasted that they'd passed the fifty-percent mark, Naaman had finally swallowed his pride and asked how much that really was.

"Master Ishmael gave me two talents," Zerah beamed. "And now I have three!"

Although Naaman couldn't understand how one talent could equal fifty, he understood that three was more than two. He silently vowed not to wait another day to put his own money to work.

He tripped over a stake in a clearing and fell back into the present. He got up and looked around. The trees went off in every direction. He looked at the hills surrounding the estate to get his bearings, but it was no use. He randomly chose a direction and walked into the grove to look for his stone.

He searched the base of a dozen trees, finding nothing but sensing something amiss. He stooped and felt moist, broken dirt at the base of a tree. Then another. And another.

Naaman jerked upright, his face as white as the moon. *The trees! They've dug around the trees!* He rushed from one tree to another, frantically searching for the stone. He looked around wildly. The earth was turned at the base of every tree, and his stone—his precious, valuable stone—was nowhere in sight.

He stumbled along, a terrible mental image forming: Zerah and Hanock laughing and pointing at him, while the entire household watched as Ishmael beat him bloody with the crop, then sent him away to starve.

Then he saw something. Was it a vision? A mirage? No, it was a pile of stones as tall as a man. He stumbled toward it and slammed his shin against something. He hit the earth and heard a crash behind him. He turned just in time to see a wooden scaffolding fall into a large hole. He rubbed his barked shin, finding blood, and crawled toward the excavation. He squinted into the hole, but the darkness was complete.

He rolled onto his back, his heart thumping. If not for the scaffold, he would have run headlong into the pit. He would be dead or dying right now. He rubbed his aching shin, a small price to pay for his life. Then he looked at the pile of stones and all hope fell away. He stood and went over to it. A thousand gray rocks formed a gray pyramid. He turned one over, looking for the **X**. Nothing. Then another, and another, until he was turning them over without the least bit of hope.

He took a step backward and stared bleakly at the stone pile for a long time, then turned and blindly stumbled through the orchard. He didn't hear the black dog barking from the shadows as he crested the rise and disappeared over the hill, his feet finding their way home when his mind could not.

TWELVE

Accusations

Jeshua stood looking at the ruined scaffold. It had fallen into the well hole and broken into pieces. He climbed down the ladder and began cutting the ropes that bound the pieces together, then lugged the timbers out of the well. He was at the bottom, untangling the rope, when a face appeared up top. "Good morning! How is it going?"

Jeshua looked up and held out the rope jumble as an answer.

"Not too good, I see," said the man.

"Not too good," repeated Jeshua, hoisting the rope over his shoulder and scaling the ladder. The man stood back as Jeshua heaved himself over the lip of the well and stood.

Naaman was about to accuse him right there, but when he saw the knife tucked into the man's belt he reconsidered. "Looks like it broke," he said as pleasantly as he could.

Jeshua nodded. "It fell into the well last night. Can't figure it out." He bowed his head. "Peace be unto you. I am Jeshua."

Naaman bowed and said, "And unto you, peace. I'm . . . Zerah."

"Pleased to meet you, Zerah," said Jeshua, withdrawing his knife and cutting the twine that bound a length of rope. "Is there something I can do for you?"

"I was just wondering if you were working alone."

Jeshua tossed the rope into a pile and put the knife back in its sheath. "Yes, but I'm always looking for help," he said pleasantly.

"Hmm," said Naaman, looking at the rock pile, certain his stone was in there, and certain that his talent was in the possession of this thief before him, the lie written all over his dirty face. "I was wondering why a man as prosperous as yourself would even need to work."

Jeshua laughed and turned back to the well. "Maybe someday."

The statement burned Naaman like fire. He considered rushing Jeshua then, pushing him into the well. But then he'd never find his money. And this Jeshua might be lying about working alone; he might have an accomplice. He knew carpenters were liars. They used inferior materials and lied about the time it took to build something. Naaman looked around for another worker but saw no one. Besides, there was the knife. The carpenter knew how to use it, and he was much bigger than Naaman. He'd probably just slit his throat and laugh while he did it.

"Well," Naaman finally said, after considering his options. "You'll get what you deserve, I'm sure."

Jeshua smiled. "I hope not." He saluted Naaman, then disappeared into the well.

Oh, I hope so, thought Naaman as he turned toward the house.

"There is someone to see you, sir," said Elisabeth, as she bounced her baby on her hip.

"I'm busy," said Esau, bent over the tally board.

"He insists."

"Well, he can insist all he wants. Tell him I'm busy."

"Certainly," said Elisabeth, turning and walking back into the great room, where Naaman stood impatiently. "I'm sorry, sir," she said. "Master Esau is busy right now. May I inquire what this concerns?"

"None of your business, woman!" Naaman sputtered. "Tell him I represent Master Ishmael. You know who he is, don't you?"

Elisabeth looked at the man through slit eyes. Then she smiled and said, "That name is not familiar to me, sir. I am so sorry."

"Oh, shut up!" shouted Naaman, pushing past her, startling the baby, who cried out. Elisabeth started after him but thought better of it. Esau would quickly put him in his place.

Naaman burst into the room and stood with his hands on his hips. "Esau? Can you not take one minute to receive a guest?"

"Depends on the guest," said Esau without looking up from the tally board.

"It is most urgent!"

Esau looked up. "Do you have a name?"

"Naaman."

Esau put his stylus down and leaned back on his pillow. "What can I do for you, Naaman?"

"I have a theft to report."

"Report it to the centurion, young man; I am not a jailer."

"The theft was perpetrated by one of your servants," said Naaman, hoping he used *perpetrated* properly.

"My servants? Who? And what did they supposedly steal?"

"The man who is digging the well in your orchard."

Esau laughed. "Jeshua? First of all, he's not a servant. He's a hireling. And second, Jeshua wouldn't steal even a minute of my time, as you are!" He waved Naaman away and bent over the board again.

Naaman took a step forward. "I must remind you this is a serious charge, and if you are protecting this thief, you are also guilty."

Esau jumped up and strode toward Naaman, who backed away, surprised at the quickness of the man. Esau hissed, "Sir, your tongue needs tightening. You accuse me of harboring a criminal? Do you know who I am?"

Naaman felt the wall against his back. "I don't care who you are. There has been a theft. What are you going to do about it?"

They stood that way for a moment, nose to nose. "If it will get rid of you, I'll ask Jeshua about it," said Esau fiercely. "Seems a small price to pay to be rid of such a pest." He left.

Naaman started after him, but Elisabeth, who had been standing outside, filled the doorway before he could get through. She was a full head taller and thirty pounds heavier than Naaman, and she had no baby on her hip now to inhibit her movement. She glared at Naaman. "Wait here."

For another long moment Naaman stood, unsure if he should get into a scuffle with a woman or just let it go. Then his pride got the best of him and he pushed his way past her, stomping into the great room and out the front door.

"Esau!" shouted Elisabeth.

As Naaman stepped into the dooryard, he saw three menservants coming toward him. He turned and angled toward a tree with a bench under it, where several children were playing. Shooing them away, he made a great show of sitting down on the bench and looking back at Elisabeth, who was conferring with the men by the front door. To his right, Esau disappeared into the orchard.

Elisabeth went back into the house, but the three men remained, watching him. Naaman raised his chin and looked away, crossing his legs nonchalantly.

After twenty long minutes, Esau returned. He motioned to the three servants and strode toward Naaman, who remained seated out of spite. He could tell the servants were angered by his rudeness, but he didn't care. That is, until Esau barked, "Get out of here."

Naaman jumped up. "He denied it, of course."

"He said you had already spoken to him and if you truly believed he had taken something from you, you should have asked him directly."

"I knew it would be useless. A thief is also a liar."

Esau laughed. "That's good, coming from you, *Zerah*."

"I told you my name was Naaman."

"Yes, of course," said Esau. "But you told Jeshua you were Zerah. So, which is it: Zerah or Naaman?"

"My name—"

"Careful," cautioned Esau, raising his hand. "Whatever you say makes you a liar."

Naaman shot angry looks at the servants, who simply smiled back. They were all conspirators. Maybe this Jeshua had already promised them a share of the money if they would take his side. He pushed past Esau and the servants, shouting, "You're all thieves. And you will all pay!"

Esau laughed again. "By the way, Naaman or Zerah or Beelzebub or whatever your name is, what exactly did he steal from you?"

Naaman whirled around. "None of your business. I see you are not disposed to help me regardless."

"Maybe he stole your manners or good temper, for you have neither," retorted Esau. The servants laughed.

"This is not over!" shouted Naaman, stomping off.

Esau and the servants watched him go. And they laughed again when Master Jacob's big black dog darted out of the barn and chased Naaman out of the dooryard.

THIRTEEN

The Synagogue

Benjamin slowly rolled the Torah onto its spindle, being careful not to worsen the tear along the bottom edge. He let his son Asher carry the scroll in the procession last week, and the boy caught it on a pew, tearing the parchment. Everyone gasped, and Asher might have dropped the scroll except for Benjamin's quick reaction.

Asher was sick about his misstep, and he quickly disappeared from the service. When the procession was finished, Benjamin allowed his assistant to read from the Torah while he went searching for Asher, whom he found sitting on the back steps, his cheeks wet with tears.

Benjamin put a bony hand on his son's shoulder. "There is a reason for all things."

Asher looked up. "You mean God made me tear it?"

"Of course not," said Benjamin, sitting. "But God allows things to happen for his own reasons. You and I are straws in the wind, Asher. The wind is God. Maybe there is a reason why you damaged the Torah."

"I can't think what that would be," said Asher.

Benjamin squeezed Asher's shoulder. "I'm sure there is one. We should be watchful so we recognize it when it appears. Come, the service is almost over, and we must join the men in song."

Returning to the present, Benjamin looked down at the scroll on the lectern. It was a hundred years old, hand copied from the original Jerusalem scroll by Rabbi Eshek himself. He carefully unrolled it, holding the pieces together where it was torn, and read the passage from Isaiah that was split in half:

"For he shall grow up before him as a tender plant, and as a root out of a dry ground; he hath no form nor comeliness; and when we shall see him, there is no beauty that we should desire him."

How unfortunate! Isaiah's prophecy about the Messiah, damaged. Benjamin stared bleakly at the parchment, wondering how it could be repaired. As a tailor, he could work miracles with cloth, but no needle and thread would restore the parchment as before. He carefully rerolled the scroll and placed it in the velvet sleeve he himself had sewn. Then he opened the repository doors and placed the Torah inside. He was making his way down the aisle between the facing pews when the door burst open, revealing a small, slender man, shaking with rage.

"Stop!" commanded Benjamin, raising his hand. "Leave your anger outside, friend. I will hear you there."

The man stepped inside anyway. Benjamin cataloged him in an instant: short, thin, a sharp nose under dark, angry eyes, his cloak dusty from the road. Benjamin, nearly a foot taller than the man, took his arm and gently led him out of the synagogue. "Peace be unto you," he said pleasantly.

"Are you the rabbi here?"

"I am. My name is Benjamin. What can I do for you?"

"I have been robbed!" When Benjamin reached for his arm to console him, he jerked away and walked a tight little circle. "Robbed!"

"By whom, sir?"

Naaman pointed eastward. "A man who is working at Jacob's orchard, there, over those hills. Do you know him?"

"Master Jacob? Yes, I do."

"No!" Naaman immediately regretted his outburst and lowered his voice. "No. The man who is digging the well. The overseer said he was a hireling. His name was Jeshua, I think."

Benjamin pursed his lips. "It is a common name—"

"He's a carpenter. A well digger. A thief!"

Benjamin shook his head. "I'm sorry. But no matter, what did he steal from you?"

Naaman studied the rabbi. He must be careful or Zerah and Hanock would surely hear about this. He would say no more than he had to. "It is very personal," he said, looking at the ground. "It was a gift, a very private, valuable gift."

Benjamin studied the man. Something about him was not right. "And you say this well digger robbed you of it?"

"Not exactly. It was hidden, and he took it."

"And what can I do for you, sir?"

"You can help me get it back. Why do you think I'm here?"

Benjamin shrugged. "I'm a rabbi, not a centurion or a judge. What can I do?"

"Master Jacob's household attends synagogue here, don't they?"

"Yes. But so does almost everyone in Cana," said Benjamin.

"You're the spiritual leader of those people!" exclaimed Naaman. "They might lie to a centurion, but they'd never lie to you!"

Benjamin nearly smiled at the man's naïveté. "Sir, are you a Jew?"

Naaman looked at Benjamin. "Why does that matter?"

"Well, I've never seen you before around here. From where do you hail?"

Naaman pulled his cloak around him and stood taller. "I am a traveler. From the Decapolis, across the Jordan. And I have been robbed by one of your synagogue."

Benjamin noticed Naaman's black horse. "Sir, if you've come all the way from the Decapolis, where are your provisions?"

Naaman threw up his hands. "What difference does it make? I have made a complaint. What are you going to do about it?"

Benjamin crossed his arms across his chest and looked evenly at Naaman. "The first thing I will do is ask you your name, sir."

Naaman looked at the ground and thought hard before answering.

Esau looked at the piece of parchment and shook his head, then refolded it and shoved it in his pocket. He dismissed the courier and walked into the orchard, threading his way between the thirsty trees. He was torn. On one hand, he had a good idea that Jeshua was honest, since he was Joseph's son. But on the other hand, the young man had ignored his advice about where to dig the well, and the location he had chosen was proving to be a mistake. So at the very least he apparently had bad judgment. But Esau had watched him secretly from a distance on several occasions. Jeshua was a steady worker, starting early, taking short lunches, and never complaining. He'd seen him with his younger brother James and had smiled in approval as they joked and worked together, even though he had outwardly disapproved of their horseplay. Esau had enjoyed a good friendship with his older brother, too, and he couldn't help but think of Daniel when he saw Jeshua with James. Daniel, long dead and long missed. No, it wasn't possible. Jeshua was not a thief.

Esau watched from his usual place. There was no one near the excavation, but when the wind died, and the dry leaves quieted, he heard singing. Jeshua's clear tenor echoed from the well shaft. He was singing an old song Esau hadn't heard in years.

We know not where our path will lead,
Nor from whence we've come.
But we must choose which signs to heed,
Until our journey's run.

Esau enjoyed listening to anyone sing, for he himself had a terrible voice. It was his greatest disappointment. He walked to the well and leaned on the rebuilt tripod. "Jeshua?"

Jeshua looked up. "Just a minute," he said and put one more shovel-ful into the bucket, then grabbed the rope and hauled the bucket up. "Would you grab the bucket, please?"

Esau did so and set the bucket on the well edge. He was thinking about how hard it must be to dig a well alone when Jeshua appeared at the top of the well, pulling himself up over the lip, and standing up, dusting himself off. "Master Esau. What can I do for you?"

"I was enjoying your singing, Jeshua," said Esau, who always felt odd around the young man, as if he kept meeting a new person each time.

Jeshua shrugged. "It passes the time."

Esau handed the parchment to Jeshua, who opened it carefully, doubt on his face. A long moment passed as he read the accusation, then he looked up. "It's not true."

"I know, Jeshua." Esau took the parchment and tore it into bits, scattering them in the hot wind. "But you must still defend yourself before the elders of the synagogue."

Jeshua looked at his dirty, torn tunic. "I have nothing proper to wear."

"And I'm afraid I can't loan you anything, Jeshua," said Esau, pinching his robe, as small as a boy's. "But it doesn't matter. We will go and defend your name against this liar."

Jeshua sighed. "He seemed desperate."

Esau patted Jeshua's arm. "Don't worry. We'll take some men, just in case."

"No," said Jeshua, "I meant that he seemed very upset, like he was in trouble."

"He is now," said Esau, offering the waterskin to Jeshua.

Jeshua drank, then handed the skin back. "I think he was in trouble before he came here."

"And he will have trouble when he leaves," said Esau evenly. "Come, they are waiting."

Elders of Israel

B enjamin stood behind the lectern and bowed his head, thinking. Before him stood a young man, recently bathed, but in ratty, dirty clothes. He was disappointed that someone would enter the synagogue dressed that way. The young man's face was clean, though, as were his hands, which were clasped together in front of him.

Benjamin surveyed the room. The synagogue was large, enough seating for almost a hundred men, as well as a balcony where the women sat. Normally the windows were open, but this evening the tapestries were let down, and a stifling heat filled the room. The doors, usually open, were also shut, for this was no ordinary meeting. It was a council meeting, and only the elders of the synagogue were present.

Rows of benches faced each other on either side of the room. Ten men sat on each side, wearing their prayer shawls and head kerchiefs, waiting silently.

Behind the young carpenter stood his accuser, a traveler named Naaman or Zerah—they could not be sure which. He maintained that Naaman was his true name, and so Benjamin had addressed him thus. Naaman never took his hate-filled eyes off Jeshua. It must have been some priceless thing Jeshua had taken, to instill such anger.

Benjamin looked at Jeshua again, pondering. He was from Nazareth, a nearby village. His father was known to be one Joseph, also a carpenter, who had married a young woman many years ago who had already been with child. People had whispered that the child was Joseph's, in which case Benjamin thought he had done the right thing in marrying her. Others believed their firstborn, the young man standing before him now, was fathered by another, unknown man. Benjamin thought that if such was the case, then this Joseph was an even better man than if the former rumor was true. But either way, the family was under a cloud of gossip and innuendo, and the young man before him was illegitimate. Benjamin knew from experience that people born into troubled circumstances often made bad decisions.

He focused on Naaman. "We have heard your accusation, sir, but you have shown no evidence."

An elderly man, sitting on the first row, stood. "Yes. He refuses to tell us what exactly it is that he has lost."

"It wasn't lost," said Naaman firmly, pointing at Jeshua. "He stole it!"

"So you have said, a dozen times now," said Benjamin. "We still must know what you allege this man took from you, so we can see if he has it."

"I told you before," said Naaman, the color rising up his neck. "It's private. I was traveling and spent the night in this man's orchard." He pointed at Esau, who sat at the rear of the room.

"Without payment!" said Esau cheerily, and the men laughed.

Naaman scowled at Esau, then turned back to Benjamin. "I left early the next morning, and when I had gone some distance down the road, I checked my pouch, which I keep around my neck, and my possession was gone."

"Where is your pouch now?"

"It's gone!"

"But you said you 'checked your pouch,'" said Benjamin.

"I said I checked *for* my pouch, and it was missing!" said Naaman.

Esau was about to correct him, but Jeshua caught his eye and shook his head. Naaman saw the exchange and a perplexed look crossed his face.

"So how do you know he took it?" queried a well-dressed man, obviously a merchant.

Naaman wheeled around. "I retraced my steps, seeking the pouch. When I returned to where I had slept, I saw this man working nearby, digging a well. He is the only one who could have taken it."

"But what was *in* it?" said another man irritably.

"That is none of your—"

"Rabbi Benjamin?"

Benjamin looked at Jeshua, who had not said a word before now—a remarkable feat, considering what was at stake. The young carpenter had listened patiently for more than an hour as Naaman accused, threatened, and ridiculed him, yet he had said nothing. Benjamin was beginning to think the young man was either an idiot or a sage.

"Yes, young man, you wish to speak?"

"I have a question for Naaman, if I may."

"Go ahead."

Jeshua turned to Naaman and said, "I know what was taken from you is valuable, but I did not take it. You do not believe me. I can understand that. We do not know each other, so you don't know if I am lying."

"I know you are lying," spat Naaman. "My pouch is missing."

"I understand," said Jeshua, and turned to Benjamin. "I have an idea that might resolve this problem. Naaman has lost something very valuable to him. I have lost my brother, who was helping me dig Master Jacob's well. My suggestion is this: we might be able to help each other. If Naaman agrees to help me dig the well, I will pay him the value of whatever it is he lost."

"It was stolen!" yelled Naaman.

"Sir!" said Benjamin. "You will not shout in this place."

Naaman glared at Benjamin, who turned to Jeshua. "Go on."

"But," interrupted the well-dressed merchant, "he won't tell us the value. So how can you pay him an amount he won't divulge?"

"I will satisfy him, you have my word," said Jeshua.

"The word of a liar," said Naaman quietly.

"We have just heard!" laughed Esau from the back of the room.

Benjamin frowned. Strange proposition. He looked at Naaman. "What do you think?"

Naaman was astonished. "You can't be serious. I am a merchant, not a common laborer. I will not be sold into servitude to the very man who robbed me!"

Benjamin sighed. "But since you have produced no evidence, we have nothing to hold against this man. I believe he has been generous— overly generous—with his offer."

"I will extend it further," said Jeshua. "If Naaman does not agree that what I will pay him is fair, I will submit to the elders again and suffer your judgment."

Naaman looked around in amazement. The men were nodding. "This is outrageous!" he shouted. "This man is a bastard. Yes! I know! I've been talking to people around town. You know an illegitimate's word is presumed invalid in a court of law!"

Voices erupted in discussion of the charge. From the noise level, Benjamin guessed it had been on the minds of many. He pounded the lectern for quiet and pointed a slender finger at Naaman. "We are not judging his parentage, sir. We are judging him. You accused him of being a thief, but you have produced no evidence. It's your word against his—"

"Rabbi."

Everyone turned. An old man, very tall and very broad across the chest, with a long gray beard, stood and removed his kerchief. He looked at Jeshua evenly.

"Yes, Eli," said Benjamin.

"I have something to say." He nodded at Jeshua. "I know this young man. Whether he is illegitimate or not I do not know. What I do know is that he is a fine carpenter. He worked for me last year, remodeling my house. The front door. Many of you have seen it."

There were nods all around.

"So what?" said Naaman. "So he can hang a door."

Eli's voice boomed. "Sir, you know not to whom you speak! I have listened to your bleating for over an hour, and now you will listen to me! The man you accuse is above reproach. I watched him as he worked at my home and was impressed with his fidelity, to master and servant alike. I never saw anything that would indicate that he could have done what you have accused him of. He is an honest man. And therefore you, sir, are a liar."

Eli sat down and silence filled the room. Naaman was speechless. He looked around for a sign that someone—anyone—believed his side of the story. Every man sat with his head down, thinking about what Eli had said. Naaman looked at Benjamin, his eyes pleading for help. Benjamin met his gaze evenly. "I think you should take Jeshua's offer."

Naaman's jaw dropped.

Benjamin turned to the others and said, "All in favor, raise your right hand."

All hands were raised.

"All opposed?"

Naaman was so surprised that he forgot to raise his hand.

"It is unanimous. Let the record so show." He nodded toward Naaman. "If you desire recompense for your loss, you will work with

Jeshua until the well is finished, at which time he will pay you for your labor. If you are not satisfied," he sighed, knowing this man never would be, "you may return and we will consider this matter further."

The men immediately stood, glad to have this over. Naaman remained frozen in place as they passed him without a word. The old man Eli glared at him until Naaman looked away. Jeshua stood to one side in his dirty tunic, his head down and eyes closed. Naaman made a disgusted sound.

"We'll see you at the orchard tomorrow," said Esau, from behind him.

Naaman whirled around. "You will not. I am done with this place. You're all criminals. I should have known not to trust a bunch of super-stitious liars!"

Esau laughed and clapped Naaman on the shoulder. "See you tomorrow." He turned and walked away. Naaman stared after him, then walked alone out of the synagogue into the night.

"Jeshua."

Jeshua turned and saw Eli. "Thank you for your kind words."

"I normally don't speak much in synagogue, but they were true, and slipped out."

"How's Reuben?"

Eli smiled. "A changed man. We are glad to have him home."

"And Simeon?"

"His wife Rachel had a son. Can you believe it? Another grand-child!"

Jeshua smiled. "Please give him my best. I'm sure he's a good father."

Eli nodded. "He's a great man, my Simeon."

"How is our door holding up?"

"As beautiful today as it was when you finished it."

"And the hinges? Do they squeak?"

Eli shook his head. "Your apprentice, Arah, oils them regularly. You really made an impression on that boy."

"Please tell him I asked about him."

"With pleasure. He asks about you all the time. For once, I have something to tell him."

"I hope it won't include this," said Jeshua, gesturing around.

Eli put his arm around Jeshua and led him out of the synagogue. "You might be a stranger in this town, but you are not a stranger here," he said, touching his chest.

He left Jeshua on the steps of the synagogue and walked over to his horse, mounted, and slowly made his way down the street.

FIFTEEN

Enemies All About

Naaman rode home in the darkness. He should have known that taking this man before the elders was a stupid idea. They were all against him. Well after midnight, when he passed Jacob's estate, he tied his horse and crept over the rise of hill. He looked down at the household buildings. Again, no candle burned in the window tonight. He thought of sneaking down there and cutting the carpenter's throat. If he could not have his treasure, no one would.

The thought gave him some comfort until he remembered the black dog that patrolled the grounds. Anyway, Jeshua would take precautions, now that he'd been caught stealing. He probably bribed every one of the synagogue elders. And Naaman couldn't just hang around, hoping Jeshua would reveal his treachery. He would have to be doubly clever to get his money back.

And he'd better come up with something soon. An hour later, when he crested the rise and Ishmael's huge estate spread out in front of him, surrounded by the stone wall, he wondered why he didn't just hide the talent in the wall in the first place. Why had he gone so far, just to lose the thing?

He shook his head. *Now they've got me saying it,* he chided himself. All those religious fanatics. Hypocrites. Sitting there in their fine clothing, judging him. He might be a stable keeper, but at least he earned an honest living. He didn't just loll around, getting fat, judging others. Judging people they didn't even know. And why they thought Jeshua was more believable was beyond belief. Didn't they see how he was dressed? One look at the man, his dark, furtive eyes, and the way he stood there mute—it was obvious he was lying.

Naaman dismounted and kicked a stone angrily, stubbing his toe. He remembered the barked shin, which was still trying to scab over. He had gone to great pains to keep his traveling cloak on to hide the cut. And he'd almost been caught in a lie with his name. It would have been a catastrophe if they'd seen the leg injury and begun asking him about it.

When he arrived at the servants' quarters, the eastern sky was brightening. He tiptoed into the room he shared with Zerah and got into bed, pulling the covers up and letting out a weary sigh. Moments later, Zerah opened his eyes and yawned. He stood and kicked Naaman's wooden bed frame. "Get up, lazy bones!"

Naaman rolled over, ignoring him. Zerah kicked the bed again. "I said, get up!" He gave the bed a solid kick, and the slats holding the tick mattress slipped from their ledge. Naaman fell to the ground with a thump. "Why'd you do that?"

Zerah just laughed and walked outside.

Naaman got up, looked at his bed, and cursed. He was too tired to fight now, and definitely too tired to put the bed back together. He crossed the room and lay down on Zerah's bed and in a moment was sound asleep.

"I can't believe it," said a familiar voice, awakening Naaman, who was disoriented for a moment. Then he remembered why. He was in Zerah's bed. And that was Zerah's voice.

"I tell you it's true," came Hanock's voice, chortling with glee. "We have nearly doubled our investment!"

"Hooray!" shouted Zerah. Naaman looked around. Light sifted

through cracks in the wooden shutters, interrupted by a shadow now and then as a person moved while talking. Naaman crept to the window and listened intently. Hanock was speaking in low tones.

"Ocran—that sly fox—has loaned a portion of the money we gave him to another, and he's collecting interest, too, half of which is payable to us!"

"How do you know this?"

"You think I just lie around here all day, like you and Naaman? I'm always thinking the way Master Ishmael thinks: how can I multiply my holdings?"

"So it was your idea, for Ocran to lend the money yet again?"

Naaman guessed Hanock nodded, because Zerah laughed. "*You're* the sly fox, Hanock. You amaze me."

"That is why I'm chief steward."

"And why I'm your assistant."

Both men laughed. "And you know the best part?" whispered Hanock.

"What's that?" said Zerah.

"Naaman, hasn't done a thing with his talent, I just know it."

"That's what I think, too," agreed Zerah. "He probably just buried it."

"Oh, it's probably worse than that. You know what a poor gambler he is!"

"Either way, it's going to be fun to watch," said Zerah. "When the master returns, Naaman is going to get the surprise of his life. I've been watching. He hasn't been keeping up with his work. The stables are a mess. I can't wait to see him whipped and cast out."

Naaman's eyes narrowed to slits, his hands clawed the blanket, and his heart pounded. Blackguards! Betrayers! Everywhere, all around him, people were plotting against him!

"He had his chance," said Hanock, his voice getting fainter. "Ishmael is a man of his word. Naaman will pay, one way or another."

Laughter from both men. Naaman peeked out the window and watched them walk away. When they were out of sight, he grabbed his cloak and stomped off toward the stables.

SIXTEEN

The Ram Appears

Jeshua hauled the bucket up, scaled the ladder, and heaved it over the well edge. This evening he would have to find a way to extend the ladder. It was too short now, and he could barely get out of the well. He had to scale the rocks the last few feet just to get out. Then he had to dump the bucket, toss it back over the hole, climb back down the ladder, and fill the bucket again.

It was backbreaking work, and terribly slow. He was curious why Esau, who had seen fit to go with him to Cana two nights ago to help defend him before the synagogue, did not see fit to lend him one of the servants. There were plenty of them around.

Then he remembered how dry the orchard was and how all the servants, even the children, were working all day, hauling water from the cistern under the house, trying desperately to save the trees with what little water they had left. It was a losing battle; the summer days were scorching, and the trees were dying. If a fire caught, they would go up like tinder. But a well would solve their problems, and that is why Jeshua couldn't figure Esau out.

He climbed up the ladder and hauled himself over the well lip, then pulled the bucket up. He carried it over to the dirt pile. When he turned, he saw Esau standing in the clearing near the dowser's stake, talking to two servants, pointing at the ground and gesturing at the trees. They must have seen Jeshua, because all three turned to face him, their voices suddenly still. Even from a distance, Jeshua knew what they had been talking about. Esau sent the servants off and walked slowly toward Jeshua, who prepared himself. He couldn't blame Esau for firing him. He had hired two men to dig the well, and now there was just one. It wasn't his fault James had to leave. It was just bad luck, and Esau had a right to be angry. Besides, the well was twelve feet deep and still no water. Behind Esau, the dowser's stake stood like an accusing finger, pointing down to the spot where the water coursed, cold and refreshing. And here he stood, next to a dry hole, preparing himself to be dismissed. He bowed his head and waited.

Esau walked up and said brightly, "Jeshua! How's it going?"

"I'm sorry, Esau. I've failed you."

Esau laughed. "That fellow hasn't shown up, has he?"

Jeshua shook his head.

"Well," mused Esau, "I didn't think he would. He is a born liar. He lied about his name, as well as his profession. A 'traveler and a merchant,' my eye. Bald-faced lies. Why didn't you call him on them?"

Jeshua shrugged. "What was the point?"

Esau shook his head. "The point was defending your honor. Surely that must matter to you."

"Honor isn't something you defend," said Jeshua. "It can't be taken away or destroyed by another. Only by yourself. It's something you just have. Or don't have. Don't you think people know, either way?"

Esau looked at the pile of stones and dirt, now higher than his head. "Maybe most people. But not all. You should be careful, Jeshua. I watched you say nothing until the last minute. Why was that? Didn't you sense the danger you were in?"

Jeshua nodded, saying nothing. Finally, Esau let out a long, portentous sigh, and turned to the well. "What are we going to do about this?"

Jeshua collapsed on the rock pile, his head in his hands. "I honestly don't know, Master Esau."

From behind the trees, Naaman watched. After watching the servants head off to work, he had entered the estate in a roundabout way. He stole closer and spied the overseer and the well digger talking. It looked like the overseer was lecturing the well digger about something, because the well digger just stood there, taking it, saying nothing. How he recognized that posture! Then the man slumped down on the rock and put his head in his hands. The image filled Naaman's heart with joy. He was not a religious man, but he believed in just deserts. And watching the overseer standing over the carpenter, hands on his hips, glaring at the man, was just too wonderful to behold.

He must have laughed out loud, because suddenly both men were looking straight at him. The well digger jumped to his feet. The overseer shouted, "You there. Show yourself!"

Caught, Naaman stepped out from behind the tree. The overseer started laughing and said something to the carpenter, who didn't respond. He just looked at Naaman, a blank look on his face.

Naaman walked forward. "I'm not here to work," he said, not knowing what else to say.

"I'm sure of that," said Esau. Then he slapped Jeshua on the shoulder. "A ram indeed!" He walked off, shaking his head and laughing.

Jeshua watched him go, but Naaman was looking for the knife the carpenter usually wore. It was not there today, so he could speak freely. He pointed at Jeshua: "You know you did it. Let's get that out of the way first."

Jeshua nodded.

"You also know how valuable the thing was you stole."

Jeshua just looked at him.

Naaman laughed. It was a little forced, but he mustn't give his plan away. "So you know there is no way in the world you can afford to pay me its worth. That is why I'm here: to watch you squirm as you realize that, no matter what happens, I will have satisfaction from you. I will have my reward!"

Jeshua nodded again. "I am happy you came. Thank you." He held his hand out to Naaman, who spit on it.

Jeshua wiped his hand on his shirt and said, "Careful, water is scarce around here." He walked over to the well. Naaman was astonished at the man's denseness. He seemed too dumb to take offense. This might work out after all. Jeshua had his money and would reveal something before long. All he had to do was watch for clues.

Jeshua was preparing to climb down into the well. Naaman took off his cloak and folded it neatly. He had dressed in his finest clothes, to further the fiction about his being a merchant, but now he wasn't sure good clothing was such a great idea. He removed his leather sandals (they were actually Zerah's but he wouldn't miss them), and placed them with the cloak. He rolled up the sleeves of his tunic and looked at the carpenter. "Just so we understand each other."

"Tell you what," said Jeshua. "You may have your choice. You can either climb down into the well and fill the bucket, or stay up here and empty it."

Naaman saw how dirty Jeshua was. Even a stableboy managed to stay cleaner than this. "I'll empty the bucket, if it's all the same to you," he said flatly.

"It's all the same." Jeshua climbed down the rock wall, found the ladder with his foot, and descended into the darkness.

They worked that way for a while, and Jeshua was happy not to have to haul every bucket up by himself. But Naaman moved slowly, and it seemed that it took him forever to lower the empty bucket back down. Jeshua wondered why it took him so long.

Up top, each time he emptied the bucket, Naaman turned over a few rocks, looking for the marker stone. He also paused to take a drink or scan the sky for clouds that might provide some shade. It was miserably hot up here, and soon he was sweating streams. He took his linen tunic off and stripped down to his breeches. But it only got hotter, and the water in the bladder was hot as well. As he lowered the bucket, it occurred to him that it must be cool down in the well. It wasn't muddy because they hadn't hit water yet. All Jeshua had to do was shovel dirt into the bucket. He didn't have to raise it or carry it over to the pile. It became clear to Naaman that he had been tricked.

He leaned over the edge. "I changed my mind. I'd rather work down there."

Jeshua climbed up the ladder and scaled the wall. He pulled himself over the lip and got to his feet. "That would suit me as well," he said.

Naaman handed him the waterskin and climbed down into the well. It was slow going, but the thought of the thirsty carpenter up there trying to get a drink out of an empty skin made him smile. He reached the bottom and looked up. It was a long way, but at least the ground underfoot was dry. And hard. He tapped it with the shovel. He looked around. The stones were big, and the dirt was like stone as well. The bucket came down and rested by his feet. He looked up. Jeshua was looking in, a silhouette against the white summer sky.

Naaman started digging, but the ground was like iron. It took him five minutes just to fill the bucket, and he was sweating when he finished, even in the cool darkness. His back ached. And no sooner did he pull on the rope as a signal to raise it, than it seemed like it was headed back down, empty.

Naaman knew he'd never last a day at this rate. *Tricked me twice,* he thought miserably.

Up top, Jeshua stretched. He was glad to be out of that confining hole and up here in the sun. His feet ached from pushing on the spade. If only Naaman would say something. But he just glared at Jeshua when he lowered the bucket. And once, when Jeshua was singing to himself as he hauled the bucket up, Naaman shouted, "Shut up!" and it so surprised Jeshua that he did.

At lunch Naaman sat to one side, eating the bread and honey Jeshua gave him, without so much as a thank-you. Jeshua marveled at the energy the man was expending in hatred. If he put that much effort into working, they'd strike water within the hour.

"What's that?" asked Naaman, pointing at the dowser's stake.

"That's where the dowser said we should dig the well."

"Then why are you digging it here?"

"Because I believe the water is here," said Jeshua.

"Are you a dowser?"

"No."

"And how many wells have you dug?"

"This is my first."

Naaman cursed, threw his bread on the ground, and stomped off into the orchard.

SEVENTEEN

Distant Memories

During lunch on the second day, Naaman plucked and ate a couple of oranges. Finishing, his fingers were sticky, and he regretted draining the waterskin, but when he picked it up, he discovered it was full again. He washed his hands and lay down under a tree, closing his eyes.

Jeshua was down in the well, splitting rocks with a maul and chisel. The pounding went on for some time, a constant, pleasing rhythm that lulled Naaman to sleep. When he awoke, Jeshua was dumping a bucket of rock shards. Naaman yawned, rose, and walked over to the well, preparing to be chided. But Jeshua simply smiled and turned back to work.

Naaman looked at the sun. It was midafternoon. He had been asleep for a long time, and the growing pile of rock chips was proof. Jeshua must have made ten trips up and down the well in that time, and yet he never wakened him. If he had been Zerah or Hanock or Ishmael, Naaman would have been awakened with a kick to the head and a dozen stripes afterward.

He looked in the well and watched Jeshua fill the bucket. "You should have wakened me."

"Ready?"

Naaman pulled the bucket up. Why wasn't the carpenter raging at him? He had a right. Naaman dumped the bucket, walked quickly back, and watched Jeshua pound another large stone into bits. He saw the sweat coursing down Jeshua's bare back and said, "Hey."

Jeshua looked up. Naaman tossed an orange down into the well. Jeshua caught it. "We're not supposed to pick the fruit," said Jeshua, looking at the orange.

"I didn't know. Tell them I picked it. I don't care."

Jeshua smiled. "I guess that's true. You didn't know, right?"

"Right."

So Jeshua peeled the orange and ate it, the juice spurting onto his beard.

"Unhook the bucket," said Naaman. Jeshua did so. Naaman pulled the rope up and attached the water bladder, lowering it back down. "The oranges. They're sticky."

Jeshua rinsed his hands, then took a long drink. He motioned for Naaman to raise the bucket. "Thanks," he said, and started splitting rocks again.

Naaman almost said, "You're welcome," but caught himself. He must remember what he was doing here. Then he reconsidered. If he ingratiated himself with Jeshua, it might be easier to discover his weaknesses. He would just pretend that Jeshua was Zerah, and before long he would know all his secrets, just as he knew Zerah's. He put a smile on his face, leaned over the hole, and said, "You're welcome."

For the next two days they worked together, with little being said but much being accomplished. After a while, Naaman discovered that Jeshua didn't much care whether he worked or not, and that, somehow, made working less of a burden. It was the lack of force, he guessed, that made the difference. And the sense of accomplishment. He'd never experienced that before. In a stable, nothing stayed clean. He never felt like he was making any progress, so he quit working years ago and instead put his mind to finding ways to avoid it. But with the well, the growing mound of dirt was evidence that at least a hole was being dug.

He even quit looking for his marker stone. It was probably deep under the pile anyway. And when he noticed the dowser's stake at lunch again on the third day, he just shrugged, figuring Jeshua must know what he was doing.

He noticed that Jeshua rarely talked but mostly just worked and sang quietly to himself. He would answer questions, though. Naaman learned how Jeshua's brother James had been called away to care for his sister. When Naaman said he had no brothers or sisters, Jeshua simply nodded.

"With your large family, it must be hard to imagine not having anyone to talk to," said Naaman, reflecting on the hunger and loneliness of growing up an orphan in Jotapata.

Jeshua nodded and walked over to get a drink from the bladder. When he returned, he touched Naaman so gently on the shoulder that it felt like a whisper of wind. The touch sparked a long-forgotten memory of Naaman's mother. She was frail and very sick. He was three or four years old and spent his days begging in the doorway of their tiny, musty alcove. He remembered her hand touching his shoulder. He looked up into her tired, red eyes, which were filled with tears. He held the cup up proudly, a single shekel in it. She removed the coin and gave it to him to keep. He placed the shekel inside his rough shirt and looked over his shoulder at his mother as she slowly climbed back into the mass of rags they called a bed. She died less than a week later. That was the last time she touched him.

Naaman touched his shoulder, remembering her touch and her brown eyes, surprised at the memory, which had hidden from him all these years. When he came to himself, he felt tears in his eyes and quickly brushed them away. He stole a look at Jeshua, who was sitting on the edge of the well, his back to him, his head bent and eyes closed. Naaman had seen that pose enough times now to know he was praying. He wondered what it felt like to pray, but then turned his mind back to the image of his mother, already fading in his mind.

EIGHTEEN

A Glimmer of Hope

Naaman stole back each evening to Ishmael's estate, to check on things. Zerah and Hanock were spending most days in Sepphoris, overseeing their investment. Naaman would make it back for the fireside gathering and sit quietly, listening as Hanock bragged about their adventures. They didn't even know he was gone.

He whipped Jonah solidly the first night back because the hay had not been changed in the stalls, but when he came back the second night, the place was clean and the tack was oiled.

Working with the carpenter had been instructive, on many levels, but not in the way he had hoped. He was there to discover where Jeshua hid the talent, but he kept finding himself watching Jeshua work. It was fascinating, especially for someone who spent an equal amount of time avoiding work. At first he considered it kind of pathetic: Jeshua obviously didn't know how to get underlings to do most of the work. Naaman often drowsed in the loft on the soft, fragrant hay as the boys cleaned the barn below. He knew as long as he was up there they would keep busy. It didn't matter if he was asleep or not; they didn't dare take the risk or they would taste the whip for their trouble.

And for a fleeting moment when he started working with Jeshua, he feared he might be treated the same way. He was prepared to refuse any demands, but none came. Every time a chore needed to be done, Jeshua cheerfully did it. At first Naaman thought it was some sort of trick but couldn't think of the purpose. Then one day it came to him: Jeshua *liked* to work. It was as simple as that. *He must be an idiot,* mused Naaman, but that idea collapsed under the weight of his experience with Jeshua.

This strange idea of enjoying labor plagued him all the way home that night, under the waning moon. And when he reached the barn, it had so filled his mind that he forgot to whip the boys. Instead, he went up to the loft to think, and the next morning gave the boys his orders without threats. He was anxious to leave, to see if they would strike water today. He hurried to Jacob's estate, and at one point on the journey even caught himself whistling.

He paused on the hill overlooking Jacob's estate and wondered what it would be like to work here. He had looked into the barn where Jeshua was sleeping because Jeshua asked him if he needed a place to stay. He had said no, but he was interested in seeing how they kept things there. It wasn't bad. It was an old barn—Jacob wasn't as prosperous as Ishmael—but it was clean. He asked where the stableboy was. Jeshua just shrugged, picked up a rake, and cleaned out the stall himself.

Standing here in the morning light, he was also certain of another thing: Jeshua knew he was no merchant or traveler. Where would he be staying? It was crazy to think he might be going back to Cana each evening.

But Jeshua hadn't said anything and the overseer hadn't been around. Naaman wondered about Jeshua. He was poor, yet he seemed happy. He worked like a common servant, yet he didn't resent it. And most of all, he didn't hate Naaman, as he should. And because of that, Naaman was finding it increasingly difficult to hate Jeshua.

And that could really get in the way of things.

NINETEEN

Two Miracles

L ate in the afternoon of his fifth day working with Jeshua, Naaman was down in the well, breaking a large rock into bits. The well was now nearly thirty feet deep, and still no water. When Jeshua lowered the bucket, he had to keep hold of the end of the rope so it wouldn't slip through the block and tackle. They had scoured the estate for more rope, but couldn't find any. When he and Jeshua exchanged places in the well, one had to lower the other down, hanging onto the bucket. The ladder was now useless, so they left it in the barn.

"Okay!" he called, looking up. "Go ahead!"

Jeshua hauled the bucket up. The sun was hot, and he felt the sweat trickling down his back. He emptied it, then lowered it back down. He heard Naaman chiseling on a large stone, the strokes ringing out rhythmically. Jeshua had noted a great improvement in Naaman's work, and he smiled when he heard Naaman singing: "We know not where our path will lead, or from whence we've come. . . ."

Jeshua turned his face to the sun, enjoying its warmth and Naaman's singing.

"Jeshua!"

Jeshua leaned over the hole. The sun was so bright he could see nothing in the darkness below.

"We did it! There's water!"

"Water? How much?" asked Jeshua.

Naaman scooped rock shards into the bucket. He had swung the maul, and the large stone cracked in two. A trickle of water emerged. He dipped his finger and tasted it. Cool and refreshing. He cheered. "Not much, but the water is good!"

Jeshua shouted happily. Naaman saw him silhouetted in the triangle of blue sky between the tripod legs.

Jeshua looked around, wanting to share his joy. In the distance, almost lost in the trees, he saw Esau talking with two servants. "Master Esau! Come!"

Esau waved back absently. Naaman's chisel continued to ring, and Jeshua felt the ache in his shoulders vanish with the news of the water strike. He tied a knot in the rope end and loped off toward Esau.

Naaman placed the iron wedge into the rock fissure and gave a mighty swing. The wedge disappeared between the halves of stone, then popped out, followed by a gushing stream of water. Within seconds, he was soaked. The water was clear and very cold. He looked up, but Jeshua was gone. He emptied the bucket of stone shards and placed his spade, the maul, and the iron wedge in the bucket and looked up again. Still no Jeshua. The water had already risen to his calves.

Naaman looked up again and shivered, amazed that just a minute ago he was sweating like a thresher. He wondered how high the water would rise. He tugged on the rope. It seemed solid. The water was licking at the backs of his knees, sending chills up his spine. "Jeshua!"

Jeshua's face appeared up top. "Esau wants to know how much water there is."

"Plenty!" said Naaman, trying not to show his fear, which was creeping up, along with the water. "Get me out of here!"

"Send the tools up first, then I'll pull you up."

Without thinking, Naaman took hold of the rope and pulled.

"No!" yelled Jeshua, reaching for the rope as the knot came undone. It slipped through the block and disappeared in the darkness.

Naaman fell backward into the freezing water as the rope coiled down on top of him. Jeshua's face could be seen, far above. "Are you all right?"

Naaman fought his way clear of the rope. "Guess I'll have to climb up."

Jeshua called down, "We need to get the tools out, too. We'll need another rope." By now, Esau and the two servants were standing around the well opening.

In the darkness, the water seemed to rise suddenly. Naaman felt it on his thighs. "There isn't time."

"What?"

"The water is rising too fast!"

Esau motioned for one of the servants to go find a rope. He peered into the darkness. "Can you climb out?"

"I think so," came Naaman's voice.

"So there's water?" asked Esau.

"More than enough." Naaman decided not to wait for another rope. He placed his foot on a rock protruding from the wall. When he put his weight on it, it slipped and he barked his injured shin, drawing blood.

"Are you coming up?" It was Esau's voice.

Naaman grunted. "Yes, but if I'm not fast enough, by all means come on down and meet me halfway."

Esau turned from the well. "He's coming up. Congratulations, Jeshua." He held out his hand, but Jeshua was still looking into the hole, concerned.

"How's it coming?" Jeshua asked the darkness.

"Just great," said Naaman, tired of questions. The water was still rising. He grabbed a rock protruding from the wall, but his hand was slippery. He wiped it on his wet breeches and reached up again, lifting himself up a foot. Above him a stone as big as a man's torso protruded from the wall.

"Jeshua?" he called out, his voice trembling from fear and cold. "I'm not sure I can make it."

Jeshua scanned the work area for an idea. He leaned over the edge. "They went for another rope. You don't have to climb all the way up. Just stay above the water. We'll get you out."

Naaman held himself above the water with his back against one wall, his feet against the other. But he was tiring, and his bare feet kept slipping. He saw a crevice in the big rock above him and forced his fingers into the cleft, feeling the skin tear and the warm stickiness of his own blood. He pulled himself up but lost his grip and fell back into the water.

Jeshua called out, "What happened? Are you all right?"

Naaman got to his feet. The water was waist deep. He looked up and, to his horror, saw the big stone above him move, dislodging dirt, which cascaded down onto his upturned face and blinded him. He threw water on his face, and then felt, more than heard, the stone give way. He looked up just as it popped loose from its socket and dropped toward him, shrieking as it bounced off the walls. It hit him squarely in the chest, pinning him to the well floor.

"Jeshua!" he croaked, his chest so constricted he could barely speak. The sound of the water filled his ears and the edges of his vision began to go gray. The water level lapped at his neck.

"Did you feel that?" asked Esau, leaning around Jeshua. They both looked into the darkness.

"Naaman!" No sound returned. Jeshua yelled again, "Naaman! Are you hurt?" No answer. Jeshua looked around. By now there were a half dozen workers standing around the well, looking in. One almost fell in and was caught by another. They all took a step back. Jeshua turned to Esau. "We have to climb down and get him."

Esau shook his head. "But he isn't answering."

"We've got to try."

In response, a servant shook his head. "That was a stone falling, wasn't it?"

Jeshua nodded. "Where is the rope?"

They all looked toward the house. No one was coming. Then they all looked back at Jeshua. He began peeling off his tunic. Esau shook his head. "He's probably dead, Jeshua."

"We don't know that," Jeshua said as he kicked off his sandals.

Esau called into the well. "Naaman! Naaman!" No answer. He turned to Jeshua. "He isn't answering."

Jeshua pointed at Esau. "Find a rope. I'm going down."

Esau caught his arm. "Other rocks might be loose. You'll be killed, too."

Jeshua pulled his arm loose from Esau's grasp and lowered himself over the edge. Esau bent toward him, their faces inches apart. "What good are two deaths?"

"No better than one," said Jeshua.

"He wouldn't risk his life for you."

Jeshua looked evenly at Esau until the overseer looked away, then he lowered himself into the well. Esau and the servants ringed the opening, watching. Jeshua almost slipped, then caught himself just in time. One servant turned away, murmuring, "God help him." Another shook his head and looked at Esau, whose face was dark with fear.

"Even if he's alive, you'll never be able to carry him back up," said Esau.

Jeshua squinted down into the darkness. "Just find a rope."

Esau motioned for another servant to run to the house.

Jeshua could hear the water coursing below, but he could not see Naaman. He gingerly lowered himself past a big rock, then saw well below him the gaping hole that moments before held a large boulder. He inched his way past the socket, his fingertips struggling for purchase, but sweat made them slippery and he fell, cracking his head on a rock and plunging into the cold water below.

He found his feet and pulled his head out of the icy water. His eyes hadn't yet adjusted and it was completely dark. The hole this deep was only about five feet across. He knelt and felt around under the water. There! A leg, a large stone, and beyond it, his hand brushed Naaman's face, barely above the water. He couldn't tell by touch whether he was alive or dead. Jeshua pushed against the stone pinning him, but it wouldn't move.

"Help! I need help!" he called. No faces appeared in the white circle above. He pushed the stone again, but it still wouldn't budge. The water now covered Naaman's mouth and nose.

"Adonai!" he cried and heaved against the stone with all his might. "Help me, Father!"

It moved. An inch.

He hurled himself against it again, the water's cold sapping his strength but not his resolve. "Lord!" he pleaded as he pushed, and the stone moved a tiny bit. Then, with one final push, it rolled off Naaman. Jeshua pulled him up out of the water, hugging him tightly around the chest from behind, expelling a burst of water from his lungs. Again. More water. And again.

Jeshua continued pumping Naaman's chest until no more water came out. After a long time, Naaman sputtered, spittle jumped from his blue lips, and he made a desperate inhalation. Jeshua held him against a rock just above the water. Naaman coughed repeatedly, but each time his breath was stronger, until he lay, still unconscious, but breathing.

The water was up to Jeshua's chest now, and he wondered how they were going to get out of the well. He looked up. "The rope!" he called weakly, tasting blood in his own mouth.

"Just a second!"

Jeshua looked up and saw a rope falling toward him. He reached for it.

It was ten feet too short.

"It's not long enough!"

"That's all we have!" came a servant's voice.

Jeshua pulled himself up, one hand pressing a limp Naaman against the wall, the other seeking a handhold. He raised a leg and forced his toes into the muddy underwater wall. He was able, for just a second, to put his weight on that foot and lift himself before it gave way. He reached up, found another cleft, and lifted Naaman up another foot. His lower foot cleared the water, and he pressed it against the wall, hauling them both up another few inches.

Jeshua looked up. There was a big rock a couple of feet above him. If he could get past it, the rope might be in reach. But as he touched the stone, it moved. He could see a large scuff on it, gouged when the first rock hit it. Now this rock was loose as well.

Here, though, the well wall narrowed a bit and Jeshua had his first good foothold. He slowly maneuvered Naaman's body until he got him onto his shoulders, the way a shepherd carries a lamb. He reached up for the loose rock, hoping it would hold his weight long enough for him to get above it.

"Can you reach the rope?" Esau called out.

Jeshua was too tired to answer. The rope was still out of reach by a couple of feet. He groaned under his burden and moved up a bit, pushing against the loose rock to hold it steady as he inched past. He grasped for the rope and grazed it. It swung across his field of vision.

"The rope moved!" someone said above.

"Jeshua! Jeshua!"

He wanted to answer, but it would take too much energy. Another inch higher. He steadied himself for another grab. Suddenly, the loose stone shifted and gave way. He lunged for the rope and managed to grab it. The stone fell from the wall, and Jeshua ran across its surface as it fell into the darkness below with a terrible crash.

Jeshua hung from the rope by one hand, holding Naaman on his shoulders with the other. He took a deep breath and whispered hoarsely, "Pull."

The rope moved, inching upward. He found the rock's empty hole with his foot and was finally able to reach up with his other hand to grab the rope. It moved slowly upward. He kept Naaman on his shoulders by leaning him against the wall as he climbed with his feet.

"There he is!" yelled a servant, sitting on the well edge, hauling on the rope. Behind him, the four other servants pulled as well.

"Slowly," cautioned Esau. "Hang on, Jeshua!"

Jeshua looked up. The surface was just ten feet above him now. Naaman was a small man, but he was heavy. Jeshua tried to feel the rise of his chest, hoping he was still alive.

Another minute and hands were reaching for him. They lifted Naaman off his shoulders, and pulled Jeshua from the well. He lay on his back, panting. Someone held out a calfskin bladder of water to him. He pushed it away, rolled over, and saw Naaman lying there motionless. Esau stood over him, his face drained of hope.

Jeshua crawled over and took Naaman's face in his hands. Several of the servants took off their head coverings. Jeshua put his arms around Naaman and rocked him slowly, his face turned upward, his eyes closed, crying silently. Esau reached out to comfort Jeshua, when suddenly Naaman coughed and opened his eyes. He blinked up at Jeshua and asked weakly, "Am I dead? Are you the Lord?"

One of the servants laughed, and the others shook their heads in wonder. Esau clapped Jeshua on the shoulder. Everyone thought Naaman was out of his head, but Jeshua put his mouth to Naaman's ear and whispered, "He is with you, for he has saved your life this day."

Naaman looked up at Jeshua, tears welling in his eyes. "Forgive me."

Then the servants pulled them to their feet and helped them back to the house, where Elisabeth prepared a feast to celebrate the two miracles: the new well, and Naaman's rescue.

TWENTY

Paid in Full

That night, Naaman slept in the house. His wounds were dressed and he was given a soft, warm bed. He awoke during the night to see Jeshua sitting to one side, watching over him. Their eyes met, but Naaman was ashamed and turned away. When he awoke in the first light of morning, he saw Jeshua sleeping in the chair. Naaman studied the carpenter, feeling a fullness in his chest. He promised himself he would never forget what happened yesterday.

When he awoke again, Jeshua was gone, and Elisabeth brought him a breakfast of figs and dates and thick bread slathered with butter. He ate, ravenous, then slept some more. By late afternoon, he felt strong enough to get out of bed and stumbled out into the dooryard. He wanted to see Jeshua.

As he approached the well, he saw Jeshua working, building a low stone wall around the well mouth, using the rocks from the pile. Jeshua looked up and saw Naaman, then came over and led him to the shade of a nearby tree.

"I'm all right," said Naaman, sitting, feeling like an old man. His bruised ribs ached, and he felt woozy from the bright sunlight.

"You're done here, Naaman," said Jeshua. "Our agreement was that you'd help me find the water. That you did."

"But the well isn't done yet," said Naaman. "I'll help you finish it—if you want me to."

"Of course I do," said Jeshua. "You can help me tomorrow, if you're up to it."

"I will be," said Naaman.

For the next two days they worked together, finishing the well. Esau bought more rope, and Jeshua climbed into the well and retrieved the tools. Standing up top, waiting for him to reappear, was the longest ten minutes of Naaman's life. He could hardly bear to look over the lip into the darkness, and when Jeshua finally appeared, he was so relieved he almost shouted for joy.

Several times during those two days, Naaman almost apologized to Jeshua, but he couldn't find the words. Guilt had tied his tongue. And yet somehow he knew that whatever apology he gave would be accepted by the carpenter with a smile. So he said nothing, and the more they worked, the less his heart ached.

Using some of the dirt they had removed from the well, they raised the ground level around the well mouth, sloping it away so the rain and mud from the surrounding hills would not flow into the well and contaminate it. Then they used rocks from the pile as pavers, creating a stone floor radiating ten feet out from the well. As a finishing touch, Jeshua built a wooden cupola over the well and finished the roof with palm leaves. They stood back and admired their work.

"It's the most beautiful well ever," said Naaman proudly.

Jeshua cast the waterskin into the well and heard the hearty splash. Naaman pulled the rope up, and the skin appeared, overflowing with sweet, clear water. They each had a mouthful.

"Jeshua?"

They turned. Esau stood in the clearing, by the dowser's stake. "May I speak with you?" Jeshua handed Naaman the waterskin and walked over to Esau, who said, "You're finished, I see."

"Yes."

"Most impressive."

"Thank you," said Jeshua. "We thank you," he said, nodding toward Naaman.

Esau pulled out the dowser's stake and cast it aside. "I underestimated you. I imagine I am not the first. Nor will I be the last."

Jeshua smiled and Esau continued. "You have earned your wages and my respect. You will forever be a friend to this household." He bowed formally, then reached into a pouch hanging from his belt. He removed two large silver coins and held them out.

Jeshua gasped. Two talents! He opened his mouth to speak, but Esau spoke first. "Now don't question my addition. Your well is providing so much water that not only are we able to water our trees, we will also be selling water to the surrounding orchards. You have multiplied yourself, and you have earned this."

Jeshua took the coins. "You are generous, Esau. But I fear now that I am in your debt."

Esau laughed. "Well, something tells me that there is no man in this world I would rather have in my debt than you." He winked and strode away, calling out to a servant to stop lagging in his work and commanding another to move faster, summer wouldn't last all year.

Jeshua turned back to the well. Naaman was sweeping the flagstones. When he heard Jeshua approach, he turned.

"We just got paid," said Jeshua.

"You just got paid," said Naaman. "I've been paid already."

"I believe this is the value of what you lost," said Jeshua, handing one of the talents to Naaman.

Naaman stared at the coin in disbelief. How did Jeshua know? He never revealed the value of what he'd lost. He tried to give the coin back, but Jeshua shook his head.

"Esau gave me two talents," Jeshua said. "One is more than generous for digging the well. The other is yours. I hope it will cover your loss."

Something loosened inside Naaman. He had never cried in front of anyone before, but he was going to now. He slumped down on the well wall and great, wracking sobs escaped him. He finally got control of himself, wiped the tears away, and looked up, embarrassed. Jeshua was standing there, looking at him and smiling proudly.

Naaman got to his feet and hugged Jeshua, tears flowing again. He knew he was sweaty and dirty, but he also knew he was—for the first time in his life—clean. From the inside out. Years of pain and anger flowed out of him along with his tears. The heaviness of heart that had always pressed down on him began to lift, until he felt his feet would leave the ground. Then a brilliant, warm feeling poured into his heart: he had a friend, his very first friend. His grateful tears soaked Jeshua's tunic, but Jeshua just held him quietly until there were no more.

When Naaman finally pulled away, Jeshua said, "We have one more chore." He picked up a spade. "Come. Follow me."

Naaman followed, the silver coin pressed into his palm, his heart full, but his mouth still empty of words. They walked past several rows of trees. The sun balanced on the western hills and the trees cast long shadows. The heat of the day was dissipating. As they passed an orange tree, Naaman reached out to pick one but stopped, remembering Esau's rule. He smiled to himself, thinking that this might be the first time in his life he had ever willingly obeyed a rule.

Jeshua stopped in front of a tree and started digging. It took a moment, but then Naaman realized what was happening. He caught Jeshua's arm and gently took the shovel from him. Jeshua stepped back, and Naaman began digging. Nothing was said for several minutes as Naaman dug rhythmically. He could barely see the hole for the tears in his eyes.

Then the shovel struck something. Naaman knelt down and unearthed a dirty cloth bundle. He unwrapped it, and there was his leather money pouch, musty but intact. He opened the pouch, and the talent rolled out onto his palm, glistening in the last rays of the setting sun. He reached into his tunic and brought out the other talent and laid them side by side on the ground.

There are two! I multiplied them! Then he thought again, *No. I did no such thing. I received a gift, a gift I did not earn. I don't deserve one of these coins, let alone two.* He turned from the hole. "Jeshua—"

But Jeshua was gone. Naaman stood and looked around, and there, through the trees, he saw Jeshua at the well, placing his toolbox on his donkey's back.

Naaman stowed the coins in his tunic, filled in the hole, then walked briskly back to the well. But by the time he arrived, Jeshua was gone. Naaman climbed up on the well wall and scanned the orchard. He caught sight of Jeshua leading his donkey up the path, nearing the summit of the hill. The breeze brought him the sound of Jeshua's clear tenor as he sang the old traveler's song:

> *We know not where our path will lead,*
> *Nor from whence we've come.*
> *But we must choose which signs to heed,*
> *Until our journey's run.*

When he reached the top of the hill, Jeshua turned and waved. Naaman waved back. Then Jeshua disappeared over the hill. Naaman sat down on the well wall. The orchard was quiet, and a light, warm wind sifted through the trees. The sky was a deepening blue, and the shadows lengthened as he watched. They climbed to the eastern horizon and flowed together as the sun disappeared over the western hills.

Naaman studied the two talents in his hands until it was dark, then he placed one inside his tunic and turned to face the well. He held the other talent out over the dark well mouth and looked heavenward. "Master of the Universe," he said, "thank you for my life, and for Jeshua bar Joseph, who, with your help, saved it."

He let the coin slip from his fingers. It rang, once, twice, and a third time, bouncing off the rocks, before splashing in the water far below.

TWENTY-ONE

Just Deserts

They bowed low before Ishmael, who looked them over with disdain, impatiently tapping his crop on his leg. "Hanock, how has the household fared in my absence?"

"Wonderfully, Master," said Hanock, immediately regretting the answer. At his side, Zerah snickered. "I mean, passably, sire. We did our best, but of course we cannot—"

"Oh, shut up!" Ishmael reached out and felt the fine weave of Hanock's new cloak. "I see you have prospered in my absence."

Hanock shook his head, but Ishmael detected pride nonetheless. "I trust this has something to do with our agreement?"

Hanock nodded and motioned for a servant boy to approach. The boy held up a small carved wooden chest. Ishmael took it from him. "Very much like mine," he said.

"But much, much smaller, sire," said Hanock.

Ishmael opened the chest to reveal ten shiny silver talents lying on a bed of velvet cloth. Hanock bowed and said, "You gave me five talents and I have multiplied them."

Ishmael nodded. "Wisely have I chosen you as my chief steward. You have not disappointed me, and I shall not disappoint you." He handed the chest back to Hanock. "The ten talents are yours. You have just become a rich man."

Hanock gasped and his knees almost buckled at the news.

"Keep your money working as hard as you do and you will prosper," said Ishmael. Hanock nodded furiously, but his eyes never left the chest in his arms.

Ishmael turned to Zerah, whose hands trembled with anticipation as he held out a fine embroidered pouch with a golden drawstring. Ishmael opened it and poured four silver talents into his hand.

"You gave me two talents, Master," said Zerah proudly. "I also have multiplied them."

"And made enough to buy yourself something as well," said Ishmael, nodding at Zerah's crimson cloak.

Zerah was alarmed. "I did not think it would be improper—"

"I am not angry," said Ishmael. "You earned your fine cloak, Zerah. Enjoy it. You will wear much finer apparel in the future." He gave Zerah the pouch. "You, too, are now a wealthy man, Zerah. How does it feel?"

Zerah was clutching the pouch tightly and didn't hear.

Ishmael grunted and Zerah looked up, finding his voice. "Your generosity, sire, is legen—"

Ishmael raised a hand and silenced him.

Ishmael looked at Naaman, who stood before him in his threadbare brown tunic, his head bowed. He held a small bundle wrapped in a piece of dirty linen.

Ishmael frowned. "Not quite so prosperous, I see . . . ah . . . "

Naaman looked up. "Naaman, sire."

"So, you have found your voice," said Ishmael. "Did you also find a profit?"

Naaman nodded. "A marvelous profit, sire. Perhaps even priceless."

"Priceless?" Ishmael grunted and motioned for Naaman to unwrap the bundle. Naaman removed the cloth and opened the dirt-encrusted leather pouch. A single silver talent rolled out onto his hand. He looked up at Ishmael, whose eyes moved from the talent up to Naaman's face. A muscle angrily worked in Ishmael's jaw.

Zerah nudged Hanock and whispered, "I told you."

Hanock took Zerah's elbow and pulled him back a step. "He'll need room." He nodded at Ishmael's crop, which had quit tapping.

Ishmael scowled at Naaman. "Are you a fool, or are your counting skills so meager that you cannot tell one from two?"

Naaman shook his head but said nothing.

"Then explain!"

Naaman bowed his head and said, "I knew you were a hard man, sire, who reaps where you do not sow, and gathers where you do not strew."

Ishmael took a step back, astonished. "Why you—"

"I was afraid," continued Naaman, looking directly at Ishmael. "So I hid the coin in the earth. Here," he said, handing the coin to Ishmael, "you have once more what was yours."

"You wicked coward!" screamed Ishmael, hurling the coin against the wall. "You traded a profit for a sharp tongue, a bad trade indeed. You say I am a hard man? You will see how hard!" He moved a step closer to Naaman, his fist clenched angrily around the crop.

Zerah and Hanock took another step back.

Naaman stood his ground, though he badly wanted to run. But even more badly, he wanted to be a man, a man like a certain carpenter he knew.

"I am sorry—"

"Silence!" bellowed Ishmael. He looked over at Zerah and Hanock, who were holding onto each other, trembling. His disgust multiplied. He nodded at Zerah to pick up the talent he threw. Zerah did so and gave it to Ishmael, who held the coin up before Naaman's face. "You should have at least given this to the lenders. I would have had interest on it!"

He gave the coin back to Zerah, who showed it to Hanock proudly.

"Give it to Hanock," said Ishmael absently. Zerah's face fell, and

Hanock had to pry the talent out of Zerah's fist. They glared at each other as Hanock placed the coin in his wooden chest.

Naaman tried to stand tall, while still being respectful of his master. Ishmael leaned forward and whispered angrily, "Why didn't you multiply the talent?"

"I didn't know how, sire."

"And these," said Ishmael, nodding at Zerah and Hanock, "did not help you?"

Zerah spoke. "We—"

"They offered, sire," interrupted Naaman. "But I was afraid."

"You know nothing of fear . . . yet," said Ishmael fiercely.

I've known fear all my life, thought Naaman, watching the crop tap angrily against Ishmael's leg. *But today, I am not afraid. For the first time in my life, I am not afraid.*

Naaman turned and pulled up his tunic, exposing his back to the crop. "Yes, Master."

As the blows rained down, the inevitable tears came. But today they were different. Instead of instilling rage and a seething bitterness, a feeling of peace settled over him. He had seen a great deal of injustice in his life, and had meted out more than his share. He had even known justice, and was feeling its power now. But Jeshua had shown him something greater than justice, something that shielded his heart from the piercing sting of the crop on his bloody back, something that had changed him forever.

That something was love.

THE CARPENTER TEACHES

Several years later, Jeshua traveled to Jerusalem for the Passover feast. He knew his time was near. He had entered the city in triumph, cheered by crowds who laid palm fronds before him so his feet would not touch the ground.

But now, just three days later, he had to leave the Temple suddenly, because the same people who had so honored his arrival wanted to tear him apart because of the hard things he had said to them.

Once away from the angry mob, he turned to his friends and said:

"The kingdom of heaven is like a man traveling to a far country, who called his servants before him. To one he gave five talents, to another two, and to another one; to every one according to his ability, and he charged them to multiply the talents, and he would return and make an accounting. And then he embarked on his travels.

"And he that had received the five talents went and traded with them, and gained five more talents. And also he that received two talents, likewise, and gained two more. But he that received one talent went and hid it in the earth.

"And after a long time, the householder returned and called his servants before him for a reckoning. And he that received five talents came with five other talents and said, 'Lord, you gave me five talents. Behold, I have gained for you five talents more.'

"And his lord said unto him, 'Well done, my good and faithful servant. You have been faithful over a few things. I will make you ruler over many things.'

"Then he that received two talents came and said, 'Lord, you gave me two talents. Behold, I have gained two talents more.'

"And his lord said unto him, 'Well done, my good and faithful servant. You have been faithful over a few things. I will make you ruler over many things.'

"Then he which received one talent came and said, 'Lord, I knew you were a hard man, one who reaps where you do not sow, and gathers where you have not strewn. And I was afraid, so I hid my talent in the earth. Here, I return it to you.'

"And his lord answered and said, 'You wicked, slothful servant. It is true, I am a hard man who reaps where I do not sow, and gathers where I do not strew. Therefore, you should have at least given my money to the lenders and I would have received interest on it. I will take, therefore, the talent I gave to you, and give it to the servant with ten talents.'

"And the lord continued, 'For every one that multiplies his talent shall receive more, and he shall have in abundance. But he that refuses to multiply his talent shall lose even that which he has, and the unprofitable servant shall be cast out, and there shall be weeping and gnashing of teeth.'"

Part Three

—⚶—

THE
MONEY
POUCH

ONE

The Mighty Merchant

Elam looked around at the marketplace. The thin sunlight of this late fall day was dissipating and the merchants were gathering up their goods. Next to him, a woman was carefully placing pomegranates back into her wicker basket. She hadn't sold a single one today. As he folded his silk cloaks, Elam wondered how she made ends meet.

Yet he'd had a gloriously profitable day. The long, dusty journey from Joppa on the coast and, before that, from Egypt by boat had been worth it. His store of fine cloaks, richly embroidered with red and blue thread and tiny glass beads, had proven very popular. At first he wondered if his wares would find buyers in Jerusalem, but he comforted himself knowing that he didn't need everyone in the city to buy a cloak; just a few would suffice.

As a Jew, he was well aware of the constrictions on what was considered appropriate clothing. It couldn't be too fancy or elaborate. Colors had to be muted. No renditions of people or animals. He made sure Napthet knew which burnt reds and blue-greens were acceptable. Napthet laughed, never having been to Canaan, and asked if the people there were as dour as their clothes.

"Certainly," said Elam. "It's a desert. Nothing like this." He gestured about at the port city of Alexandria, with its myriad date palms and green rushes crowding the banks of the mighty Nile. "I wonder why they left Egypt in the first place."

Napthet had laughed at that, too, but Elam knew it was just a polite response. Napthet would know nothing about the captivity of the Jews so many hundreds of years ago, about Moses' adamant demands on the Pharaoh, the plagues of falling frogs and hungry locusts. Or even about the drowning of the Egyptian army in the sea to the east. No, Napthet knew nothing about history. But he knew about thread and soft silken fabrics, woven by dark-eyed women on enormous looms. And he knew not to gouge Elam, who was perhaps his best opportunity to open trade with Jerusalem.

Elam folded a midnight blue cloak across his lap, being careful not to let it touch the ground. He sighed. Such a dirty land. He looked up at the Temple wall, the brilliant alabaster facade glistening gold in the sunset. So much superstition.

The Jews believed their God would deliver them from bondage—a day Elam knew would never come. They were slaves to a mirage, like the glint of mica on a faraway hillside. They dreamed of a mighty city on a hill, which didn't exist. Not in this world. Not for Jewish slaves.

Elam knew the truth. He had traveled the world. Galatia, Egypt, Syria, and even Rome. And now he was back in the city of his birth, feeling like a stranger, seeing his own people as they couldn't bear to see themselves: as insignificant slaves of a mighty empire, bickering like children over who was most chosen of God and, indeed, over who God even was.

If this means we're chosen, he thought, looking around at the marketplace with its poor selection of hard quince, rotten walnuts, and mealy barley flour, *then I'd rather God ignored us altogether.*

He placed the blue cloak on top of the other two and lifted the corners of the canvas square, securing it with a length of twine. His day had gone well: five cloaks sold at a good profit. He was a gifted merchant; he'd made his first profit at a young age, selling a sickly calf to a neighbor, who discovered his mistake too late. When the calf died just three days later, the neighbor came back, demanding his money. Elam, just twelve at the time, shrugged, saying he'd lost the money gambling. The neighbor raged and cursed him but finally gave up, stomping angrily away. As Elam watched him go, he fingered the three shiny coins in his pocket, his heart full of dark power. He knew it was the man's own fault he'd been cheated by a mere boy. He deserved it, and as Elam's father used to always say, "Sheep get sheared."

He'd sheared a few today, and the coins were nestled in the leather pouch inside his tunic. As he hefted the bundle of cloaks, he could feel the pleasant plumpness of the pouch against his chest. Walking across the marketplace, lost in the swirl of merchants and last-minute hagglers, he wondered if anyone had been watching him today. If they were, they knew he'd made a small fortune. He forced himself to slow down and lowered his chin and eyes, affecting the pose of a less prosperous merchant.

He retrieved his donkey from the livery, tied the bundle to the pack frame, and led the donkey out of the marketplace, wondering if he ought to stop and visit his father, whom he had not seen in five years. He decided against it. The old man would probably just ask him for money.

Passing lit doorways, he smelled cooking fish and fresh barley cakes. He considered stopping but wanted to leave the crowded, smelly city and get out into the countryside. There he could curl up in his warm cloak, look up at the stars, and enjoy his solitude. As he passed through the Damascus gate, Elam saw the first star twinkling in the southern sky. He was headed for Jericho, where a wealthy sultan would certainly relieve him of his last three cloaks.

Achish lounged against the stony curve of the archway, watching the people leave the city. A beggar sat close by, grinning toothlessly up at him, the stumps of his legs poking out like signposts. Achish placed his sandaled foot on the man's shoulder and pushed him away. The man continued to smile stupidly up at him, his cup held in a knotted mass of scarlet knuckles. Achish met his gaze. "Don't touch me," he hissed.

But the beggar still smiled, and Achish figured he was probably insane. One thing was certain: he was a leper, and Achish took a step away from the ruin of sinewy flesh and sunken eye sockets. He turned his attention back to the stream of people leaving the city.

"P-Please," stuttered the leper, brushing his cup against Achish's leg.

Without looking, Achish turned and kicked him hard in the chest. The leper rolled down the steps. He came to a stop and lay there, motionless. Several beggars had witnessed the kick, but no one, except for a young boy, appeared shocked. Achish scowled at the boy and clutched an invisible rope, slowly twisting it. The boy turned and ran away.

Tired of this side of the gate, Achish entered the stream of people. He was a man of average height, broad across the chest. His deep-set eyes and tangle of long dark hair gave him a fearful aspect, and the same hands that twisted the imaginary rope had twisted a neck or two. He had once killed an ox with his bare fist, smashing it in the snout, driving bone into the brain. But though he could fight when necessary—his misshapen nose was a testament to a scuffle with a centurion three years ago—he preferred the finesse of picking pockets. As he threaded through the feckless crowd, his hands brushed gently against packs and cloaks, seeking the coins men carried in bulging money pouches.

A tall, elegantly dressed man passed through the gate. Achish started toward him, then stopped when he noticed a looming bodyguard walking a step ahead of the man. In the guard's hand was a large, knobbed sap.

Achish waited for the tall man to pass and looked back to the gate. There. A fat merchant, wearing much too fine a cloak, leading a donkey. His corpulent face was topped by a curly mass of graying hair. Achish passed close to the man and saw it: the telltale bulge of a fat coin pouch under his tunic.

From the other side of the street, Achish turned and watched the merchant move with the crowd. He had something that now belonged to Achish; the transfer of wealth had occurred the moment Achish noticed him. All that remained was taking possession.

TWO

Priests of the Most High

In the darkness of the dressing chamber, lit only by a single oil lamp, Kohath shook the dust from his white robe and folded it carefully, then sat and took off his white leather slippers. Dipping a rag in water, he carefully cleaned the brushed leather, shaking his head. It was useless, but he must try anyway. After all, he was a priest, and it was his calling to teach a dirty people about the holiness of cleanliness, about how to behave in God's house, the earthly throne of Jehovah himself.

He'd spent the last twenty years in this thankless endeavor, working his way up from worker to assistant to officiator to priest, where now he walked the darkened halls and sunny courtyards in a perfectly white silken robe, his eyes downcast piously, his hands clasped behind his back, his head bent at an appropriate angle. People fell silent when he approached, and he felt proud when they quietly studied him.

After he had gifted them with a discreet smile for their edification, however, there were often hushed whispers emerging in his wake. He knew they were mocking him. At such times he was tempted to turn around and point a slender finger and say, as they quavered before him, "Thus sayeth the Lord . . . ," and then intone some awful condemnation, punishing them for their evil speaking of the Lord's anointed.

But in the Temple, as in life, Kohath did not give in to temptation, no matter how sweet and just the fantasy might be. He concentrated instead on being an example to the very people who derided him. Kohath sighed, placing his moccasins in the storage space below his robe.

Nearby, a young Levite priest was changing clothes. His robes were splattered with blood like a common butcher, and his face was tanned brown from the heat of the sacrificial fires. Kohath noticed the freckles on the young man's forearms, tattoos from scalding oil spit from the burning flesh. He rubbed his own forearm, where some of those same marks remained after all this time, even though he himself hadn't offered a sacrifice in a dozen years.

The Levite placed his stained robe in a pile of clothing and turned to Kohath, his head bent respectfully. "Sire," he said quietly, his eyes never leaving Kohath's feet.

"God's grace," said Kohath mechanically, "be with you."

The Levite picked up the bundle of dirty clothing and exited. The young man had worked in the Temple for five years, and Kohath still didn't know his name. Like most of his brethren of the high priesthood, Kohath did not fraternize with the Levites, who held the lower priesthood. The distinction maintained the order of the Temple, which was a microcosm of eternity. All had their place, and all were ruled by the high priest, who was God's representative on earth.

Nevertheless, he was glad to be leaving all that order for a while. He was going to Jericho for a month to visit relatives and relax among the green things that grew there, away from the cold, barren stone of the Temple. His lungs ached to breathe air not billowing with the black acrid smoke of burning flesh, rising from the giant copper braziers. And he yearned to look men in the face and not fear their looks at his back.

Kohath exited the Temple and stood on the wide marble steps, looking out over the Court of the Gentiles, now emptying of vendors with their sacrificial lambs and fowl, the money changers, and the Temple clothing merchants.

Kohath had not been off the Temple grounds in more than seven years. Even though he was nearly forty, he still had a boy's anticipation of the larger world. As he descended the Temple steps in his borrowed cloak, his heart lifted with a giddy, growing fear. An adventure awaited, and he must be very careful.

From behind a fluted marble column, Lamech watched Kohath descend the stairs, looking odd in his street clothes. He'd never seen him in clothing that wasn't Temple issue, and seeing him now, strutting like a rich man in poor man's clothing, he knew the disguise would fool no one.

Like the other Levites, Lamech lived outside the Temple walls, in a small, spare compound of single-room apartments. The priests lived in splendor inside the Temple itself and never let the Levites forget they held the higher priesthood. Lamech imagined Kohath was also a Levite (most of the priests were), but they might as well have been direct descendants of Moses himself, the way they acted.

Nevertheless, Lamech admired the priests' dedication and came to their defense when occasion required. Lamech felt lucky to have been chosen to serve in the Temple. On the day he was dedicated to the Lord, twelve other boys were also offered up, and Lamech still remembered the tears on his mother's cheeks when the news came that he was the only one chosen.

"You belong to God now," she had said quietly. His father had placed his rough miller's hand on his shoulder and nodded gravely, proud beyond words.

Lamech still saw his family on occasion, but he wearied of questions about the Temple. They seemed convinced that there were great miracles and intrigues in constant motion inside the white stone walls. Of course he could tell them nothing. It was a sacred place, after all, but the truth was his duties at the braziers were so demanding that he knew nothing of what went on elsewhere inside the complex.

For his diligence, Lamech indulged himself in one private fantasy:

one day he would wear the blue linen robes and golden breastplate of the high priest and preside over the Feast of the Tabernacles, the year-end celebration of the harvest. To be chosen, he must be diligent, and so he was always on time, always hardworking, and always respectful. But no one seemed to notice, and he wondered if his faithfulness would ever be rewarded with position.

Watching Kohath descend the marble steps, Lamech held his bundle of blood-spattered robes and reflected on their encounter in the dressing area just moments before. He wondered if the old man even knew his name. He doubted it. And so he also doubted he would ever become a priest. Choosing priests was fiercely political, and he knew nothing of politics, only killing and burning lambs and rams.

But that would have to wait. Lamech was leaving this very night to visit his uncle's family, who were shepherds near Jericho, that mystical oasis of sweet figs and grape wine. He'd never been there before and was excited. He yearned to swim in the cool Jordan River, to play with his cousins, and to act like the young man he still was.

Lamech exited the Temple via the western viaduct, along with the stream of patrons, vendors, and sightseers. Dressed only in a brown tunic and gloriously barefoot, he headed for his quarters, where he would have his clothing washed and dried, and then he would set off for Jericho. He knew it would be late before he got going, but no matter. He could taste the sweet grape wine already.

THREE

Four Journeys, One Destination

Elam reached up to feel the bulge of the money pouch inside his tunic. When he returned to Jerusalem next year for the last time, he would do so in a large caravan, weighted down with precious gems and silken fabrics, for one last trip through Judea and Samaria and Decapolis and Galilee. Attired in silk and gold and silver and precious gems set in rings on all his fingers, he would stop in to see his father in his hovel and magnanimously invite him to come visit him in Rome, if he was ever in the neighborhood. The thought made him dizzy with bitter joy. The look on the old man's face would forever be a prized possession.

And then he would leave Judea, never to return. He would hand the reins of his camels to the stable master, receive their value in empire *sestertii,* and set sail for Rome, to live in luxury at the center of the world, to enjoy the sport, the theater, and the women, and not in that order, either.

Elam had to laugh. He could think of no better place to be than in Rome when the mighty Jewish army, according to his superstitious father, came marching into the city to vanquish it. Elam himself would toast their arrival with a cup of red wine and would laugh as they stood aghast at the splendor of his adopted city and the power of her legions.

Elam's step quickened and he tugged the donkey forward, passing the last few houses, finally clearing the city.

Achish followed the fat merchant and his donkey at a distance. The day had tilted into evening, and the darkness would be complete in another hour. As he passed the last inn of any quality, the happy voices and clink of cups beckoned him. But the merchant continued on into the darkening night.

Achish was not in such a hurry. He entered the inn, figuring he'd have just one drink, and then he'd go skin the fatted calf. He scooped a handful of figs from a tray and popped one into his mouth. Fortune had smiled on him. The merchant did not live in Jerusalem, and neither was he staying inside the city. The only other possibility was that he was going to camp on the Jericho Road, a twisting, narrow trail that wound down the barren wadis as the rolling hills gave way to the rugged cliffs and ocher-colored canyons that overlooked the Jordan River Valley. There were a thousand places to ambush a traveler on that road, and an entire night in which to do it. Achish settled back against the wall and ordered a drink. He had all the time in the world, and besides, there might be a pocket or two to pick in this crowded inn.

Kohath stumbled, bumping into a man standing just inside the inn door. The man growled at him, his dark eyes piercing him and leaving behind a curtain of dread that settled over Kohath's heart. As he moved deeper into the room, Kohath could feel the man's hot gaze on his shoulder blades. He walked to the far side of the room and took an empty table, finally daring to look back at the door.

The muscled, dark man stood near the door, speaking to the innkeeper. Kohath wanted to escape this all-too-tiny room, but he'd have to pass the brute again. He noticed his hands were shaking, and he placed them on his lap, clasping them tightly. When a servant approached him, asking what his pleasure was, all he could say was, "Food."

The servant nodded and waited.

Kohath finally regained his composure. "What are you serving tonight?"

"What we serve every night," said the servant, bored. "Bean stew. Barley cake."

"That will be fine, young man," said Kohath, turning his back to the dark man by the door. "You can bring me—" but the servant was already gone.

Kohath shook his head, chiding himself for his cowardice, and tried to think. Was it really wise to continue on tonight? He glanced over at the dark man, who was leaning against the wall, scanning the crowd from under hooded eyelids. His black eyes were about to reach Kohath, who turned away, staring fearfully at the stucco wall before him, his heart pounding. He felt the man's eyes move across his back, felt the prickly needles of their malevolent intensity, and then, gratefully, felt them move on to another.

No, it was not a good idea to travel the Jericho Road tonight. When the servant returned with his clay bowl of stew and a flat barley cake, Kohath inquired about accommodations. The price seemed high, but he really had no choice.

"Where is she?" demanded Lamech, holding the bundle of dirty clothing under his arm.

"I don't know," said Gad. "She hasn't come yet. Just leave it."

"I need them washed tonight. I'm going on a journey."

Gad yawned. "So you've been saying."

"For two weeks," said Reuel, appearing in the doorway. He was a small, skinny boy, barely fifteen, with an air of superiority that was somehow well founded. "You'll just have to do the laundry yourself, Lamech. It won't kill you."

Lamech shook his head. "I'm a Levite. I don't do laundry."

Reuel shrugged. "You do now." He disappeared into the other room.

This isn't fair, Lamech thought to himself as he walked outside. He trudged toward the stone basin in the far corner of the courtyard and dumped his clothing in it. Turning back to the well, he bent and began hauling the waterskin up.

That's a whole day I'll lose, he thought angrily, dumping the water into the clay jar. *One less day in Jericho.*

He dropped the waterskin back into the well and considered the dirty clothes in the basin. He had never washed clothes in his life. He looked around at the tiny rooms that opened out on the courtyard. Most of them were dark, the men having left for dinner. Lamech walked toward the dining hall. He needed a full stomach before he tackled this problem. Jericho would have to wait till morning.

FOUR

A Dark Journey

E lam looked back over his shoulder. The last houses of Jerusalem were amber lights on the horizon, the outline of purple all that was left of the day. A pall of smoke from cooking fires hung over the city like a gray blanket. Golden light shone through a distant window but winked out when he took a few more steps. When he looked back once more, the city was gone, replaced by blackness.

Elam listened to his own breathing and the clip-clop of the donkey's hooves. The road was wide, gray under the darkening sky. He sucked a sage twig, enjoying the faint licorice taste, looking upward, trying to catch the stars as they appeared. But they came on so slowly that no matter how long he stared at a particular spot, knowing that there would be a star there soon, when it came, it came during an eye shift or a blink. Suddenly, there it was, twinkling, laughing at him for trying to witness its magic.

Elam patted the donkey on the withers. "Come on, just a few more miles tonight, then we rest. Besides, you've been resting all day."

Achish downed several flagons of wine and half a loaf of warm spelt, but his true appetite remained unsatisfied. The only interesting thing in the inn was a man sitting at a table across the room, facing the wall. He didn't talk to anyone but the servants and didn't even turn around when someone dropped a glass with a crash. Achish figured he must have something to hide. His clothing covered a body too well fed for a laborer, and his skin was too white and soft for anyone but a merchant. Achish watched for a long time, hoping he would turn and see him glaring at him, but he was disappointed. He was doubly disappointed when he overheard the innkeeper rent the man a room for the night.

Achish didn't mind, for down the road another, fatter, animal was ready for slaughter. He picked up his bedroll and tossed a shekel to the innkeeper. Time to go to work.

Elam sat on a large rock and removed his sandal, shaking a stone out. He wanted to get as far away from Jerusalem as possible. Then Jericho would be just a couple of days away, and his tour of Canaan that much shorter.

Two hours later, well past midnight, he finally slowed. He had been nodding off, trudging alongside the donkey, lulled by its snuffled breathing and the cadence of its hooves. Awakened suddenly, he looked around, wondering for an instant where he was. It had been hours since he had passed anyone, and he had seen no one on the road either before or behind him. There was no moon—the night was as black as a kettle bottom.

The road was descending into the gorge. Elam let the donkey lead; his own eyes had long since lost the path in the darkness. But the road was narrowing, and a false step would send him tumbling over the precipice into the craggy abyss. They had gone far enough; it was time to find a place to camp.

The trail curved around a corner, then down a series of switchbacks. Elam became impatient, peering into the darkness, trying to find a place to rest for the night. But the trail wound down and down, and now the Judean hills were far overhead, indistinguishable from the sky, which burned with a million stars but gave off no light. It was too dangerous to travel farther.

Elam goaded the donkey. "Find us a place to rest," he whispered. "I'm tired."

From above, Achish watched the merchant make his way slowly down the switchbacks. He wondered why the man hadn't stopped yet. What was his hurry? If he would just camp, then it would be a simple matter to lift his pouch while he slept. That would be much less bother than attacking him on the trail. Achish tiptoed along, wary of any loose stones he might dislodge, alerting the merchant to his presence.

Achish wondered about his prey. Who would travel the Jericho Road at night, alone? Only a fool, but perhaps the man was not as he seemed. Perhaps he knew he was being followed, and was waiting for a chance to turn the tables on Achish. Perhaps he had a sharp sword under that fine silk cloak. And perhaps he knew how to use it.

Achish touched the dagger tucked in his belt, wishing he had something bigger. On the trail below, the merchant had stopped and was looking up at the moonless sky again. Achish looked up, seeing nothing but stars. Perhaps the man was a sorcerer, traveling on some evil necromancer's errand, casting spells as he walked, calling forth demons to do his bidding.

The thought made Achish shudder. He had killed a man once, and as he died, the man looked at him and hissed, "Cursed." Achish had withdrawn the knife and wiped it on the dead man's cloak. The man's cloudy eyes stared heavenward, causing Achish to look up as well. He saw nothing and had backed away then, holding the coins he'd obtained, knowing it was far too little a reward for the risk of being cursed by a sorcerer.

Over the next week the man's staring eyes had floated in and out of Achish's dreams, the mouth repeating the word over and over again. Achish knew it was true—his life had been cursed, yet when he realized that, he laughed. The dying man hadn't cursed him, he was just stating a fact: Achish *was* cursed, and the only way to dispel its effects was to curse others as well. So as he plundered and stole and killed, he began to feel a blessed darkness filling him, as if he were standing neck-deep in a silent, black lake. A few more sleights of hand, and the water would rise and cover his mouth and he would never again cry out in his sleep, remembering the beatings his masters had given him. A few more thefts, and it would cover his nose, so he would never smell the wheat mush his mother made him before taking him to the door of a stranger, where she left him, never to return. A few more murders, and the darkness would cover his eyes and he would never again see the men having their way with his sister as he stood by watching, too small to do anything to stop them.

A few more victims and the darkness would be complete. And then he would find peace.

Elam was gratified when the path widened. They were rounding a shoulder of gray rock, and the trail flattened out for a time before dropping off into the canyon again. The donkey was moving slowly. Elam looked up at the night sky.

Suddenly a black shape lunged at him. A knife haft smashed his nose, and in an instant he was covered with blood, reeling, one hand clutching at his money pouch and the other flailing for the donkey reins. He stumbled back and raised his free hand to ward off the next blow, which came down heavily on his left eye, spilling a sticky warmth onto his cheek. He rolled over, tasted dirt, and scrabbled weakly away.

A hand grabbed him, rolling him over. A silhouette loomed, and something shiny glinted in the darkness. An icy coldness stabbed him in the shoulder, and he cried out in pain. He wanted to touch the wound, to see how bad it was, but that would mean letting go of the money purse, which he still held through his tunic, his knuckles white with effort.

Someone laughed. Elam opened the eye that wasn't full of blood and saw the shape of a man's head, moving slowly back and forth. "Must be quite a prize," said a deep voice.

Elam removed the purse from his tunic and held it out, his hand shaking. "Take it. It's yours."

The man chuckled. "Yes. I know."

A fist was raised, then fell thunderously, over and over again. Elam tried to fend off the blows that rained out of the clear night sky, sending him into a darkness deeper than sleep.

Achish sat back on his haunches, out of breath. He armed sweat from his forehead and felt the stickiness of blood. Cursing, he rolled the fat merchant out of his cloak and used it to wipe his face. Then he stood, amazed at the fury he'd felt just moments before. It still sizzled through his joints, making his fingers hot with white fire. The merchant's face was covered with blood. His donkey stood quietly by, chewing on a clump of grass.

Achish pulled the pack off the animal's back. A canvas bundle contained a few silk cloaks. Worthless. He heaved the bundle into the canyon. Then he bent and pried the money pouch free of the dying man's fingers. Opening it, he counted, eight, nine, ten, eleven. Eleven gold denarii. He laughed out loud. "Eleven!"

Eleven denarii was several years' work for Achish but just one sales trip for this fat swine. He shook the coin purse at the man. "How did you make this much money?" he asked incredulously. "You must be an even bigger thief than I!"

The man lay there, his ragged breath bubbling out of his broken nose, one eye socket pooling blood. Achish wondered what other possessions he might have. He unbuckled the leather belt and hoisted the man's tunic over his head, revealing his white fish-belly, but found no more money purses. Achish tossed the tunic into the ravine. The man lay in his loincloth, pale as a piece of marble. He looked at the man's hands. No precious stones set in gold rings.

Achish held the money pouch tightly, wondering what to do next. He felt uneasy, as if he had forgotten something. He looked around. The donkey quietly nibbled at the bunchgrass. Achish pulled his knife and walked toward the animal. Gently taking the reins, he led it toward the edge of the trail.

"Nothing to worry about," he whispered, patting the donkey's withers. "Nothing at all."

Achish felt the cool, dark waters gathering about his chin and placed the blade under the donkey's neck.

FIVE

The Road to Jericho

After dinner, Lamech got to talking with the other Levites and forgot all about his laundry. When he stepped out into the courtyard hours later, he was actually surprised to see his dirty clothing still lying on the granite washbasin.

He roused the laundress and insisted she wash his clothing tonight. She followed him to the basin, murmuring at his back the entire time.

He watched as she angrily washed his tunic, smashing it against the stone, wringing it fiercely, and whopping it again. When he could stand no more, he turned away to finish packing. When he returned, she was hanging his clothing on a line in the courtyard.

"That won't do," said Lamech testily.

The laundress turned. "What, sir?"

"I need it now, I told you that. Dry it over the fire."

She let out a long, bitter sigh, gathered up the clothing, and trudged inside. He went to his room and waited. Hours later (he must have dozed off), he heard a knock at the door. When he rose to open it, there were his clothes, folded and still warm from the fire's heat. Lamech pulled them inside and fell back into bed.

At dawn, Lamech shouldered his pack and walked along the cobbled streets, munching a piece of goat cheese and feeling the waterskin slapping at his side in syncopation with his footsteps.

He examined his palms, still stained red with sacrificial blood, even after a hard scrubbing last night. Just then a girl stepped out of a building, a bundle perched on her head, black hair framing a pretty face. She smiled at him. Lamech looked away, thrusting his red hands deep into his cloak pockets. He could feel himself blushing.

Then he realized something. The girl's smile added another layer of adventure to the day. The sun was warm on his face, his stomach was full, and his legs were strong. An adventure awaited him, and he'd never been more ready for it. He smiled at the girl as he passed.

Kohath rose early and stepped out into the street, turning toward the morning sun, just now peeking above the distant hills. He walked briskly, stopping only to refill his waterskin at the well and purchase a few hard rolls from a passing vendor. He was now ready for his march, and he set off down the road.

Once out of sight of the inn, he began to search for a secluded spot where he might offer his morning prayers. A promontory overlooking the canyons presented itself. A lone olive tree, bent with age and long since barren, stood sentinel. Kohath took off his sandals, spread his prayer blanket under the tree, and knelt facing Jerusalem, which glistened gold in the sunrise.

Kohath bent his head to the ground and repeated his usual morning prayer: "Lord God Almighty, Master of the Universe, look upon Thy servant with mercy as he serves Thee this day in Thy Holy House. . . ."

He stopped, baffled. This was not the proper prayer. He wasn't in the Temple; he wasn't serving God today. What prayer would suffice?

"Lord God Almighty," he began again, "look upon Thy servant with mercy as he . . ." Nothing came. He let out a frustrated sigh and lifted his head, studying Jerusalem's city walls, bright as the sun itself.

Here I am, a priest of the Most High, and I don't even know the proper prayer for the occasion. He bent again, closing his eyes. "Lord God Almighty, may my travels be consecrated to reflect Thy holiness, and may I be an example to all as a representative of Thy power."

He was unsatisfied with the prayer, but it would have to do. He stood and rolled up the blanket. He would have to ask the other priests about the proper prayer for traveling. There surely was one; there was a prayer for most things. He should have checked on this before leaving. Now his journey might be under a cloud of Jehovah's disapproval. He tucked the blanket under his arm and continued down the road, shaking his head at his ineptness.

By midmorning, Kohath had traveled several miles down the sloping canyons. He had been watching a fan-tailed raven arcing overhead, ranging far away, then returning. Dust rose from his feet and he gave up hoisting the hem of his cloak. It was already dyed brown; a little more dirt wouldn't hurt it. The rough tunic scratched against his shoulders. He shifted it, but it still irritated him. He couldn't imagine wearing crude clothing like this every day. He smelled the fabric. His own sweat, mixed with the inn's cooking smells and the dirt of the road, made him recoil. He needed a bath, and soon. Jericho was miles away and wouldn't be reached for two days, at least. He forced himself to drink sparingly from his waterskin and had eaten only two of the hard rolls in his pocket. He meant to ask a fellow traveler about the accommodations on the trail, but he'd passed no one yet this morning.

Then he turned a corner and stopped suddenly. Lying on the path was a man, stripped of clothing, covered with bruises and the face so bloody Kohath couldn't tell his race. "Lord save me," he said hoarsely, clutching his breast. A cloud of bottle flies circled the bloody body, and Kohath turned away, his gorge rising.

He looked around, fearful that the men who did this might still be nearby. The trail disappeared from sight just around the next corner.

Every rocky outcrop seemed a perfect hiding place. Kohath's heart beat wildly, and the sudden caw of a raven made him jump.

He was about to check the body to see if the man was alive when he remembered the purity laws: priests were rejected from service in the Temple if they were ill with a disease or if their skin was blemished. And of course the touching of corpses was strictly forbidden.

Kohath looked at the body. If the man was dead, he was prohibited from touching him. And if the man was not dead, what could he do? He touched his waterskin. He didn't have enough to spare, and more important, Kohath knew no medicine.

But what disturbed him most was all the blood. Human blood was different from the animal blood that coursed down the Temple sacrificial braziers. Human blood was holy, and yet, when shed, it was the filthiest stain of all.

Kohath turned away and hurried down the trail. At any moment he expected the murderers to step out from behind a boulder and fall upon him, like that poor man back there. When he rounded the corner and saw no one on the trail, he let out a deep sigh of relief and looked heavenward, praying, "Thank You, Lord, for protecting Thy servant."

Shortly after noon, Lamech stopped for a drink from the waterskin. The cool liquid rinsed the dirt from his mouth, and the dried fish was pleasantly salty. He hadn't seen anyone on the trail in hours, although he had walked briskly past several people, also heading eastward, including a caravan of several camels led by a giant dark-haired man who was nearly as broad as he was tall. Lamech had almost spoken to him as he passed, but then he noticed the man's clothing. He lowered his head and passed quickly, ignoring the man's hearty "Good morning!" Lamech half raised his hand to acknowledge the greeting, but then let it fall, keeping his eyes on the trail.

Samaritans. The mixed-race people who inhabited the rocky hill country north of Jerusalem, up to the Jezreel Valley near Galilee. Loathsome and dirty in their habits and traditions, they were the result of intermarriage between Jews and pagans from Babylon and Assyria. They had even gone so far as to build a rival temple on Mt. Gerazim, where they claimed to worship Jehovah, but their ordinances and sacrifices were unauthorized and unholy copies of the true Temple.

Jews were forbidden to have anything to do with Samaritans, not by holy writ but by long tradition. As far as he knew, Lamech had never actually looked a Samaritan in the face, and he was glad of it. The thought of talking to one made him shiver through the sheen of sweat on his back.

A couple of hours later, he came around a corner so quickly that he almost tripped over a body. He had noticed circling birds for quite a while but hadn't been able to make out what kind of birds they were.

Vultures, he thought, stumbling, gaining his feet and stopping, his heart racing. A large raven sat on a nearby rock, watching Lamech as he gawked at the man.

The body was covered with blood. From where he stood, Lamech couldn't tell if the man was alive or dead. He lay on his side, his head resting on his extended arm. A gash in the shoulder oozed blood. The man's other arm fell behind his back in an unnatural way, obviously broken. And the man's left eye looked like it was missing, lost in the sunken blackness under his crushed brow.

Lamech turned away and vomited. When he looked up, his eyes met the raven's, and the bird extended its huge wings and lifted off, beating its wings against the hot canyon air.

The bird's flight gave Lamech's feet wings as well. He stumbled down the trail and did not stop until he was sure the body was well out of sight. He collapsed on the path and looked over his shoulder. He knew he should go back and help the man.

But he couldn't. The man might be unclean: a foreigner or a gentile. Or a Samaritan, doubly so. He stood on wobbly legs and lurched down the path. He'd had as much adventure as he could take for one day. Trying to clear the man's bloody face from his mind, he concentrated instead on an image of the cleansing waters of the Jordan.

SIX

A Savior

Zebulon watched the young man hurry past. Was he deaf? Hadn't he heard his greeting? But, no, he must have, because he had half raised his hand in response.

Zebulon shook his head. Of course he knew what had just happened. He'd seen it all his life. Many people of his homeland, knowing their clothing gave them away long before the features of their faces could be scanned for the correct lineage, had ceased wearing Samaritan clothing. Even the braided belt of seven colors had been discarded in favor of the thick, heavy leather belts of the Jews.

But not Zebulon. He proudly wore the braided belt, which he tied across his light brown tunic with the golden gamma shapes in the corners. The enmity with which the Jews had treated his people for hundreds of years was not lost on him, but neither was its mirror image found in his own heart. He had no time for bitterness. It was too much effort to take offense from every passing Jew, when there were so many of them freely giving offenses away.

So Zebulon decided to greet all travelers warmly, even if their disdain was more often the rule than the exception. He traveled much of the year on Judea's dusty roads, selling grapes and raisins and plump figs grown in his own orchards, and had met enough people to know that deep inside they were all alike. They had the same fears, joys, and dreams. His own dream of his wife and children sustained him on the road, especially now, when he was only a few days from home.

Hearing birds squawking, he looked up and saw a number of vultures wheeling in the sky. "Hut hut!" he said, goading his camel forward. As he rounded a large rock, he saw what the birds were after, down in the gorge. The half-eaten carcass of a donkey was burst open on the rocks below. A wooden pack frame was shattered nearby, and several colorful swatches of fabric lay about, torn to pieces by the carrion birds.

Zebulon turned and saw a man lying at the side of the trail, near a wall of rock, covered with blood. A raven was nipping at a large, bloody wound over the man's ear.

"Shoo!" yelled Zebulon, rushing forward. The raven lifted off and coasted away. Zebulon rolled the man over and put his ear to the man's open mouth. For the longest time there was nothing, and then the tiniest, weakest breath wheezed out, and another equally insignificant breath went in.

Zebulon rushed to his camel and grabbed a waterskin. He returned and poured water over the man's face, wiping the blood from the nose, eyes, and mouth. One of the man's front teeth was broken, and the other was perilously loose. Zebulon tipped the waterskin into the man's mouth. Most of the water came back out, but he kept at it until a little bit went in, causing the man to cough weakly. He opened his right eye, looked at Zebulon for a moment, then closed it again.

Zebulon went back to his camel and fetched a bottle of wine and a jar of oil. He poured the antiseptic wine over the shoulder wound and salved it with the olive oil before binding it with a piece of cloth. He broke his walking stick over his knee and placed the pieces on either side of the man's broken arm, binding it gently. Then he lifted the man onto his camel's back. The man was limp as a sack of beans, and Zebulon had to hold him on with one hand while he goaded the animal forward with the other.

SEVEN

The Inn

Kohath was nearing the end of his strength when the road curved and the inn came into view. It was a squat, flat-roofed building constructed of sandstone blocks, plastered the same color as the tan hillsides of the wadi. Two large palms stood on either side of the arch, which led into a courtyard. Kohath's empty waterskin had bounced at his side for three hours now, and he was parched. A trough half full of water stood by the arch, and Kohath rushed to it, scooping several handfuls into his mouth.

The innkeeper watched Kohath slaking his thirst, his muscled arms folded across his chest. "Peace be unto you," he said, holding out a towel for the dripping man.

Kohath took the towel and buried his face in it. "And unto you, peace," he managed, looking around. "Where is everybody?"

"I am Caleb. This is my inn on the wadi Qelt," he said, apparently unwilling to answer Kohath's direct question. "I am at your service."

Kohath nodded. "Have you no one staying here? And what is that noise?"

"You are early . . . ah . . . "

"Kohath. I'm traveling to Jericho."

"Where else?" laughed Caleb. "You are early, Kohath. But there will be many arriving soon. It is a busy road."

"It wasn't today," said Kohath absently, then, remembering the wounded man, looked away and asked, "What is that racket?"

"The stonemason. We are expanding the inn."

"I hope he doesn't raise that din through the night," said Kohath, irritated.

"No," said Caleb. "But he does start early. I can't talk him out of it."

"Well?" said Kohath. "You have a room for me, then? Seeing as I am the first."

"Yes, sir," said Caleb, bowing low. "We have a room. For you alone."

"Very good," said Kohath, picking up his things. "Show me, then."

Lamech had run for two miles after seeing the man on the road, not slowing down until his side ached and he thought his lungs would burst. He sat panting on the edge of the trail, disgusted with himself for fleeing like a scared child. After all, he'd seen death before.

Indeed, in the Temple he was even the instrument of death. He would hold white doves in his hands, swiftly wring their necks, then pitch them into the crackling fire. Or he would pull his sharp blade across the neck of an unblemished sheep, then hoist the animal using the block and tackle, allowing its blood to drain into the huge silver chalice. Then he would dip his finger into the blood and dab it onto the tip of his right ear, the thumb of his right hand, and the big toe of his right foot, symbolizing obedience to God's voice and activity in his service. As he repeated the ritual prayers, eyes closed in concentration, Lamech knew the people at the foot of the stairs were looking up at him with rapt attention as he invoked the name of Jehovah on their behalf.

Lamech considered the blood shed in the Temple to be God's will. But out here, on the road, the blood he'd seen covering the man was so out of place that he had to flee. And now the humiliation of doing so weighed heavily on him.

He got up and trudged down the trail, wishing he were back in Jerusalem or already in Jericho, skipping this day entirely. Thinking about blood, in the Temple or elsewhere, was the last thing he wanted to do right now.

So he was surprised and gratified when he turned a corner and there it was: the Qelt Inn. If it was an adder, as his father would say, he'd be praising Jehovah to his face. Lamech walked under the arch between the two palms. The innkeeper greeted him, and Lamech asked if there was an extra room.

"Perhaps," said the innkeeper, grinning.

"I'm going to the Jordan," said Lamech. "I've never been there." He knew he sounded like a boy, but he wanted to hear the sound of a voice, any voice, even his, saying something, anything, so long as it didn't concern blood.

"Ahh!" said Caleb. "The oasis, yes? Water, rich food, . . . and"—he smiled conspiratorially at Lamech—"the women."

Lamech gave him a perfunctory smile. "Yes. The women."

"The women," repeated Caleb. "And wine. Red wine!"

"Yes," said Lamech flatly, the bloody image returning. "Red wine."

EIGHT

A Light on a Hill

It was well past dark when Zebulon arrived at the inn. The going had been slow, and he'd been passed by a number of travelers, all of whom had ignored his plight. Ordinarily, he wouldn't have asked for help, but the wounded man would not stay on the camel's back. Finally, Zebulon had to hoist him onto his own shoulders and carry him like a spring lamb—a fat, bleeding spring lamb. He'd even gone so far as to directly ask a group of men who overtook him on horses if they might lend him a hand. They had judged his race and had goaded their horses into a gallop, raising a cloud of dust as they passed. Zebulon had broken a commandment then, and cursed them.

But he was finally here, and his charge was still alive, though who knew for how long. He rarely stayed at roadhouses in this part of Judea because they usually refused him lodging, but he hoped that, just for tonight, they might make an exception, if not for him, then for the injured man.

A small, skinny boy appeared bearing a torch and took the reins of the camel, his eyes never leaving Zebulon, who stood there, his feet planted widely, holding the injured man in his arms like a child. "We need a room, son. And a doctor, if there is one."

The boy ran back into the lamplit courtyard, disappearing into the crowd of people inside. Zebulon bent under the arch, carrying his unconscious burden. The courtyard quieted and every face turned toward him. A table was cleared and Zebulon placed the wounded man on it and stepped back. A man who was bringing a pitcher of water saw Zebulon's braided belt and quickly set the pitcher down on the table. Another whispered, and Zebulon heard an epithet coupled with the word *Samaritan.*

Zebulon looked around. No one said anything. A tall, thin man pointed at the wounded man and asked Zebulon, "Did you do this?"

Zebulon fought the urge to throttle the man right there. Instead, he turned and reached for the water pitcher. It was gone. He looked up. "He needs a doctor."

"An *animal* doctor," muttered someone. Zebulon's head snapped in the direction of the sound. No one moved. Even the innkeeper, identified by his dirty apron, stood stock-still at the rear of the crowd. Zebulon bent his head, disgusted. "I have money."

The innkeeper didn't move, except for his eyes, which looked away.

Then a young man, darkly tanned with dark curly hair, stepped forward, handing a crescent of bread to Zebulon. "Here."

Zebulon took a bite of the bread. The young man held out a flagon of wine. "You must be thirsty," he said, and Zebulon took a long, slow drink of wine, his eyes scanning the crowd as he drank. Most of the men were looking hatefully at the young man, who was looking at the injured man with concern.

When Zebulon finally drained the flagon and wiped his mustache with the back of his hand, the young man bent and snaked his arms under the injured man. Zebulon grasped the young man's hands under the traveler in a ladder carry. The crowd reluctantly parted as they carried the traveler back out under the arch.

"Where are we going?" asked Zebulon.

"Back here," said the young man, leading the way. They chose their steps carefully in the dark, followed the rounded wall of the inn, and soon Zebulon saw a doorway. They entered a small dark storeroom, which had been rearranged so there was space for a sleeping pallet in the corner. Hanging lentils, sacks of grain and beans, and casks of wine filled the room, floor to ceiling. They laid the injured man down on the pallet. The skinny boy appeared in the doorway with a torch and lit a wall sconce. The young man nodded to him. He disappeared, then returned with a pitcher of water and clean rags. The young man set to work on the man's cuts and bruises. Zebulon's knees were suddenly weak and he sat down on an upturned wine cask.

"Who is he?" asked the young man as he gently dabbed at the injured man's face.

"Don't know," said Zebulon. "Is he still breathing?"

"Barely."

"You can't bring him in here!" came a voice. Zebulon turned. The innkeeper stood in the doorway, fists on his hips, his bald head shiny with sweat. The young man continued working, wiping away the blood on the man's face.

"Jeshua!"

Jeshua turned, and the look on his face would have frozen fire. It was emphatic and absolutely nonnegotiable. Zebulon looked at the innkeeper, who was equally surprised. "Okay," he finally responded to the silent reprimand, "but he's your responsibility. You pay for him."

Zebulon said, "I said I had money."

"I don't want your money. Or you," said the innkeeper.

Jeshua turned. "Caleb, I don't have any money. Yet," he said, smiling.

"But I do," said Zebulon. "Please." He held out his money purse as proof. The innkeeper scowled at Jeshua, ignoring Zebulon. "Please," repeated Zebulon.

Caleb shook his head and snatched the purse from him. He looked through it, then looked up. "I suppose you'll want a room as well?"

Zebulon nodded.

"We're full," he said, extracting a coin and handing the purse back to Zebulon.

"He can stay here with me," said Jeshua, bending forward and cupping his hand over the unconscious man's ruined eye, whispering silently to him.

"I'll be leaving tomorrow," said Zebulon wearily.

Caleb folded his arms across his chest. "Yes. You will." He turned and left.

Zebulon turned to Jeshua again. "My name is Zebulon. I'm a Sam—"

"Jeshua bar Joseph," interrupted Jeshua. "I know. I saw your belt and cloak."

"So did everyone else," said Zebulon, shaking his head angrily.

"I've always liked those braided belts your people wear," said Jeshua, carefully wrapping the injured man's head in a long piece of linen, covering the damaged eye but leaving the other one exposed. "They're beautiful. The colors represent the seven seasons, don't they?"

Zebulon nodded. "Yes. They remind us of how things change. Or how they do not." He scowled at the empty spot where the innkeeper stood moments before.

Jeshua nodded again to the servant boy, who stood like a sentinel at the doorway. "Food and wine for our guests, Timothy."

The boy fled the room as if bitten. "Your servant?" asked Zebulon.

"No, just a boy who works here, like me." He pulled the wood chip from behind his ear, a sign of his trade, then replaced it, where it was eclipsed by the dark curly strands. "I'm a carpenter. I'm working on an addition to the inn."

"It is lucky I found him," said Zebulon. "And lucky you were here, too."

Then Jeshua looked at Zebulon so intently that Zebulon felt suddenly exposed. "I don't believe much in luck," said Jeshua mildly. "But I do believe in kindness." He paused a moment and said, "When you leave in the morning, I will look after your friend."

"He isn't my friend," countered Zebulon.

Jeshua smiled. "Of course he is."

Kohath excused himself from the dining area, threading his way past the men still talking about the Samaritan and injured man. "Was he a Samaritan, too?" "They both were," assured another. "Didn't you see his cloak?"

Kohath shivered, thinking how close he had come to touching a Samaritan on the road today. Once again, his intuition had saved him. He didn't remember any cloak, though, when he saw the man lying there. All he had on was a loincloth.

And who was the dark giant who had brought him in? Kohath hadn't passed him on the road; he hadn't passed anybody the entire day, gratefully. It occurred to Kohath after he'd traveled a few miles past the wounded man that if he should encounter any other travelers coming in the opposite direction, they might think *he* had attacked him.

Spared by the hand of the Lord, he thought. Kohath was innocent, of course, but it was good to avoid even the appearance of evil. And speaking of evil, that Samaritan had looked like the embodiment of the Adversary himself. Every part of the man was dark: his greasy black hair, his bristling black beard, even his deep-set eyes, ringed with dark circles. He must have been hiding in the wadi when Kohath came upon the injured man. Gooseflesh lifted on Kohath's arm as he thought of how the Samaritan had probably watched him as he examined the wounded man.

Kohath shut the door to his room, then knelt by his bed and thanked God for saving his life and promised him that he would always listen to the still, small voice, the voice that God had said would always protect his servants, if they would but listen.

He lay down in the hard, bumpy bed, feeling the warmth of understanding. His life had been spared today. The prayer he offered this morning was accepted by the Lord after all.

When the man entered the courtyard, Lamech's view of him was obscured, but he heard someone say, "He's injured!" and he knew instantly that it was the wounded man he had passed on the road. He'd jumped up, grabbed the pitcher of water, and moved decisively through the knot of people, wanting to be of help.

And then he had found himself face-to-face with the Samaritan, the same one he'd passed on the road. He tried now, back in his room, to remember the condition of the wounded man lying on the table in the courtyard. Was he still alive? He couldn't remember; it was all a blur. But the face of Darkness had stared down at him in frank hatred, and that he did remember. The Samaritan obviously knew Lamech was a servant of God; his look had said it all. Lamech's disguise had proven incapable of hiding him from the Evil One.

Lamech pushed his pallet to block the door. He might not sleep tonight, but if he did, the opening door would awaken him in time to defend himself. He knelt down and tried to pray, but he was too scared. Just knowing the Samaritan was in the building was enough to keep him awake all night.

Hours later, Lamech's fear of the Samaritan shifted into a deeper dread that the injured man would survive and recognize him as having passed by without helping him. As sleep beckoned, his memory grew confused. Out there on the road, did the injured man open his eyes and look at Lamech? Would he now point his finger and accuse him? And would the accusation get back to the Temple priests?

Lamech tossed and turned throughout the night, exchanging one fear for another, until finally he slept, dreaming once again of the cool waters of the Jordan. But for some reason, the waters were red.

NINE

He Who Hath Eyes

Zebulon lay on the hard stone floor, his cloak a pillow under his head, hands folded across his chest, thinking well into the night. Jeshua slept next to him. In the starlight falling through the high window, he studied the carpenter's features. Zebulon had never seen such a man. He wasn't handsome, but there was something arresting about him. As he ministered to the injured traveler, Zebulon had asked him if he was a doctor. Jeshua had laughed and said, no, he was a carpenter. Zebulon was the last person to denigrate a laborer; he'd been one most of his life, but he'd never really been proud of it, and when his circumstances changed and he found himself a wealthy merchant, he never again admitted to dirtying his hands.

But the way Jeshua had said, "I'm a carpenter," had filled Zebulon with a kind of sweet envy. When he walked outside during the night to relieve himself, he surveyed the stone foundation Jeshua was working on. Though there was no moon, he could see well enough to tell that this young man was a competent builder. Apparently, he was working alone, moving the huge sandstone blocks by himself.

Zebulon looked at Jeshua's hand, draped over his chest. It was rough and callused, a long cut on the forefinger just now scabbing over. He couldn't help thinking that this was not the hand of a common laborer. It was the hand of a nobleman or even a king. He shook his head, wondering how he knew this, yet he was rarely wrong about people. *That comes from people being so wrong about me,* he thought.

Another way he knew something was different about Jeshua was that when he was talking with the innkeeper about payment, his eyes had caught the young man leaning over the injured traveler, gently sponging the blood from the man's face. Jeshua had placed his hand over the man's crushed brow and had whispered something. Then he had wrapped the man's head in a long strip of cloth, covering the damaged eye.

Zebulon looked over at the injured man lying on Jeshua's pallet. His face was white in the low light, but he finally seemed to be resting peacefully. Something had happened right before Zebulon's eyes. He had ministered to the traveler with wine and oil, but he knew the real healing had occurred when Jeshua cupped his hand over the man's eye and whispered to him. What had he said? Much of the afternoon, as he carried the injured man, not knowing if he was alive or dead, he had wondered what he would do next. He needed to be getting home again after his long absence. Where could he leave the traveler? Who would care for him? He had no answers.

But as he lay there, he knew his steps had been guided today. The carpenter with the nobleman's hands would see to it that the traveler was cared for, and Zebulon could continue his journey with a clear conscience, knowing he had done what he could for the poor man.

Then Zebulon's eyes once again lit on Jeshua's hand, and he knew the injured man would live, and more than that, he would be healed. The carpenter's hand, callused and injured itself, had healed the traveler with a touch. Zebulon had witnessed something miraculous, and as he drifted off to sleep he reminded himself not to forget what he'd seen today.

"Take care of him," said Zebulon as he handed over five gold coins to the innkeeper. "And whatever you spend more, when I return, I will repay."

Caleb scowled at the money. He looked over at Jeshua, who was chiseling on a block of sandstone. Jeshua had implored him to accept the Samaritan's money, and he had finally given in. He knew the Samaritan's money was as good as anyone else's, but the truth was he didn't want anyone to see him accepting it. But since the injured man was Jewish, and the money was meant to help him, Caleb saw no conflict. Plus, they were alone out here in back of the inn and no one else saw the transaction. He put the coins in his apron pocket.

"If you don't return, I'll dock your friend's pay," Caleb said, nodding at Jeshua.

Zebulon shook his head. "I will return. You can trust in that."

Caleb shook his apron, jingling the coins. "I will trust in this," he said, and turned away.

Jeshua came over to Zebulon. "Travel safely."

Zebulon nodded. "And you. Work safely." He pointed at Jeshua's cut finger, which was bleeding again.

Jeshua sucked on the cut. "I'll try, but of the three, the stone and the chisel and me, I'm afraid I'm made of the softest material."

Zebulon shook his head. "I don't believe that for a minute, young man." He walked toward his camels, then turned back. "I hope we meet again, carpenter."

Kohath adjusted his tunic and the secured the wide belt around his waist. He couldn't get used to this rough clothing. He looked at his dirty feet. He must get a bath this morning before setting out again.

Then he remembered that the Samaritan would be on the road today. He didn't want to meet him on the emptiness of the trail. One casualty on that road was enough. Kohath sat down on the bed, thinking. No, it wouldn't do to be hasty. He would give the Samaritan a wide berth, waiting long enough to be sure the man was well out of the area. Besides, a day or two at the inn would be restful.

Last night the place was full of cursing drunkards, boasting of their prowess with women and all manner of base things. Kohath had kept to himself, saying nothing to anyone, and then a dirty, foul-smelling man sat down across from him and tried to engage him in a conversation. Kohath had feigned ignorance of the man's language, and after a few attempts the man gave up and left. Kohath felt guilty, lying like that, but he was afraid that if he spoke to the man he would be recognized as a Temple priest and subjected to ridicule. Or worse.

And when the Samaritan arrived, he had seized the opportunity to leave the courtyard, escaping to the safety of his room, which had become a sort of cell. He had missed breakfast and now it was nearing noon. He couldn't stay in here all day. Just another hour or so, he decided, and then he would emerge, stretching and exulting to the innkeeper about the good night's sleep he'd had, when the truth was, he hadn't slept a wink. He had stared at the barred door for hours, expecting the Samaritan to come bursting in at any moment.

Kohath lay back on the bed and closed his eyes. He needed some sleep, and when he awoke, hopefully, this nightmare would be over.

Lamech rose early, eager to be on his way. Unfortunately, there were many others of the same mind, and it took forever to get even a crust of bread and a cup of juice. He sat in the great room on a cushion next to a low table and watched the servants bringing food to the travelers, waiting his turn. Lamech listened as men talked of their journeys and destinations, and he was filled with envy. They had journeyed far, seen sights he would never see. Carved palaces in Babylon, fantastic stone monoliths in distant Egypt, and colonnaded marble porticoes in Greece.

But they had never seen the high priest emerge from the Holy of Holies, his face translucent with the sure knowledge of God, either. They hadn't felt his cool hand on their forehead as he blessed each of the Levites and priests in turn; hadn't felt their souls expand at the touch, knowing that the high priest had just been in the presence of the Lord.

No marble column or Greek temple or Egyptian pyramid could compare with that.

Lamech finally got his breakfast and was eating it when it occurred to him that he hadn't seen the Samaritan or the injured man. The thought made him uneasy. Perhaps the Samaritan would be on the road this morning, and should Lamech meet him, Lamech would have to explain why he passed the injured traveler yesterday without helping him.

Lamech munched the barley bread and pondered. It would be a good idea to wait a little while before continuing on. Maybe he could learn some more about the big world right here, at the inn. Maybe today wasn't such a good day to rush off toward Jericho after all.

"He's awake," said Timothy. Jeshua put down his chisel, and they walked toward the storeroom. The traveler was indeed awake, perspiring heavily. One eye was bandaged, and the other, blackened and swollen from the attack, was circling wildly. He saw Jeshua and raised his unbroken arm. "Don't!" he moaned weakly.

Jeshua approached him slowly. "It's all right. You're safe." He intercepted the man's arm and lowered it to his side. His broken arm was bound between two wide barrel staves. The wound on his shoulder had bled through the bandage. Jeshua lifted it and peered at the wound, shaking his head. "You've torn my stitches," he said.

The man shook his head weakly. "Who are you?"

"Jeshua bar Joseph."

The man looked around, noting the stores and casks of wine. "I am Elam." Then, remembering something, he looked around. "Where are my goods?"

"You had none. What happened?"

Elam closed his eye. "I was set upon by thieves. It was dark; I never saw them." He reached up to find the bandage over his left eye. "What happened to my eye? It hurts."

"It is healing."

Elam reached up with his good arm and touched his tender shoulder. "Feels like the knife is still in there," he said.

"It shouldn't be, but then I'm not a doctor," said Jeshua, smiling.

"Where am I?" asked Elam,

"At the Qelt Inn. A good man found you and brought you here last night."

"Where is he? I must thank him."

"He continued on his journey. But he left money with the innkeeper to take care of you. He said he'd return in a few days to see how you are doing."

Elam shook his head slowly. "So you're not the innkeeper."

"No, I'm just working here." He lifted the cup of water to Elam's mouth. "Now, rest and heal."

Elam took a mouthful of the cool water and leaned back. Gone. All his fine cloaks. His hand moved reflexively to his chest. The pouch was gone, too. He moaned.

"What is it?" asked Jeshua.

"My money. Everything, gone." He started to cry.

"Not everything. You are alive."

Tears coursed down Elam's cheeks. "Everything. Gone."

For the rest of the afternoon, Jeshua carved stone. Two full courses of tan sandstone were already in place, forming the wall of the addition, a large room that would be roofed with cedar timbers. The room would be subdivided into a half dozen sleeping chambers, each with a small window and a drape across the doorway.

Caleb had designed the addition. Jeshua was impressed with his understanding of building, along with the man's prodigious knowledge of cultures and people, which he had shared with Jeshua on several occasions. Tales of distant lands, of famed travelers and wicked warlords, all of whom, it appeared, had stayed at this very inn. It was interesting as well; Jeshua's family had passed the inn many times on their way to Jerusalem, though they had never stayed here. It was too expensive. Besides, Jeshua's father, Joseph, came this way reluctantly because it was the long way to Jerusalem from Galilee. It was much faster to travel south through Samaria, but Jews generally avoided Samaria altogether, traveling east to the Sea of Galilee, then south along the Jordan River until reaching Jericho, then up through the dusty wadis to Jerusalem.

The travel route was a source of contention between Joseph and his brother Abiah, who preferred to avoid Samaria. To maintain harmony, Joseph usually acquiesced, and his family had accompanied Abiah's family along the Jordan and past this inn on their travels several times.

One year, however, Abiah was ill and his family did not go to Jerusalem for the Feast of the Tabernacles. Joseph steered his own family down the green, rocky hills south of Nazareth, across the broad Jezreel Valley, past the majestic cone of Mt. Tabor, and then up the rolling hills of Samaria. They had passed many orchards and vineyards, and the children (Jeshua included) had marveled at the beautiful country. They discovered a people much like Galileans: quick to laugh, generally honest, and pleasant if they knew they were not being judged.

Jeshua had even worked in Samaria once with his brothers Joses and Juda. They had dammed a river for a Samaritan named Ismaiah, who had proven to be the hardest taskmaster they had ever known, but while he was not generous, neither was he cruel or a cheat. At the conclusion of their work, they left Samaria, young Joses wondering aloud why there was such enmity between the Jews of Jerusalem and the Samaritans.

"Perhaps, " said Juda, "it's because Jerusalem is so far away."

"Why would that matter?" asked Joses.

"Why are you so dumb?" chided Juda, shaking his head.

"I'm not dumb."

"That's true," said Jeshua, stepping between his two younger brothers. "When he talks, it might sound foolish, but that's because he is so smart. We cannot hope to understand how his mind works."

Juda smirked at Jeshua. "Or if it works."

"Go ahead," said Jeshua, prodding Joses. "Tell us what you think Juda meant when he said people hate the Samaritans because Jerusalem is so far away."

Joses pursed his lips, thinking. "There goes that great mind," said Juda. "You can almost hear the wheel turning, threshing an idea into dust."

Joses scowled harder. Finally, he brightened. "Is it because they don't know the Samaritans like we do?"

Jeshua clapped him on the shoulder. "See?" he laughed, nudging Juda. "Exactly right."

Juda shook his head. "Slow as the coming of spring."

Joses cuffed Juda on the back of the head and broke into a run, shouting, "Who's slow?" He bolted down the path. In an instant Juda was on his heels, reaching for his little brother, but Joses wove and turned, narrowly escaping Juda's grasp. Jeshua laughed, running after them.

Now, several years later, Jeshua wished he could avail himself of his brothers' boundless energy. As they had grown older, they worked together less often. Conflicts inevitably arose, as no one wanted to take orders from another. They built a kiln together a few years ago, and Jeshua had never seen so much bickering in his life. When it was finished he asked Joseph why he had to oversee the work when his expertise was clearly not needed, or his labor either. "And they don't listen to me," he said, shaking his head.

Joseph had smiled and handed Jeshua his hammer.

"What's this for?" asked Jeshua.

"You're ready, son. Go build a world of your own."

Jeshua had looked at the hammer. "With this? It's awfully old."

"And you're awfully young. Any hammer, in the hands of a competent journeyman, will build a fine house. It isn't the hammer that matters—it's the man swinging it."

Jeshua grasped that same hammer firmly now, his mind returning to the present, hunched over a chunk of rock that was starting to look more and more like a cube. He steadied the chisel and struck it firmly. A shard of sandstone fell away, revealing a smooth plane of white stone. Jeshua sat on the stone, looking at the hammer and wondering how long it would be before he knew all there was to know about building a world.

TEN

The Priest and the Levite

It was late afternoon before Kohath finally ventured out of his room. He entered the great room and took a seat on a cushion by a low table in the corner. The inn was nearly empty of last night's travelers. A few new ones were straggling in, dirty and tired from the road. Kohath eyed them all with disgust, knowing the evil that lurked in their hearts. After all, he spent his days performing atoning sacrifices for such people. They came to the Temple, hearts heavy with sin, to purchase atonement. They would approach the altar and humbly hand the offering to the Levite, who would prepare the sacrifice while they stood, their eyes never leaving the priest's hands as he worked, hoping for absolution.

Over the years, he'd come to recognize two types of people. On the one hand, there were the godless pagans, who violated the Law indiscriminately, spoke with unclean mouths, and sinned at every turn. Bawdy houses like this inn were their temples.

And on the other hand, there were the Jews, who should know better, but even they were disobedient, slow to hearken to the words of the prophets and eager to follow the wickedness of the world.

Kohath had all but rejected both groups. His solace was the Temple. There, he avoided the evil of the world and the wickedness thereof. After what he had seen yesterday on the road, he wondered why he had thought going to Jericho was such a good idea after all.

Lamech had been hanging around the inn all afternoon, watching for the Samaritan. When he was satisfied the man was gone, he felt better. He decided that tomorrow he would continue his journey to the Jordan, and his heart lifted for the first time all day. He walked into the great room and was shocked to see Priest Kohath sitting in a corner.

Kohath felt eyes on him and looked up. A young man was looking at him, mouth agape. Kohath looked away, trying to place him. He seemed familiar, but how could he be? Kohath barely knew anyone in Jerusalem; how would he know anyone at this place?

"Priest Kohath?"

The young man was standing before him. But how did he know his name?

"I am Lamech, sire. A Levite. From the Temple."

Kohath blinked, then it fell into place. A Levite. One of many, and yes, he did recognize the slender, sandy-haired young man. He nodded. "Yes. Of course."

"May I join you?" The young man pointed to a cushion opposite Kohath. When Kohath didn't object, he sat down and leaned forward, whispering. "It's amazing, seeing a priesthood holder here, of all places."

Kohath nodded, still perplexed. What was this boy doing here? As if he heard, Lamech spoke up. "I'm on holiday, as I guess you are. I'm going to the Jordan."

Kohath found his voice. "I'm on my way to Jericho."

"Wonderful!" exclaimed Lamech. "Imagine. We're on the same road at the same time. And we didn't even know it."

Kohath nodded. He didn't want company, not here, not now, and not from a Levite boy. And the familiarity with which he addressed him. He knew Lamech would never have invited himself to sit with a priest at the Temple. So why was he doing so now?

Lamech motioned for a servant girl to come and asked her for some dates. When she left, he turned back to Kohath and smiled as if they were old friends. Kohath looked away, mind racing, thinking of how he might excuse himself from this uncomfortable situation.

"Would you like some dates as well, Priest Kohath?" asked the young man.

Kohath shook his head. "No, thank you."

Lamech looked around, then leaned toward Kohath. "It's nice to find a man of God on this wild road. Perhaps we might journey toward Jericho together. It's dangerous out there; a man was brought in last night who was nearly killed by thieves."

"I know," said Kohath, the memory renewing his concern about traveling alone. He looked at the Levite. He was young and strong. He might be of some protection on the road. The servant brought a plate of dates. Lamech held one out for Kohath, who took it gingerly.

"What did you say your name was, young man?"

Elam awoke again, moaning. It was daytime, but he'd lost track of which day. His left eye throbbed horribly, sending sharp needles into the center of his head. His other eye was so swollen he could barely see out of it. And the fingers at the end of his broken arm were so swollen he couldn't bend them.

He looked up at the ceiling and listened again to the rhythmic sound of a hammer striking metal. Occasionally, the pounding would stop and Jeshua would appear, carrying a dripping waterskin, which he would pour into a basin and then gently sponge on Elam's body.

At such times Elam closed his eyes and turned his head away. It was humiliating to be cared for in the most personal of ways. Jeshua would roll him onto his side, and he would feel the cool wet cloth on his body, a helpless infant. During such times, Jeshua would talk idly, asking questions at first, but when Elam didn't answer, he resorted to telling him about the inn, the travelers he'd met, and what he was working on.

Jeshua left him again. Here he was, a shoulder badly injured, an arm broken, and a good chance he would lose an eye. The hazy darkness he moved in and out of seemed endless. Even night was no darker than the inside of his heart. A thought came to the fore at such times and often stayed with him until he fell asleep. That evening, as Jeshua was spooning broth into his mouth, he let it slip.

"I fear God has punished me."

Jeshua looked at him.

"Do you believe God punishes us?"

Jeshua put the bowl down and helped Elam to a drink of water. Elam was about to repeat the question when Jeshua said, "If you had a disobedient child, would you harm it?"

"Of course not. It's just a child. It might not know any better."

"But if the child knew better, would you harm it for disobeying you?"

"No, but I might punish it. That's what I'm saying."

Jeshua leaned back, thinking. "Look." He held up his hand. There was a long, scabbed gash running the length of his forefinger. "Who do you think did this to me?"

Elam smiled. "The god of sharp things?"

Jeshua laughed. "I don't know that god, and I don't think I want to."

"You're saying we punish ourselves, like when you cut yourself there."

Jeshua nodded.

"But even if God doesn't punish us, he might withhold his love."

"Elam, would you ever cease to love your child?"

Elam thought of his own father and the many times the old man had tried to make peace with him. The last time he saw him, he had begged

Elam to stay overnight so he could arrange a feast in his honor. Elam had just shaken his head and left.

Instead of answering, Elam turned his head away so Jeshua couldn't see the pain in his eyes.

At dinner that evening, Jeshua walked into the kitchen, an empty bowl in his hand. He handed it to Laisha, the servant girl. "Some more of the stew, please. For Elam."

"Is he getting better?" she asked as she filled the bowl and handed it back to Jeshua.

"Yes," said Jeshua. "Maybe you should visit him."

The girl shook her head.

"He's a good man," said Jeshua.

She shook her head again. "He scares me."

Jeshua placed a flat circle of bread over the steaming bowl. "Well, you think about it."

She nodded, then scurried off to deliver a plate to two men sitting in the corner of the great room. Jeshua watched as they received their food and bent to eat, talking low, with furtive glances at the other travelers. When Laisha returned, Jeshua handed her the bowl of stew and said, "Would you take this to Elam?"

Laisha's face went white.

"Just give it to him and tell him I'll be in shortly."

Laisha sighed. "All right." She carried the bowl through the doorway at the rear of the kitchen. Jeshua walked toward the two men in the corner.

"Peace be unto you."

Kohath and Lamech looked up. "And unto you, peace. The food is fine. Thank you," said Kohath.

"I'll tell the cook," said Jeshua.

Kohath looked perplexed, but Lamech understood. "You are not a servant?"

"I'm Jeshua, a carpenter. I'm working here."

"You're the one making all the racket at dawn," said Kohath flatly.

"That's me. I apologize for waking you."

"Please sit, Jeshua," said Lamech suddenly. Kohath shot him a surprised look.

"Thank you," said Jeshua, sitting cross-legged on a cushion.

"I am Lamech, a Lev—"

"And I am Kohath, of Jerusalem. We are traveling to Jericho, to see family."

Lamech gave Kohath a strange look, then, "Yes. To see family."

Jeshua nodded. "That's wonderful."

"You are a Galilean, aren't you?" asked Kohath.

"I fear my speech gives me away."

"I've never been to Galilee," said Lamech. "I hear it is beautiful."

"Quite beautiful," said Jeshua. "But so is Jerusalem."

"You've been to Jerusalem?" asked Kohath.

"For the feasts, of course."

"Don't forget the taxation," said Lamech, warming to the young man, who was just a few years older than he.

Just then Laisha tapped Jeshua on the shoulder. "He says he's too weak to tear the bread. And I was . . ." She hung her head in embarrassment.

Jeshua nodded. "All right, Laisha. I'm coming."

She ran off and Jeshua turned back. "A man was injured on the trail to Jerusalem, nearly killed by thieves," he said.

"Yes, we heard," said Kohath carefully.

"You did? Well, he's in the back. He was near death, but a kindly traveler brought him to the inn. He will heal, God willing."

Neither Kohath nor Lamech offered the usual "God willing" rejoinder, and the silence stretched out. Finally, Jeshua said, "When did you arrive here?"

Lamech looked at Kohath, who had been expecting this. Kohath cleared his throat. "This morning. Is this man a friend of yours?"

"Yes," said Jeshua.

"The world is a dangerous place," mused Kohath solemnly. "Our best wishes for your friend. We hope he recovers fully."

"Thank you. Your prayers would be appreciated," said Jeshua.

"Of course," said Kohath, nodding.

Jeshua stood and said, "It was nice meeting you. I wish you a safe journey." He turned and walked toward the kitchen.

Lamech turned to Kohath, shocked. "But, sire, we came in last—"

"Never tell anyone your business," hissed Kohath. "You don't know this man. You have no idea what his intentions are."

Lamech looked toward the empty doorway. "He's just a carpenter. He seems—"

Kohath gave Lamech his most withering look, and Lamech shut his mouth. "You will learn, young man," Kohath whispered, "that people are not always what they seem."

Lamech leaned back, rebuked. He dipped a piece of bread into the bowl. What was bothering Kohath? Had he seen the injured man on the road as well? And if so, had he seen Lamech pass the injured man without offering help?

When he finally spoke again, it was to change the subject.

ELEVEN

Face-to-Face

Achish stood on the promontory overlooking the trail as it snaked around a bend in the canyon wall. Last night he'd slept in the desert, and he spent today hiding in shallow cave. Only after dark did he venture out. He was tired and dirty and ready to spend some of his newly acquired money. Down below, hunched in the darkness the old inn sat, two date palms on either side of an archway leading to an enclosed courtyard. Wisps of smoke curled up from the chimney, and Achish could smell meat cooking. He looked forward to a hot meal, a bottle of wine, and a soft bed. He felt the money pouch inside his tunic. He had done well this time and would be rewarded.

Nearing the inn, he passed a number of camels and donkeys tied near a low trough. The torchlit courtyard was full of people. Achish searched for an accusing look on a familiar face. He saw no one he recognized and relaxed.

"Pardon me. Could I ask you a favor?"

Achish turned. Behind him was a man with dark, curly hair and brown eyes, a small chip of wood tucked behind his ear. Sweat had drawn tiny clean rivulets down his dirty cheeks. Achish squinted at him, noticing the leather apron and the man's filthy tunic.

Achish shook his head and turned back to the courtyard, scanning for the innkeeper.

"Please. It will just take a minute."

Achish ignored the request. When the man came around to face him, Achish considered punching him and getting it over with. But the fool was just standing there, and Achish was suddenly amused. Why was he angry? Wasn't he the richest man at the inn? Didn't he have a minute, as the man had requested? Maybe it was time for him to play the part of the wealthy man he had so long aspired to. He nodded expansively and smiled. "What can I do for you?"

"It will take just a moment, then I will introduce you to the innkeeper," said the man. He led Achish around to the back, following the curve of the building. A door stood open and the man walked inside a dimly lit room.

In a corner lay a little fat man on a low pallet, his head bandaged thickly and one arm bound between two barrel staves.

Achish froze. It couldn't be. He'd left him for dead. What was he doing here?

"Elam! This is . . ." The carpenter turned to Achish. "I'm sorry. I didn't get your name."

Achish had turned away, his mind racing. He turned back slowly, head down, and mumbled, "Hanan. My name is Hanan."

Elam looked up at the man with his bruised, bloodshot eye. He still couldn't make anything come into focus. He lifted his unbroken arm. "Thank you, Hanan."

The man was actually smiling through his broken teeth, the very teeth Achish had knocked out just last night.

"Elam," said Jeshua, kneeling down by him, "would you like to go out into the great room? Perhaps enjoy some company?"

Elam's eyes teared up with gratitude. "Yes. Thank you, Jeshua."

The display turned Achish's stomach, and he almost turned and walked out when Jeshua caught his eye, and the intensity of his gaze held Achish immobile.

Achish shook his head to clear it. Maybe this Jeshua was a sorcerer and was casting a spell on him. The important thing—if that was the case—was not to meet his gaze directly. He found his voice and croaked, "Let's get on with it, then."

"Thank you!" wailed the little fat merchant again.

Jeshua and Achish bent to pick Elam up. He smelled of urine and seeping wounds and poultices. As they lifted him, Achish's heart stopped. The money pouch! It hung from its leather drawstring around his neck, underneath his tunic, but now it was being pressed against the little merchant. Achish wanted to drop him and run from the room. Surely he would be found out. This was some kind of trick. His heart beat thunder in his chest. The bulging pouch pushed hard against his ribs; he knew it was pressing into the merchant's side as well.

"Ready?" said Jeshua.

"Ready," mumbled Achish.

"Here we go," said Jeshua. They carried Elam through the doorway. They had to turn sideways to transit the narrow hallway that ended in the kitchen, which meant Jeshua was looking right at Achish as he backed down the hall. Achish looked elsewhere.

"Thank you," said Elam quietly. "I'm sorry I'm so fat. . . ." he trailed off under sniffles.

As they moved through the kitchen, Achish couldn't avoid Jeshua's eyes any longer. The money pouch, bulging with coins, was digging a furrow between his ribs. He was certain the little fat man could feel the pouch as well, but Elam just lay in his arms, eyes closed, whimpering quietly.

If this is all an act, thought Achish, *I'll kill them both.* He looked at Jeshua, but Jeshua's head was turned, looking over his shoulder at where they were going.

They passed under an arch, and then they were in the great room. It was crowded, but people gave way, looking curiously at Elam.

"Almost there," said Jeshua, leading them toward a pile of pillows. They set Elam down and Achish turned to go.

"Hanan?"

Achish didn't turn. He'd forgotten the name he'd given them. But the man's thin, quavery voice had somehow silenced the entire room, and every eye was now on him. Achish turned back. Elam smiled. "Thank you, Hanan."

"Don't mention it," said Achish, hoping no one would. Was this the moment of truth? Was he going to be unmasked right here? Is that why they were all smiling at him?

As he headed for the door, several men patted him on the arm or slapped him on the back.

Outside the inn, standing in the darkness, he wondered if he should just keep going. He looked back. Everyone had gone back to their own business.

All right, he thought, relaxing, *no one knows who I am or what I did. I held the man in my arms and even he didn't recognize me.*

But he knew he'd been lucky. It was foolishness to stay here, with the merchant here as well. He turned away from the inn and walked a few paces, thinking.

"There you are," came a voice, and Achish turned, prepared for the worst. It was the carpenter. "I'm glad you're still here."

Steady, thought Achish. *Don't panic.* "Just getting some air."

Jeshua looked up at the stars twinkling in the cold desert night. "I'll introduce you to the innkeeper now, if you wish."

"I was thinking of moving on," said Achish, gesturing to the road. "It's too crowded in there."

"It's not safe on the road at night. You saw what happened to Elam. He was beaten by thieves."

"I can take care of myself," said Achish flatly.

"They stole everything he had and left him for dead."

Achish decided enough was enough. If he had to face it, it should be now, out here, where he could throttle the carpenter and then make his escape into the dark canyons. He frowned at Jeshua and asked, "Who did it?"

"We don't know," said Jeshua mildly. "He never saw his attackers."

"I hope they are brought to justice."

Jeshua nodded. "I am sure they will be."

Achish relaxed. "Perhaps I will stay, after all. No reason to take chances."

Jeshua nodded. "I'm so glad. You will be welcome here, friend."

Achish followed Jeshua inside. He had to smile at the irony of it all. The man he had robbed and beaten would be sitting just a few paces away as he bought food and wine and a warm bed with his money. The feeling gave Achish a wicked chill. He settled himself on a cushion near the door. Across the room, Jeshua was helping Elam sip a cup of water.

Achish ate slowly, dipping his bread into the broth and emptying the wine jug. He hadn't eaten this well in a long time, and he relaxed his defenses to focus all his attention on his meal. When he finished, he leaned back and looked across the room at Elam, who was dozing. The carpenter was sitting nearby, engaged in conversation with another man. Watching Jeshua, Achish knew he was safe. The carpenter was no sorcerer, he was just a fool, and if properly persuaded, his own wages might fill Achish's coin pouch. Thinking about robbing the man of his naïveté and his money gave Achish a shiver of joy.

Achish stood, his stomach full and his head heavy with sleep. He beckoned the innkeeper, a huge bald man, who stepped forward, wiping his hands on his apron. "I trust the meal was satisfactory?"

Achish nodded. "Acceptable."

The innkeeper nodded. "That will be five shekels, fifteen pence."

Achish frowned. "That's quite a lot."

"You ate quite a lot," said the innkeeper. "And drank my best wine!"

Achish shrugged and reached inside his tunic, grasping the money pouch.

It was empty.

He turned away and withdrew the pouch, peering inside. It was empty as a beggar's bowl; not a single coin remained. He stuffed it back inside his shirt and turned back to the innkeeper. "My coin pouch is empty."

"You have no money?" yelled the innkeeper, and the inn became quiet as death. Two men moved to block the exit. A hook-nosed man holding a long carving knife came out of the kitchen, flinging his dirty hair out of his face, his hands already bloody from cutting meat.

"I was robbed," said Achish weakly.

The innkeeper cocked his head. "Who robbed you?"

Achish looked around, knowing he was about to destroy any good-will he might have had at this inn. Everyone waited for a name, but Achish just looked at the floor. "I don't know who it was, but I had money when I came in."

"And now it's gone. Like my food."

"Perhaps we should get our food back," said the man with the knife, stepping forward.

Then Achish said something he had never said before in his life: "Please."

The innkeeper laughed. "*Please* is for cripples."

"He will be," said the man with the knife.

"I'll pay his bill, Caleb," said Jeshua, appearing at Achish's side.

Caleb laughed. "You? Why, you've less money than he has!" Everyone laughed, and Achish felt the tension loosen its hold on his neck. He started breathing again.

"True, Master Caleb," said Jeshua. "But you can take it out of what you owe me."

Caleb shook his head. "You're a soft touch, carpenter. How did you survive this long?"

Jeshua placed his hand on Caleb's arm. "I've always been lucky in friends." He leaned toward Caleb and whispered, "He helped me tonight. Please let me help him."

Caleb frowned. "All right, Jeshua. But if you keep this up, you'll end up owing me money." He shook his head and walked away.

Jeshua gestured for Achish to follow. They sat across from Elam, who had been awakened by the altercation. Achish leaned in and said, "Truly, I have no money."

"And I have no help," said Jeshua. "You could repay me by working for me. You'll get a couple more good meals in you and a good night's rest before you move on."

"But I'm not a common laborer," protested Achish.

"Things change," said Elam. "Look at me."

Jeshua said, "Hanan, I need help. You need help."

"We all need help," said Elam flatly, looking at his broken arm.

Achish looked over his shoulder. The innkeeper was still talking to the man with the carving knife, who was scowling at Achish. He was trapped; he had to agree to the proposition, for now at least. Tomorrow he would find out who stole his money. He smiled tightly. "All right. One day. Meals and lodging. And then we're even."

"Absolutely," said Jeshua.

TWELVE

Confederates

"That was stupid," said Lamech, leaning toward Kohath. "I wouldn't trust that evildoer for a minute, much less pay his bills."

"Don't be a fool," whispered Kohath, watching as the two men talked, just a few feet away. "There must be a good reason the carpenter is helping him."

"What reason is that?"

"I don't know," responded Kohath. "But there always is. You'll see."

Lamech watched Jeshua conversing with the penniless traveler, then his eyes wandered over to the injured merchant. He looked away, his conscience seared again. Yet his eyes returned again to convict him anew of his cowardice.

"I saw him on the road," said Kohath suddenly, nodding at Elam.

Lamech's jaw dropped. He whispered, "You did?"

"Yes," said Kohath absently. "I thought he was dead."

"I saw him, too," said Lamech, glad to finally admit it.

"I know. It was written all over your face."

Lamech looked down. "I thought he was either dead or a Samaritan."

"In either case, it was none of our business," said Kohath without emotion.

"Yes," said Lamech, and the heaviness in his heart that had lifted with his confession returned again. "We weren't to blame."

Kohath looked at him with genuine surprise. "Of course not," he said, and went back to his meal.

Achish settled onto the lumpy pallet in the storeroom. Caleb had refused to grant him a decent room, saying he wasn't inclined to extend him any more credit than he absolutely had to. So here he was, sleeping on the bed Elam had fouled with his poultices and ointments. Sure, they'd changed the straw and covered it with clean blankets, but it rankled Achish that he had to sleep in the very same bed as the man he'd almost killed had slept in, while they moved Elam to a private room.

Jeshua had said that Elam also was unable to pay for his lodging, so why was he getting a private room? It didn't figure, and as Achish lay there, listening to the carpenter sleeping on the floor next to him, even more questions began to present themselves.

If Elam didn't have any money, then who was paying for all this? It must be Jeshua. He was taking care of him, so he obviously had an interest in the man. But why? He had nothing with which to pay him. Achish had left Elam for dead, stripped naked and his goods destroyed.

Aah! The carpenter must have money. It was the only answer. He had to be rich, because not only was he helping Elam, he had offered to help Achish as well. Jeshua must be receiving something in return from Elam, just as he was requiring Achish to work with him. But what could he expect from the little fat man? He couldn't work to pay off his debt. He was probably blind in the one eye. Did Elam have rich relatives? No, they would have been notified already and would be on their way if he did.

So why was Jeshua helping the merchant? He could understand the economics of work for food, the agreement Jeshua made with him, but why was he caring for Elam, when no such transaction was possible?

The only logical explanation was that Jeshua must be rich. Rich men do strange things, like giving their money away, though Achish was sure they always got something in return. Maybe he was working here as a sort of vacation from his life as a wealthy man.

Or maybe he was a thief as well and his labor a ruse.

Achish looked over at the sleeping carpenter. He wondered if the man had a money pouch. Achish got up on one elbow, straining to see the telltale bulge under Jeshua's tunic. His own hand went to the now-empty pouch inside his own shirt. If this man was a thief, he was a very good one, discreet and subtle, for he had no pouch. In addition to recovering his money, Achish would have to be on the lookout for this Jeshua. He might be the most dangerous thing about this whole adventure. There was a mystery here, and he would have to unlock it.

"Life is a mystery," said Jeshua, his eyes still closed, startling Achish, who quickly lay back, his heart racing.

"How's that?" answered Achish.

"Well," said Jeshua, getting up on one elbow and looking at Achish, "Elam needed help, and I'm helping him. I needed help, and now you're helping me."

"Yes," said Achish.

"I was thinking," said Jeshua quietly. "There must be something you need."

"Just a night's sleep," said Achish irritably.

"Oh, I'm sorry," said Jeshua. "Good night."

Achish stared at the ceiling. *The only thing I need is my money*, he thought bitterly.

THIRTEEN

Worthy of His Hire

Dawn came clear and cold. Ice had formed on the water troughs. Achish stood shivering as Jeshua hauled the bucket of water up over the well lip. He poured it into Achish's outstretched hands. Ice cold. Achish briskly rubbed his face, fully awake now. Then he held the bucket out for Jeshua to wash, looking carefully to see if he had a money pouch inside his shirt. Apparently not. Jeshua ran his wet hands through his thick curly hair and buried his face in the rough towel.

"That is cold!" said Jeshua. "I'm wide awake now."

Achish set the bucket down. "Why are we starting so early?"

"It's October. The days are short and we can't work at night."

"What do you mean? It still *is* night." The sun was just a glint on the horizon. The cock had not even crowed when Jeshua had nudged him awake. Achish chided himself for sleeping so soundly. His hand moved quickly to the money pouch, and he had an instant of despair before remembering it was empty when he went to bed.

Now they stood by the building addition, munching apples and nearly frozen bread. Achish surveyed the sandstone blocks and groaned.

"I've been cutting these for several days," said Jeshua, walking around a big block. "I didn't have any way of getting them up to the third course. Then you arrived."

"Then I arrived," said Achish morosely.

Jeshua placed a plank on an incline up to the third row, then lined up three short, thick dowels at the base. "We haul the stone over here," he said, pointing at the plank, "then we roll it up the plank on these dowels. Just like the pyramids."

"You've been to Egypt?" asked Achish, certain now that Jeshua was indeed a rich man, having traveled so far.

"I lived there for a time when I was a child. Then my family moved back to Galilee."

"I've heard the people of Galilee are wealthy," said Achish, helping Jeshua push the heavy block toward the incline.

Jeshua shook his head. "The country is, but not the people. Most are laborers, like me."

They hoisted the block up onto the three dowels. Achish was already sweating. He thought about Jeshua's money pouch. Perhaps it was in the storeroom.

"Why are you staying in the storeroom?" he asked Jeshua as they pushed the block up the plank.

"Grab the lowest dowel and put it in front," said Jeshua.

Achish did so and the stone rolled onto it, moving up a few more inches. "Hey," said Achish, surprised. "It works."

"I'm in the storeroom because that's the room they gave me," said Jeshua, straining to hold the block steady.

"Why don't you get another room?" asked Achish, placing the next dowel under the leading edge of the stone.

Jeshua pushed against the stone. "If you want to pay, I'd be glad to move." He chuckled, and the stone slipped back. Achish leaned into the stone, stopping it. Jeshua kept pushing, but he was still laughing, and in another moment, Achish was laughing, too.

"Stop it," said Achish.

"I can't!" laughed Jeshua, and the stone slipped a little more. "I get this way."

"You're gonna make it fall! Stop it!"

"All right," said Jeshua, stifling a chuckle. But it didn't work, and in a moment they were both laughing and the stone was slipping back down the plank. Finally, they got their backs into it, stopping it. Jeshua wiped the sweat from his forehead. "That was close."

Achish shook his head. "It almost fell on our feet."

"That would have hurt!" said Jeshua and they both started laughing again.

"Stop it!" demanded Achish weakly. "I can't ... take it ... any longer!"

"All right," said Jeshua, forcing a frown. "It's not funny."

"That's right," said Achish. "It's not funny." They sat on the plank, their backs to the stone, winded.

"Not at all," said Jeshua finally. He laughed again.

"Stop it!" barked Achish, affecting a serious glower. "I mean it."

Jeshua copied Achish's angry look. "All right. All right."

Seizing the moment, they turned and pushed the stone up the rest of the incline. When it was settled into its place in the course, Achish wearily leaned his forehead against the cool surface of the stone. "Working with you is exhausting."

"Only twenty more to go," said Jeshua, clapping him on the back.

"It must be lunchtime," said Achish, looking up at the sun. The sky was an unbroken blue, and a group of swallows swooped around the inn.

"Timothy will tell us," said Jeshua, handing the water jar to Achish.

"Jeshua!" came a boy's voice. Achish and Jeshua looked at the storeroom door.

"Right on time," said Jeshua.

Timothy emerged with Elam, who leaned on a makeshift crutch, his broken arm draped over the boy's shoulder, a smile on his face. "Well," said Jeshua. "Look who's alive."

Elam waved weakly. "I came to supervise," he said. He sat down on a chunk of sandstone.

"We don't need a supervisor," said Achish testily.

"We've already got Timothy," added Jeshua, mussing the boy's hair. "Would you like to join us for lunch, Elam?" He nodded at Timothy and the boy ran back inside.

"Very much. Yes. Thank you," said the small man. He saw Achish's perturbed look and looked at the ground, embarrassed. "I know. I'm pathetic." No one said anything. "I've always been independent; I never had to ask for anything before."

"I understand," said Jeshua.

Elam looked at Achish for approval. Achish nodded.

Elam brightened. "So you know how uncomfortable it is for me to be . . . like this."

"There are times," said Jeshua, squinting at the horizon, "when we all need help." He looked at Achish but Achish looked away. He hated this camaraderie he was being lured into. These men were not his friends; they weren't going to be. One was already his victim and the other soon would be. He had to remember that.

Timothy emerged with three small loaves of hot brown bread in his arms and gave them to the men. Then he scooped up the water jar and ran off to the well.

"What's his hurry?" asked Achish, tearing his bread and taking a bite.

"His master beats him," said Elam, watching the boy draw water. "He told me."

Jeshua was surprised. "He does?"

"Of course he does," said Achish, shaking his head. "They all do."

Elam nodded. Jeshua turned from Elam to Achish, seeing their agreement. Then he stood and said, "I'll get the rest of the food." He walked briskly into the inn.

Elam was still watching as Timothy pulled on the rope at the well. "My father used to beat me when I was little. Said it was for my own good."

"They always say that," said Achish.

"Did your father beat you?"

"I never knew my father," said Achish. "He was gone before I was born."

"My father is dead, too," lied Elam.

Timothy ran toward them, the water sloshing out of the jar. He strained to lift it to fill Elam's cup. Achish stood and said, "Here, let me," and took the jar and filled Elam's cup, then filled his own. "Here," he said, handing the jar back to the boy. "Fill Jeshua's cup, over there."

The boy did so. Achish sat down, feeling strange. Timothy stood by silently, awaiting the next order. Achish looked at the boy, rail thin, wide, scared-looking eyes, unkempt hair, probably an orphan. Without a word, he lifted his tunic and showed the boy several long, angry keloid scars on his lower back.

Timothy nodded and slowly lifted the hem of his tunic. Achish saw several red welts on the boy's thighs. Achish tore a chunk of bread from his loaf and handed it to the boy, who took it gingerly, looking around first to see if it was permitted.

Elam silently raised his cup to the boy. Achish held his own cup out, and Timothy took it eagerly, draining it, the water coursing down his chin. When he finished, he smiled, the first one Achish had seen him offer.

Just then Jeshua came out the door with a pot of stew and, noticing the lack of conversation, said, "Are you all getting acquainted?"

FOURTEEN

Writing on the Wall

Achish looked around. He was walking on the Jericho Road, the path winding down the canyon wall, each turn a mystery in the moonless night. He swatted at the lead camel; it sped up a little, hauling the other five camels along just a little faster. They were loaded down with packs. He pulled apart the folds of the lead camel's burden, and gold, silver, and precious gems winked back at him. But instead of feeling joy at his wealth, all Achish felt was dread.

He looked up. The blackness of the sky was complete; there weren't any stars. Achish couldn't tell where the hills ended and the sky began.

Suddenly three men were on the road, blocking his way. They were giants, each a full head taller than Achish, and broad across the shoulders. One held a sputtering torch aloft, and Achish saw the glint of steel in their hands. He started to turn the train around, but two men at the rear blocked the way. Achish dropped to his knees.

"Please," he said. In a moment, all five men circled him, their shadowed faces looming over him.

"Take it," said Achish weakly. "All of it . . . is yours."

"Yes," said one, laughing. "Yes it is."

"Then leave in peace," murmured Achish, shaking with fear.

As one, the five men raised their clubs and knives and swords, holding them high over their heads. And waited.

"There is no peace for you, Achish," said the leader, who reached inside Achish's tunic and withdrew the stolen money pouch. It was full, bulging at the seams. Achish's eyes never left it as the leader opened the pouch and turned it upside down. Achish's own beating heart tumbled out of the pouch and into the man's hand, where it pulsed weakly for a moment, then stopped. Achish stared in amazement at the bloody organ, feeling no pulse in his own chest.

"No dark, peaceful waters," said the leader, and the blows started raining down. They hurled their clubs against his ribs, slashed his arms and legs with their swords, and jabbed him with their daggers. Achish fell to the ground, tasting blood.

The men circled him, chests heaving, weapons dangling from tired hands. Achish slowly rolled over onto his back, feeling his life flowing from his body, and looked up at the sky. A million stars lit the scene like day. Five distinct silhouettes loomed over him. "No peace," he said weakly, looking past his attackers at the brilliant sky.

"Not for you," laughed the leader. He was joined by one, then another, until they all were laughing, heads lifted toward the blinding night sky.

And each upturned face, white in the starlight, was his own.

Achish awoke suddenly. It was still night and he was safe in the storeroom. He lay clutching his chest, trying to feel his heartbeat. Instead, he felt only the empty money pouch. He stared at the ceiling, willing the terrible images from his mind. The faces of the men, all his own, looked down at him, smiling.

When dawn came, Achish stumbled out the door, toward the well. Splashing his face with the icy water pushed the images back somewhat, but not entirely. The men were still there, smiling wickedly at him. Achish dunked his head into the water trough. Blinding pain in his forehead dropped him to his knees, and he lay there, head pounding, icy water trickling down his back, fingertips numb, hands pressed against eyes that would only see his own face. He struggled to his feet and staggered toward the storeroom door. Inside, Jeshua was awake, kneeling by the pallet, praying silently.

Achish leaned against the doorway, head aching, out of breath, dripping freezing water. Jeshua opened his eyes and turned. A look of surprise crossed his face, and he got to his feet and helped Achish lie down on the pallet. Achish placed his forearm across his eyes, and still the image of the faces would not leave him.

"What is it?" asked Jeshua.

"A terrible dream." He removed his arm and looked up at Jeshua. "A dream haunts me even now, in the light of day, like a spirit."

"Tell it to me," said Jeshua gently.

Achish related the dream. The empty road, the camels loaded with riches, the five attackers, and the bright, starry sky. "They all had my face," said Achish. "What does it mean?"

Jeshua looked away, thinking. For a long time he said nothing, then he looked at Achish. "Can a man rob himself?"

Achish considered it. Clearly, that is what the dream meant. "But why would I rob myself? And what could I steal from myself?"

Jeshua stood. "Only you know that, Hanan," he said, and left the room.

Achish pondered the dream. No man would, or could, steal from himself. A man might injure himself or even kill himself, but why would he? The purpose of life was to survive, so why would a man take his own life, as he had done to himself in the dream?

Then he realized what he'd done. He'd shared his dream with a stranger, someone who could link him to the attack on Elam. He might as well have confessed. Achish chided himself and the faces appeared again, each one his own, and each one smiling at his predicament.

Just then Caleb entered. "Still here? That's twenty-five shekels you owe me now."

"For what?"

"Yesterday's food, three meals, and lodging, two nights. And don't even think about leaving without paying. I have a fast horse and I'll find you." He stared down at Achish, who lay with his forearm across his eyes. "What's the matter with you?"

"Nothing."

Caleb looked outside. Jeshua was working methodically with the hoe in a wooden basin, mixing plaster for the wall. "Jeshua is a trusting fool," said Caleb, squinting at Achish. "But if you try to hang your debt on him, I'll hunt you down. Now get to work!"

He kicked the pallet and left. Achish put his hands over his eyes. The pain in his forehead was still there, and growing worse.

Last night, before the nightmare, Achish had planned to rise early this morning and slip away. Now he was too sick to do so, and Caleb would chase him anyway. He had no choice but to stay a little longer.

But the pain grew worse, and he struggled throughout the day. They finished moving the last of the blocks onto the higher courses. Jeshua enlisted a number of other servants to help place the last blocks on the top row. When they finished, they had a lunch of flatbread and fish, and Jeshua thanked everyone for their help, even Achish, who hadn't been much help at all.

Timothy noticed that Achish was feeling poorly and brought him several drinks of water, each time leaving him with a shy smile. Achish had never felt kinship with anyone, but he knew Timothy's future. He would grow up, fearing and hating the world, as Achish did. And the scars on the back of his legs might heal, but the scars on his heart would not.

———————

That evening, in the great room, Kohath sat with Lamech in their usual spot, apart from the others. Dinner was finished, and there were few guests in the inn tonight. The day had been unexpectedly warm, and the doors and windows were thrown open.

"I'm enjoying this place," said Kohath, looking around. "Not the people, of course, they're filthy and uncouth, but the inn itself is rather interesting."

"Yes," said Lamech, leaning back on his pillow. "I know what you mean. We rarely get to see such people in the Temp—"

"Shh," said Kohath, nodding toward Achish, who stood in the doorway, dirty from the day's work, talking to the servant boy.

Lamech surveyed Achish. He had looked more dangerous before, when he first arrived, but now, tired and dirty from working out back all day, he just looked like another laborer: uneducated, unskilled, and uninteresting. He turned to Kohath, who was still looking at Achish. "Do you know him?" asked Lamech.

"Of course not," said Kohath. But then his worst fear came true: Achish looked right at him and began walking toward them. Kohath averted his eyes.

Momentarily, Achish stood before them. He pointed at Kohath. "You were looking at me."

Kohath shook his head.

"Yes, you were," said Achish, squinting at him. "Do we know each other?"

Kohath shook his head.

"Who are you?"

Kohath shook his head again. "Kohath," said Lamech, drawing a surprised look from the priest.

"And you don't know me?"

Kohath shook his head. Lamech said, "I'm Lamech."

Achish considered the younger man. "I'm Achish. I mean Hanan. Hanan is my name."

Lamech said, "Achish Hanan?"

"Just Hanan," said Achish, his eyes still on Kohath, who had the look of a frightened deer.

Then Achish snapped his fingers. "I know! Jerusalem, a few nights ago. You were eating at an inn, right?"

Kohath shook his head.

"Sure you were. You were staring at the wall, like you're staring at me now. What's wrong with you?"

Kohath just looked at him.

Achish turned to Lamech. "Is he deaf or something? Can't he talk?"

Lamech was surprised, too. He'd never seen Kohath scared. Suddenly the man was no longer a near-deity. "He can talk. I guess he just doesn't want to talk to you." He smiled at Kohath, whose eyes popped open even wider.

"Why is that?" asked Achish evenly. He'd just come to make conversation, but this was getting interesting. What was this man afraid of? Achish surveyed his clothing, looking for the purse bulge under his tunic. "What do you do in Jerusalem, Kohath?"

"He's a priest at the Temple," said Lamech and Kohath's mouth dropped open in surprise.

"Well, now, a priest," said Achish. "Is that right?"

"Yes. It's true," said Kohath finally. "I am a priest of the Most High God."

"It seems he has a tongue after all, at least for boasting," said Achish, winking at Lamech. "And you?" he asked the young man.

"I am a Levite, a Temple worker as well."

"And what are you two boys doing out of the sanctuary?"

"Traveling to Jericho," said Kohath. "Not that it is any of your business."

"Aah. You're feeling better," said Achish, smiling. "Good."

Lamech was sure Kohath would tongue-lash him later for revealing their identity, but it was interesting to see the priest humbled this way. Kohath was clearly unfit to travel by himself. He would need Lamech. And they might even become friends, which couldn't hurt Lamech's future in the Temple.

The dream that had plagued Achish all day returned with ferocious intensity, causing him to turn, blinking away the image of his bloody heart in the man's—his—hand. When his vision cleared, he turned back, knowing why he felt drawn to these two men. He needed an answer or this dream would certainly drive him insane. And since he'd already revealed the dream to Jeshua, the damage—if any—had already been done. Surveying the two soft-bellied priests, he knew they had posed no threat to him, and they might even be able to explain the terrible images that still hung in his mind's eye.

"Since you two are men of God," said Achish, "I'd like your opinion on something."

"Certainly," said Lamech.

"Good," said Achish. "I had a dream, and priests are supposed to know about the interpretation of dreams, isn't that right?"

"Well," said Kohath, "dreams are sometimes difficult. . . ."

"Yes, they are," said Achish. "So I need help, you know, the way Daniel interpreted the king's dream."

"Daniel was a prophet," said Kohath. "We're simple priests, not qualified—"

"Oh, you'll do just fine." And Achish related the dream to the two priests. When he was finished, he asked, "So, what does it mean?"

Kohath shook his head. Achish looked at Lamech, who was also shaking his head.

"Neither of you? Nothing?" asked Achish. "Why, Jeshua out back gave me a fair interpretation, and he's just a carpenter. You two are supposed to be priests of the Most High," he said sarcastically.

"It might be a warning," said Kohath finally.

"Really?" said Achish, standing. "Thanks for your insight. I'll be sure to drop by the Temple next time I'm in Jerusalem and let you cook up a chicken for me."

Lamech said, "We don't offer chickens—"

But Achish had already left. Lamech turned to Kohath, who was shaking his head. "Well," said Lamech, as Kohath gave him a look of disgust, "we don't."

Elam feared his heart would stop. He had hobbled out to the courtyard to watch the sun go down and was lying on a divan, covered with a blanket. And through the open window he had heard the entire exchange between Hanan and the priests.

Elam hadn't missed the slip. The man's name was Achish, not Hanan, and that was just the beginning of the lie. The story he'd told, the supposed dream, revealed the rest.

Elam looked down at his hand. It was trembling. His unbandaged eye was still cloudy, but his mind's eye was clear. He remembered the attack, and the emptiness of his attacker's face now become Achish's. He was sure of it. Achish had been the one who had robbed and nearly killed him.

Elam looked at the dark sky and felt a chill moving up his spine. But how could he prove it? What evidence did he have? His hand went reflexively to his breast, feeling for the missing pouch. Yes! Achish would have the pouch. He might have thrown the cloaks away, but he would have kept the money. Today a traveler arrived at the inn carrying the shredded cloaks. He'd seen them in the ravine and had climbed down to retrieve them. Nearby, he said, was the carcass of Elam's donkey and the broken pack frame. Elam had sorted through the cloaks but there was nothing to salvage. He gave them to a servant woman who said she might be able to make something from them.

But he would wager the money pouch was still intact, and at this very inn. The thief was hiding it somewhere. Elam had watched Achish working with Jeshua, but he couldn't remember if he'd seen the pouch hanging around the man's neck, secreted under his tunic. He was sure he hadn't, which meant the man had hidden it, probably in the storeroom, where he was staying.

And tomorrow, while Achish was working with Jeshua, Elam would find his money and bring his attacker to justice.

FIFTEEN

Common Threads

Achish awoke. He was so anxious about having the dream again that it had taken him several hours to fall asleep last night. But the dream did not return, and this morning, except for his tired back, he felt much better. The needlelike pain in his forehead was nearly gone.

He rolled over and saw Jeshua kneeling at a wine cask, praying. Achish thought he must have a clear conscience to talk to God that often. Not that he believed in God; the world Achish had seen was evidence enough that all was random, cruel chaos. But if there was a God, people were in big trouble anyway, for there was no way, as far as Achish could see, that people could possibly please any sort of god, even the loving God Jeshua had spoken of.

When Jeshua finished praying, Achish couldn't help noticing how translucent his face was. He was surprised others didn't notice it, but then Achish's business was reading people, looking for their weaknesses. It occurred to him that Jeshua was skilled in exactly the opposite way: he looked for people's strengths, found them, commented on them, so that when people left his presence, they were as refreshed as if they'd had a long, cool drink of water.

Achish had felt that way around Jeshua, when he permitted it. He had to remind himself that this man was not his friend, but it was a useless exercise. He knew that no matter what he did, Jeshua was going to treat him like a friend. He had no defense against such kindness.

The tarnished coin of his selfish world had been turned over, revealing its shiny reverse. And Achish discovered he was pleased that such a world existed at all.

Jeshua continued praying, and Achish got up. He tiptoed across the cold stone floor, picked up his sandals, and crept outside, closing the door quietly behind him. His muscles ached, but he didn't mind. An aching back was better than an aching heart. Achish almost laughed out loud at the quaint observation, but he knew it was still true. And he hadn't slept that well in years.

Jeshua had both a strong heart and a strong back. The only weakness he'd shown was for Timothy, for whom Achish felt a growing affection as well. Achish followed Jeshua's lead in praising him, and he saw the boy's face light up. It got Achish to thinking how different his own life would have been if anyone had ever said anything kind to him when he was a boy.

But they didn't, and here he was, working for a carpenter who alternatively amazed him and made him feel like crawling into a dark hole for shame. He wanted to hate Jeshua, but when he saw him talking to Timothy, he knew Jeshua meant harm to no one. He didn't judge Achish or that stupid Elam or the greedy innkeeper. Apparently, he didn't judge anyone.

"You dropped this," said Jeshua, appearing in the doorway. He handed Achish the embroidered leather money pouch. Achish quickly tucked it inside his tunic.

"You still with me today?" asked Jeshua.

Achish felt the pouch against his chest, again amazed. Jeshua hadn't asked why he wore an empty money pouch instead of leaving it inside. No suspicion, no judgment. Achish wanted to know how anyone could be like that, so he said, "I might stay another day, if it's all right."

Jeshua nodded and headed toward the well to wash up.

———

Elam hobbled into the storeroom, leaning on his crutch. There were a thousand places to hide something in here. He walked to the outside door and opened it slightly. Jeshua was straddling the new stone wall. Achish was handing him up a long squared roof beam. They would be occupied for a while, and Elam shut the door quietly, turning first to the sleeping pallet. He grunted as he bent, running his hand through the loose straw under the blanket. Nothing. He looked under the bed, surprising a mouse, which squeaked and scurried out of sight. He withdrew a roll of clothing. Loincloths, two tunics, a cloak, and a pair of sandals. Nothing more.

A bedroll lay on the floor, Jeshua's possessions. A couple of tunics, poor quality, a leather belt with the buckle about to fall off, and a pair of worn sandals, the latch broken on one.

Elam sat down on the pallet, wondering how two men together didn't have one decent set of clothes. He almost laughed when he realized that he didn't have one, either. But the money must be in here somewhere. He scanned the room and saw, sitting on top of a wine keg, a small wood carving in progress, a worn whittling knife next to it. He crossed and picked it up. It was a carving of a mother holding a child in her arms, gazing happily into its upturned face. The work was delicate and precise. He held it up, squinting at it.

"What are you doing?"

Elam turned. Achish stood in the doorway, holding a clay water jar.

"Just admiring this," said Elam.

"It's not for you. Jeshua is carving it for Timothy."

"I understand," said Elam, replacing the figurine and stepping away. "How are you coming out there?"

"We're working," said Achish harshly.

"I know," said Elam, feeling Achish's anger. "You're making progress."

Achish scowled at Elam, then turned and left. Elam followed, grateful he hadn't been caught. Admiring the carving was one thing, but rifling through their belongings was another thing entirely. If Achish knew what he was doing, he just might have finished the job he started a few nights ago. The thought made Elam shiver.

Outside, Achish climbed the ladder, handing the water jar to Jeshua, who took a long drink and handed it back. On Jeshua's look, Achish turned to see Elam standing in the doorway. Jeshua waved and Elam waved back.

Achish turned away. He felt a twinge of guilt at his anger at Elam for admiring Jeshua's carving. Achish himself had been looking at it just this morning, wondering how Timothy would react when he finally saw it. The feeling that came was warm and good, but now it was sullied by his anger at Elam.

When Jeshua turned back to work and Achish climbed down the ladder, Elam noticed that Achish wouldn't meet his eyes. And when Achish walked by him, he thought he saw the tiniest hint of sorrow in the man's face.

Sorrow? pondered Elam. *A murderous thief, sorry?*

He would have to think about this.

All that afternoon they worked on the roof. Achish held the notched timbers together while Jeshua lashed them with wet rawhide cords, which, when dry, would shrink and hold the beams together securely.

As they worked, Jeshua spoke of his brothers; there seemed to be about a dozen of them. He had sisters, too, and a mother and father. Hearing about a large family, with typical troubles and tensions, but also with joy and laughter, made Achish feel dark inside, even though Jeshua's pride and happiness were infectious. Timothy, between trips to the well for the cook, listened in, saying nothing, but Achish knew he felt the same kind of sadness and envy he did.

Jeshua looked at Achish. "What about your family?"

"I have no family," said Achish, glancing at Timothy, hoping this would make him feel less alone.

"None at all?" asked Jeshua, tying off a cord and pouring fresh water on the lashings.

"No," said Achish, suddenly tired. "I never knew my father."

"What about your mother?"

"She abandoned me when I was a child," said Achish, the painful memory welling up.

"Why did she do that?" asked Timothy, surprising both men. The boy rarely spoke, much less asked questions.

"I don't know. She just did."

Timothy looked down and moved a pebble with his foot. Achish looked up at Jeshua, who was watching the boy.

"I was too much trouble, maybe," said Achish, revealing a deep, inner belief.

"Maybe she was afraid," said Jeshua.

"Afraid of what?"

"Afraid of not being a good mother to you."

"She was a good mother," said Achish. "I was a bad son."

"I don't believe that," said Jeshua.

"Neither do I," said Timothy. His look revealed a deep, inner hope.

"I was an embarrassment," said Achish. "You see, I was illegitimate. A bastard." He glanced at Jeshua, then looked away. "You wouldn't know how that feels."

Jeshua looked out past the Jordan Valley, toward the distant, white hills across the river. He nodded slowly, then said, "You might be surprised what I know."

SIXTEEN

Life Eternal

By late afternoon, Achish had gotten the knack of securing the roof timbers, so he and Jeshua traded places. Achish worked on the roof, and Jeshua cut and squared the raw wood down on the ground. Achish had asked if Timothy could help him, and Caleb had approved, glad to loan them the boy if it meant the job would be finished sooner.

Elam hobbled out of the inn and settled under the lone willow tree near where Jeshua was working. For a long time he watched quietly, then his eyes moved up to where Achish and Timothy straddled a roof beam. Their conversation and laughter drifted toward Elam, and he was once again confused. Could he be wrong about this man? Jeshua seemed to like and trust him. Was it possible they were in collusion?

No, it was not possible. Was it possible, then, that Achish had deceived Jeshua? Also unlikely. Jeshua was the wisest and most compassionate man Elam had ever met. He had no possessions, no wealth, yet his very presence in a room gifted everyone with a light heart. Elam noticed at meals that Jeshua was always with people, yet he rarely spoke, preferring to listen. And when he did speak, it was always constructive. Elam had tested it; he'd said something about Caleb's exorbitant charges, and after others had agreed, Jeshua had simply said that Caleb had been generous with him. The criticism deflected, the conversation had turned to something else, and when it turned negative again, at someone else's expense, again Jeshua mentioned something positive about that person.

And Jeshua's compliments weren't idle musings; they were amazingly accurate. He got them from listening to people with an intensity that was almost uncomfortable. Elam had felt it himself. So perhaps Jeshua might know something about Achish that Elam had missed.

"How is your helper doing?" he asked, nodding toward Achish.

"Very well," said Jeshua, sawing. "He has a gift for building. Which surprised even him, because he said he'd never built anything before."

"Did it surprise you?" asked Elam, more to the point.

Jeshua shook his head. "No. He's a capable man."

"I believe you're right," said Elam, reflecting on the dual meaning of the word. "He said he was a merchant, but where are his wares?"

"He didn't say."

"Doesn't that strike you as odd? A merchant traveling without wares?"

Jeshua stopped sawing and looked at Elam. There was that intense, but kind, look again. "I guess you would know something about that." He winked.

"I started out with wares, then I was robbed and nearly killed."

Jeshua knelt by the long timber, which was now squared on two sides. Examining the wood, he said, "A few years ago, my father sent me out on my first carpentry job. It was a simple matter of repairing a piece of furniture for a neighbor, a wooden chair that had great sentimental value for the old woman. She'd held all their children as babes in that chair, and now it was old and loose and falling apart."

He started planing in long, smooth strokes. "I thought the job was simple: take the chair apart, true up the wood, reassemble it, then sand and refinish it."

"I trust it didn't go well," said Elam.

Jeshua chuckled. "It went terribly. I took it apart, planed and sanded the pieces, but when I put it back together, I couldn't make it work. I used too much water in the glue and the wood swelled, and when it dried out, it cracked. I destroyed her precious chair," he said, shaking his head.

"They must have been angry," said Elam.

"They were disappointed. It cost my father a lot to replace that chair."

"Then he must have been very angry."

"Funny thing," said Jeshua, setting the plane down and looking at Elam. "He wasn't. He saw how bad I felt; he knew I'd done my best, but my skills were still incomplete. But he believed in me—not in the carpenter I was, but in the carpenter I could someday be."

"And now you are," said Elam.

"Well, I'm a much better carpenter because my father gave me another chance."

He stood and walked over to the well to draw water. Elam looked at the shavings on the ground at his feet and smelled the cut wood. He watched as Jeshua climbed the ladder and gave Achish and Timothy the water jar. They shared a joke, and Jeshua's clear laugh could be heard.

I am a suspicious man, thought Elam. *A dream is not a confession. He dreamed about something I told everyone about. If anything, his dream is evidence that he empathizes with me. The real problem here is me.*

And then the weight of this realization fell upon him: *I've never trusted anyone. And look where it's gotten me.*

He picked up his crutch and slowly made his way inside the inn.

"Another day like this and I believe I shall be ready to travel," said Kohath, sunning himself in the courtyard. "Pity. I rather like it here."

Lamech was eager to get on the road, too. The cool waters of the Jordan beckoned him, but he felt if he left Kohath now it would be seen as a snub. He leaned back on the divan cushion. "It's all right, I guess. I am looking forward to the Jordan, though."

"By all means, then, go. Be on your way," said Kohath absently.

Lamech didn't know what that meant. Was Kohath testing his loyalty?

"I will, soon. But this place is nice, too."

"I have family in Jericho," said Kohath, closing his eyes, feeling the dappled sunlight on his face. "They will harass me with questions and false honor. I prefer the anonymity of this place."

Lamech really did want to leave. His feelings that he might have to protect Kohath on the road were dissolving. The priest seemed self-confident. But the idea that they would be safer in each other's company had taken root in Lamech's mind, and he recoiled at the thought of traveling alone, now that he'd seen some of the men who traveled the Jericho Road.

"I like it, too," he said, motioning the servant girl for another drink of wine.

Another day's worth of travelers streamed into the inn. By dinnertime, the place was full, raucous and loud. Men stood near the open doors, shouting at one another, drunk on Caleb's wine, boasting of their adventures and conquests. The area outside the archway was crowded with pack animals, and every room in the inn was taken. Caleb, seeing Lamech and Kohath together, asked if they would be kind enough to share a room, since they were friends. Kohath snorted at the idea, but when Caleb mentioned that he was short of rooms because of Elam, who still needed to be cared for, Kohath leaned forward and inquired as to what it was worth to him.

"You and your friend will not be charged for dinner tonight," said Caleb, grimacing.

"Then we would be happy to," said Kohath.

"I will tell Elam," said Caleb, turning away.

Kohath stood quickly. "Let me. It would be my pleasure."

Caleb nodded and walked away. Kohath stood and made a grand show of dusting off his cloak and straightening it. Lamech watched as he crossed the crowded room to Elam, who was dining with Jeshua and Achish.

"Master Elam?" he said, bowing low. All three men looked up at him with some surprise on their faces.

"Yes?" said Elam, looking up at Kohath from underneath the head bandage, stained yellow where his left eye was. Kohath looked away in disgust. When he looked back, he made a point to look at Elam's bruised, cloudy eye.

"I trust you are healing?"

"Slowly, thank you."

"I am so glad. I came to inform you that you may have my room tonight. I understand the innkeeper was going to toss you out into the general sleeping area."

Elam nodded.

"I told him that was quite unacceptable. A man who has suffered as you have, who has lost everything and who may very well be scarred for life . . . well, I told him that was simply wrong."

Elam's mouth dropped open. "Won't you join us . . . ?"

"Kohath, Priest Kohath. Of the Temple in Jerusalem." He sat down with a flourish.

"We are honored by your presence," said Jeshua, handing Kohath a piece of bread.

"I don't know what to say," said Elam emotionally. "I am ashamed to be such a burden."

"My traveling companion," said Kohath, nodding toward Lamech, who was watching as best he could through the crowded room, "was opposed to the idea, but I reminded him that we were representatives of the Lord and should be examples to others."

"Please extend my thanks to him," said Elam.

"Why don't we invite him over as well?" asked Jeshua. "To thank him properly?"

"Oh, no," said Kohath. "He is rather squeamish about . . . Elam's . . . condition. The result of a sheltered life, I suppose. But I will thank him for you."

"Please do," said Elam, touching his dirty and stained bandages, embarrassed.

Kohath dipped his bread into the bowl and looked at Achish. "Have you discovered who took your money, friend?"

Achish shook his head, feeling Kohath's imperious gaze on him. A tiny spark of anger flickered in his heart, something he hadn't felt for a few days, and it surprised him. He looked at Jeshua, seeking a cue as to how to respond, but Jeshua was simply looking at Elam thoughtfully, munching a slice of apple.

"I may have simply lost it," said Achish. "But thank you for your concern."

"Certainly," said Kohath, rising. "It seems bad fortune abounds in this world. We must be certain it is not deserved. Have a pleasant evening." He made his way back across the room.

"What was that supposed to mean?" asked Achish.

"I think it was clear," said Elam. "He thinks we earned our misfortunes."

"That's nonsense," said Achish quickly.

"I'm not so sure," said Elam, tearing a piece of bread. He looked at Achish, who looked down at his hands.

"I'm still hungry," said Jeshua, standing. He left.

Achish looked at Kohath and Lamech. "I don't like him," he said, narrowing his eyes.

"Was your money stolen from you, Hanan?" asked Elam, carefully using Achish's alias.

"No. I must have lost it."

"I usually carry my money in a pouch around my neck, for that very reason. Harder to lose that way, unless, of course, you're robbed. . . ."

"I suppose that's true."

"Did you lose your pouch?"

Achish looked up at Elam, wondering if the little man knew the truth. "I don't carry one."

Elam looked away, again feeling guilty for suspecting Achish. Was there no end to his suspicion? Of everything and everyone? Even the priest? "My mother Lydia used to say—"

Achish's head swiveled around. "What?"

"My mother, she used to—"

"Did you say her name was Lydia?"

Elam nodded.

"That was my mother's name, too," said Achish, surprised.

"Isn't that a coincidence?" said Elam.

"Yes, isn't it?" said Achish, feeling a sudden urge to get out of there.

"She died many years ago," said Elam.

"My mother is probably dead as well. I haven't seen her since I was a boy. It seems like everyone's mother is gone. Even Timothy over there is an orphan." Achish nodded at the boy carrying dirty dishes to the kitchen. "Like us."

"I'm not an orphan," corrected Elam. "My father is still alive."

"You told me he was dead," said Achish. "A couple of days ago."

"Did I?" said Elam, trying to remember. "He might as well be. I haven't seen him in many years."

"Why not?"

"It's not important. We just don't get along."

Achish leaned toward Elam, eyes bright with intensity. "If I even knew who my father was, I'd go see him. Doesn't matter what he did. Or didn't do. He'd be my father. And that's something, isn't it?"

Elam nodded. "It is something, I guess."

When Achish entered the storeroom, he did so quietly, knowing Jeshua had gone to bed long before. He was surprised when he saw Jeshua kneeling by the pallet, still praying. When he finished, even in the darkness Achish could see he had been crying. Achish looked away, embarrassed to be present at such a private moment, but Jeshua simply smiled, lying down on the skins on the stone floor, folding his hands across his chest.

Achish crossed to the pallet and sat down. "Jeshua?"

"Yes?"

"Who is God?"

"He's our father."

"Our father?" asked Achish, surprised. "Really?"

"Yes," said Jeshua, still looking at the ceiling. "He created the world, gave us life in it, and watches over us. As a father does."

"And when you pray, you're talking to him?" asked Achish.

"Yes. We talk."

"He talks to you?" asked Achish, surprised.

"Yes. He does."

Achish looked up, following Jeshua's gaze, wondering. He was truly surprised when he heard himself say, "Show me," and he turned and knelt by the bed.

Jeshua got up and knelt by him, folding his hands. Achish copied him, lacing his fingers together. Jeshua inclined his head and closed his eyes. Achish did likewise, waiting.

"If you want," said Jeshua quietly, "you can repeat the words I say."

"All right," said Achish.

"Father in heaven," began Jeshua.

"Father in heaven," repeated Achish, and he was pleased at how good it felt to say those three simple words.

"Thank you for my life," said Jeshua.

"Thank you for my life," repeated Achish.

"And thank you for this world."

"Thank you for this world," said Achish, noticing that saying "thank you" in this context didn't feel like admitting weakness.

"Thank you for your presence in all things."

Achish paused. Was God truly present in all things? Had he ever felt such a thing before? It would take a leap of faith to believe it, but he was breaking new ground here anyway. He took a deep breath and said, "Thank you for your presence in all things."

"And thank you for your spirit, which teaches truth."

Achish felt something old and cold and empty loosening inside, heavy blockage shifting slightly, slowly moving aside, and a glimmer of light shone in his darkness, accompanied by a wellspring of warmth, rising, displacing the cold dark waters that for so long had filled him. He repeated the phrase, marveling at the feeling.

"Forgive our sins," said Jeshua quietly, and he reached out and touched Achish lightly on the shoulder.

Achish's shoulder felt warm where Jeshua touched him. His own hands tingled, and he opened one eye to see if they were glowing. Instead, they were trembling. "Forgive my sins," he implored, and the warmth expanded up his arms and enveloped his heart, dissolving the cold, leaving peace and comfort in its place.

"Teach us to forgive ourselves, and to forgive others," said Jeshua.

"Teach us to forgive ourselves," repeated Achish, unsure if such a thing was possible, but hoping so. "And others," he said, guessing that this was the real crux of the prayer. "Teach me to forgive others," he repeated.

"For all things are possible for Thee, Lord," said Jeshua.

"All things are possible," said Achish.

"Amen," said Jeshua, opening his eyes.

"Amen," repeated Achish, tears catching in his throat. He felt a heaviness on his shoulders, a spreading mantle of warmth that penetrated his skin, soaked through his muscles, dissolved through his bones, and settled in his chest, filling him with peace.

After a long time, he opened his eyes and turned to Jeshua, unable to speak. Jeshua put his arms around Achish and held him gently. Something gave way and Achish sobbed, a lifetime of hurt and pain, both given and received, loosening inside. Jeshua looked upward and whispered, "Thank You, Father, for this gift. For this good man, Your son."

Achish heard the words and was racked with grateful sobs. He knew now he had a soul, and he also knew, for the first time in his life, that he had a friend.

SEVENTEEN

The Road Home

Afterward, Achish lay awake for hours, basking in the warmth, not wanting it to leave. He had talked to God . . . and God had talked back, filling his soul. His heart, which for so long had simply pumped blood, was now also filled with hope. Even the night seemed bright, and the quarter moon that shone through the high window seemed to light the room as noonday.

Jeshua slept, his chest slowly rising and falling. Achish wanted to waken him, to ask him to pray again, so he could feel more of the warmth, but he felt foolish and greedy. In the end, he finally dropped off to sleep, astonished at the new world he had just entered.

But when he awoke, well before dawn, the darkness had returned and doubts began to surface. Maybe Jeshua was a different kind of sorcerer, one who didn't curse people but blessed them. That was good, but if it was some sort of magic, it wouldn't last.

And what if his magic was no magic at all but simple perception? Surely all people wanted to be loved. It didn't take a prophet to know from Achish's story that he was alone in the world. Maybe Jeshua's gift was nothing more than kindness, and just as shallow. In the end, he would return to his life and Achish would return to his. Nothing lasted; all things changed, and usually for the worse.

He rose and went outside. Dark clouds obscured the stars. Dawn was close, but the day would be gray and wet. Near the well, the horses stamped their feet, snorting mists of steam. The camels sat motionless, conserving their energy.

Achish dipped his hands into the trough water and washed his face. The cold hit him like a sharp slap, and the last warm feelings dissolved. *There is always an end to summer,* he reflected, feeling foolish for believing the lies of love and forgiveness and a father in heaven.

He decided to take a walk to warm up. He climbed the hills to the east and walked across a mesa that ended in a sharp precipice, dropping hundreds of feet into the dark canyon below. Achish sat down on the cliff and hunched his shoulders against the still, cold air.

The distant mountains to the east were visible as a gray line against the black clouds. In the middle distance he could see the dark outline of the Jordan River, meandering southward to the Dead Sea. It traveled for hundreds of miles, seeking the life-giving ocean, but where did it end? In the salty and shallow Dead Sea, where nothing grew. Life was like that river, and no matter what people did, all the good and the bad, it was all for nothing. They would all end up in darkness, cold and dead.

He laughed out loud at how close he came to believing the carpenter's foolishness.

Folding his arms against the cold, he felt the bulge of the empty money pouch. Achish reached inside his tunic and withdrew it. It was made of fine calfskin, delicately embroidered with tiny glass beads and silken threads, the leather worn glossy with use.

He thought of Elam, who slept in the inn, suffering from injuries that would plague him the rest of his life. Achish thought of his bandaged eye, remembered striking him with the knife haft, feeling the brow collapse under the blow; the rage he had felt for a total stranger, the wicked cruelty that had seized his soul, urging him to snuff out a life like a candle.

What soul? he thought ruefully. There is only pain and suffering and death. But his mind would not release Elam's image, cowering on the ground, begging for mercy. Achish had wanted to kill him for simply being alive.

Achish closed the pouch and grasped it tightly in his hands. *And for what?* he thought, shaking his head. *The money I took from him—lost. Nothing gained, except a man's pain, which did not enrich me at all.*

Then Jeshua's image floated in front of him. The carpenter, stepping forward to quell a mob of hateful faces, offering his trust to a stranger, giving him food and a bed—his own bed! The carpenter, who possessed riches of peace and happiness Achish could never hope to steal. And all he asked in return was that Achish work for one day. Yet Achish knew Jeshua well enough by now to know that if he had refused, Jeshua would still have paid his bill and wished him a good journey.

And the boy, Timothy, an early reflection of Achish himself, a life devoid of love, yet not without the dim possibility of hope. He saw how Timothy watched Jeshua, and the perplexed look on his face was a younger version of Achish's surprised reaction to a man who seemed from another world, a man who never gave as he got, but always gave better.

Then Achish's mind circled back to Elam with his bandaged head and broken arm and bruised ribs. He reached back to rub the ridge of scars on his own back. Elam would have such scars to carry with him now. And so would Timothy, who didn't deserve them any more than Elam did.

Achish looked up at the horizon, still slate gray. His eyes filled with tears, and he saw his life for what it was: he was nothing more than a sluice that carried filthy water further down into darkness, returning evil for evil, adding his darkness to the already blackened water, knowing it was killing the very plants it was meant to give life to.

He pulled the money pouch from his neck, breaking the rawhide cord, and stared into the emptiness of the ravine. After a long time, an idea came. If he couldn't add clean water to the stream, at least he could direct it away from tender plants like Timothy.

End it now, came a low, rumbling voice. *You cannot change.*

Achish nodded, agreeing. *There is no peace for you,* it continued, and he knew it was the voice from his nightmare. He also knew it was his own voice, coming from his own mouth, as he loomed above himself, the glittering sword held high, preparing to let it fall.

And then Jeshua's quiet voice came: *All things are possible for Thee, Lord.*

Achish bent his head, the money pouch pressed between his hands, and asked weakly, "Is it true, Lord? Are all things possible for you? Even the forgiveness of my wicked soul?"

As if in response, a peal of thunder echoed across the canyons, and Achish saw a flash of light burst at the horizon, the first rays of the sun, splitting the clouds, striking him like a holy arrow. As he blinked, he felt warmth filling his heart again. Tears filled his eyes, prisming the bright light into a million colors.

He felt wetness on his cheeks and looked up. Plump raindrops fell from the glowering sky. Yet still the sun's rays blinded him from the horizon. He got to his feet, the rain falling on his upturned face, his heart overflowing, astonished that God would answer him so immediately and powerfully. Achish's own tears mingled with the rain, and he fell to his knees.

"Thank you," he said quietly, and an epiphany blossomed: life was like this—rain on our faces with the promising sun shining in the distance.

He stood again, resolved. Beginning today, he would turn the sluice of dirty water away from living things. He grasped the symbol of his old life, the money pouch, intending to throw it off the cliff.

But now it was *full*.

He looked down at it. The seams bulged, and a muffled jingling came from inside. He loosened the drawstring. Inside were a dozen gold denarii.

"Eleven," said Achish, counting the money. "There should be eleven!"

But there were twelve now, and Achish looked around in shock. The rain had stopped suddenly, and the world held its breath. The ground around him was completely dry, yet he was soaked to the skin. And he was holding a money pouch—Elam's money pouch—with twelve golden denarii inside.

Achish counted the money once more, then held the pouch out before him, toward the rising sun. "All things are possible for Thee, Lord," he said solemnly. "Help me to do what I know I must."

He turned toward the inn and broke into a run.

Jeshua was washing at the well when Achish ran by. "Good morning, Jeshua."

"You're soaking wet," said Jeshua, grabbing his arm, stopping him.

Achish laughed. "Yes. It's a miracle!" He continued toward the inn.

Jeshua smiled, watching him go. "Isn't everything?"

Achish entered the back door, passed through the storeroom, and strode down the hall toward the kitchen. Timothy was inside, tending the fire in the oven. Achish walked past and called out, "Good morning, Timothy!"

"Good morning!" answered the boy.

In the great room, a number of travelers were eating breakfast. Achish walked through the room and down another hall. He wasn't sure which was Elam's room, so he just opened each door in turn. When he opened Kohath's door, the priest jumped up in surprise and backed against the wall. "Don't hurt me!" he cried out.

"Sorry. I wasn't looking for you," said Achish cheerfully. He shut the door and Kohath collapsed on the bed. Lamech rubbed his eyes, awakened by the commotion.

"I feel sorry for who he *is* looking for," said Kohath.

Down the hall, Achish opened the last door. There was Elam, lying on his bed, wide awake, his splinted arm lying across his round stomach, his face a mass of yellowing bruises. When he saw Achish, he fought back fear and forced a smile. "Hanan," he said, motioning him forward. "Come in."

Achish stepped inside, his words tumbling out. "May I speak to you?"

"Of course," said Elam, motioning toward a chair. "I am glad you're here. I've been doing some thinking and I would like to speak to you as well."

Achish was too excited to sit, so he paced in front of Elam's bed. "First of all, I lied to you."

"I know," said Elam. "Your name is not Hanan."

Achish was surprised. "It's Achish. But that's not what I came to tell you. I have another confession, much more serious."

Elam slowly sat up. "I have a confession, as well."

Achish shook his head. "You?"

"Yes. I have harbored ill will toward you," said Elam, lowering his eyes. Achish sat on the chair at the foot of the bed, perplexed. "I saw your clothing and your rude manners and judged you to be of little worth. And when I heard you tell the priests about your dream, I drew unfair conclusions."

Achish looked at the floor. "They weren't unfair."

"Yes, they were. When I saw you working with Jeshua and the boy, I knew I was wrong. You are a good man. I know that now."

Achish looked up. "How do you know that?"

"My instinct tells me so, but it's mostly because of Jeshua. He is never wrong about people; I'm sure you know that."

"Jeshua is a wise man, that's true," said Achish. "But he doesn't see people as they are, just how they could be. You were right about me: I am an evil man. I've done terrible things, wicked things. I am so ashamed. . . ." He stood, unable to say more. He backed slowly toward the door, unable to meet Elam's eyes.

"Don't go, Achish, please," said Elam.

"I'm sorry," said Achish, reaching into his tunic and withdrawing the money pouch.

Elam's jaw dropped open. "Is that . . . mine?"

Achish turned away. "Yes," he coughed, unable to say more.

Elam got out of bed, ignoring his aching ribs. "Let me see." He took the pouch, opened it, and poured the coins onto his hand. He looked up. "There are too many."

Achish shook his head. "I can't explain that. When I took it from you, there were eleven denarii. Now there are twelve."

"What happened?"

"This morning, I felt so guilty that I was ready to throw myself off a cliff. Then I remembered the words of a prayer Jeshua taught me. I'd never really prayed before, but—and I know this sounds strange—somehow God spoke to me."

Elam nodded. "It doesn't sound strange at all."

"You believe me?" asked Achish.

Elam placed the coins back in the pouch. "I have seen enough miracles in the past few days to know one when I see one." He reached out and touched Achish's arm. "You and I have shared a miracle, my friend."

"What do you mean?" asked Achish.

Elam said, "You know those stories Jeshua always tells? It's like that. You and I were traveling on our separate paths, in the darkness of sin and selfishness, the promise of our lives unfulfilled. Then each of us was set upon by thieves. They stole my money; they stole your soul. And then both of us were rescued. A stranger—a Samaritan I've never even met—saved my life—"

"And a carpenter who taught me to pray saved mine," said Achish, nodding.

"And God performed a miracle, the least of which is this," said Elam, shaking the coin pouch. "For yesterday we were both dead and today we are both alive."

Achish reached out and put his arms around Elam, whispering, "Please forgive me."

Elam snuffled back tears. "With all my heart."

At that moment, a knock came at the door. Achish disengaged himself from Elam, a little embarrassed. Elam reached and opened the door.

Caleb stood in the hallway, hands on his hips. "You have a visitor." He stepped aside, and in came Zebulon, filling the doorway, smiling broadly, hands raised in greeting.

"So this is my traveling friend!" he said, crossing the room, placing both hands on Elam's shoulders, looking him up and down.

"Who are you?" asked Elam.

"Who am I?" laughed Zebulon. "Only the man who saved your life!"

"You're the . . . the . . . "

"The *Samaritan!*" crowed Zebulon, waking the rest of the inn. "Yes. I admit it. I'm a Samaritan. Does that change anything?"

Elam smiled. "Yes. It changes everything."

"Like what?" frowned Zebulon.

Elam simply stepped forward and hugged Zebulon tightly. "Thank you, dear friend, for my life. I am in your debt."

Zebulon, surprised, extracted himself from the little man's embrace. "I should say you are." He nodded at Caleb, who produced a bill, handing it to Zebulon with a flourish. Zebulon frowned at it, then at Caleb. "And these are fair charges?"

"They are," said Caleb defensively.

Zebulon nodded at Elam. "Did he treat you well in my absence?"

Elam smiled. "No. But others did, and I am mending."

"Now wait a minute," interjected Caleb. "I fed and housed you—"

"He has been fair," amended Elam, "if not kind."

"Well," said Zebulon, fishing around inside his tunic for his coin pouch. "Fair is enough, in this world."

Elam touched Zebulon's arm. "Wait," he said, opening his own pouch. "I have money."

"I knew it!" shouted Caleb, stomping his foot. "I knew you had money all along!"

Zebulon peeked into the pouch as Elam withdrew a golden denarius, handing it to Caleb. "Will this cover my expenses?"

Caleb bit into the coin, testing it. "And more. Now I'm leaving before someone figures out what's going on here!" Everyone laughed as he left.

Zebulon squinted at Elam. "This doesn't fit. When I saw you last, all you had on you were blood and rags."

Elam nodded. "That's true. But a friend," he said, gesturing at Achish, who was watching in amazement, "was passing through and repaid me a debt he owed me. So now I can repay the debt I owe you." He handed Zebulon a gold denarius.

Zebulon made a fist around the coin, shaking it. "What a happy coincidence," he said, looking at Achish, "that you should be traveling this way and able to help your friend."

Achish looked at Elam. "I don't believe in coincidences," he said. "Not anymore."

Elam nodded. "Neither do I."

Zebulon looked at them, seeing the certainty in their eyes. "I am beginning to doubt them myself," he said, and reached to shake each man's hand. "But if I'm not mistaken—and I rarely am—there is yet another miracle. May I?" He reached and slowly began to untie Elam's head dressing.

Elam reached up, stopping him. "Don't," he said sadly. "I can't bear it."

Zebulon continued unwrapping the bandage. "Faith, my friend, can move mountains," he said, and finally Elam's left eye was visible.

"Oh, my Lord," said Achish, staring at Elam.

"Is it terrible?" asked the little merchant.

"Open your eye and see for yourself," said Zebulon.

Elam gingerly opened his left eye. He saw Achish and Zebulon and little Timothy all looking at him, and all smiling.

"It's not hurt at all!" shouted Timothy from his post in the doorway.

"What?" said Elam.

"Your eye," said Achish with astonishment. "It's completely healed."

"The miracle, as promised," said Zebulon, smiling broadly.

"But how?" asked Elam.

Achish shook his finger at Elam. "You said you knew a miracle when you saw one."

"Don't question," said Zebulon, "but give thanks to God."

Elam blinked, touching his healed eye with his fingers, tears falling on his cheeks. "I cannot believe it," he said.

"Come!" shouted Zebulon, turning toward the door. "There is yet more!"

Achish took Elam's arm and led him out the door. Timothy had to jump out of the way to avoid Zebulon's giant strides. They walked down the hall and entered the great room, where breakfast was progressing.

"My friends!" shouted Zebulon, holding the gold denarius aloft. Everyone eating stopped and looked up at the coin. Someone muttered the word *Samaritan* under his breath.

"Shut up!" yelled Caleb, from behind the kitchen counter.

"Thank you, innkeeper," said Zebulon. He pulled his cloak aside, revealing his multihued belt. Proudly turning so everyone could see it, he held the coin higher. The place was deathly quiet as every man coveted the coin, which, apparently, was going to perform some wonderful trick.

"My friends," said Zebulon quietly, looking at everyone in turn, "I am a Samaritan and I wish to make a toast. I trust that is not a problem."

A few men halfheartedly raised their cups. Zebulon shook his head. "This will never do," he said, motioning Timothy forward. "You work here, lad?"

The boy nodded.

"Do you know where they keep the wine?"

Timothy nodded again.

"The *good* wine?"

Timothy looked over at Caleb. Caleb scowled, threw his towel down on the counter, and cursed. Timothy looked up at Zebulon and smiled. "Yes, sir. I know where it is."

"Then run and get it!" shouted Zebulon.

Timothy dashed out of the room. Achish helped Elam to a seat and sat down by him. Presently, Jeshua entered, carrying two large dusty bottles of wine. Timothy followed him, hauling a third in both arms.

Caleb produced glasses, Zebulon filled them, and Timothy distributed them to the crowd. In the corner, Kohath and Lamech received brimming glasses. When everyone had received a glass, Zebulon raised his own, and the room quieted once again.

"To the goodness of God," he said quietly, winking at Jeshua, then raising his eyes heavenward. "May His miracles never cease!"

Kohath and Lamech stared slack-jawed at each other as the room repeated the toast and everyone emptied their cups. Achish clinked glasses with Elam. Jeshua laid a hand lightly on Timothy's shoulder, and the boy beamed up at him. In his hand, Timothy held the polished wood figurine of the mother and child Jeshua had carved for him. When he caught Achish's eye, he proudly held out the carving. Achish waved the boy over and Timothy dropped into his lap, proudly showing off his prize.

In the corner, Lamech set his empty goblet down and leaned toward Kohath, whispering, "A toast to the Lord? Here? In this wicked place?"

Kohath nodded wisely. "You see?" he said, smiling, "We're having an impact on this rabble after all."

THE CARPENTER TEACHES

Several years later, Jeshua and his followers came to Jerusalem for the Feast of the Tabernacles, where they dwelled in booths made of the tree boughs in memory of the Israelites' wanderings in the wilderness.

One day during the feast, Jeshua was teaching in the Temple court. A lawyer stood up and asked him, "Master, what shall I do to inherit eternal life?"

Jeshua said, "What do the scriptures say?"

And the lawyer responded, "They say I should love God with all my heart, with all my soul, with all my strength, and with all my mind, and that I should love my neighbor as myself."

And Jeshua nodded, saying, "You are right. If you do this, you will please God."

But the lawyer, seeking a loophole, asked, "But who is my neighbor?"

And Jeshua said, "A man went down from Jerusalem to Jericho, and fell among thieves, who stripped him of his clothing, and wounded him, and departed, leaving him half dead. And there came down a priest that way, and when he saw the injured man, he passed by on the other side of the road. And likewise a Levite, when he saw the injured man, he also passed by on the other side.

"But a Samaritan was traveling that same road, and when he saw the man, he had compassion on him, and bound up his wounds, pouring oil and wine, and set him on his own beast, and brought him to an inn, and took care of him.

"And the next day when he departed, he gave money to the innkeeper, saying, 'Take care of him; and whatever more you spend, when I return, I will repay.'"

And Jeshua turned to the lawyer and asked, "What do you think? Which of these three was a neighbor to the man who fell among thieves?"

And the lawyer answered, saying, "The one that showed him mercy."

Then Jeshua said, "Go, and do the same."

Acknowledgments

Although the actual process of writing is a solitary one, no book springs full-blown from one person's mind. Research is, by definition, relying upon others. There are so many of these people, in fact, that any attempt to credit them is not only difficult from a memory standpoint, it is impossible from a logistical one.

But I will try, because their contributions (many of whose names I don't even know, like the man in Nazareth who explained, in engrossing detail, about carpentry in ancient Israel) have resulted in a book which has turned out to be the best writing experience of my life. I want to thank that man, as well as many others who have taught me, not only about the life and times of Jeshua bar Joseph, but also about the meaning of his teachings.

It begins, of course, with my parents, Omer and Virginia Kemp, who taught me about what it means to follow the Carpenter of Galilee, teachings I first blindly accepted, then reflexively questioned, then finally came to understand. Jeshua's words are real to me because my parents gave me the greatest gift a parent can give a child: a good example.

My friends, too numerous to mention, have also shaped the stories you have read. I am an effusive story teller, and these wonderful people have listened carefully and made constructive suggestions, and their contributions lie between every line of the story. Bill and Lisa Hansen, Bonnie and Jeff Sheets, Mark and Stephanie Griffin, Bob Rees, Lex Watterson,

Joy Young, Natalie Reed, Linda Thomson, and Douglas Page stand out most in my mind. There are many, many others as well.

I have been blessed with the fellowship of the good folks at Harper San Francisco, where they love good books and books that do good. In a previous life I self-published, and so I know first hand the job description of the following people, although I cannot hope to match their expertise and knowledge. The book you hold is evidence of their skill. The great copyediting team of Priscilla Stuckey, Chris Hafner, and Terri Leonard; talented cover designer Jim Warner; marketing and publicity gurus Roger Freet and Margery Buchanan; inspired and energetic sales director Jeff Hobbs; HSF publisher Steve Hanselman, whose vision and ideals make the offices of HSF the most delightful—dare I say *spiritual?*—workplace I've seen; and finally to Cathy Hemming, Harper Collins publisher, who shepherds the entire affair with skill and a genuine love of people. All of these people and more whose names I don't even know have made getting this book to print a joy.

Gideon Weil, my editor, is the best kind of co-worker imaginable. Honest and helpful, our near daily discussions always energize me to do my best. Unfailingly positive and constructive, Gideon is the kind of inspired editor few writers will be blessed with. He saw the potential power of these stories and his vision and insight fill these pages. I am grateful beyond words for his tireless efforts and his formidable editing skills.

My agent, Joe Durepos, is a great example of a loving husband and devoted father, and also one of my dearest friends. It was Joe's idea to ask HSF to do a series of books, and it was Joe who understood from day one what I was trying to do: to reintroduce the most famous person in history in a way that people might see his teachings in a new light. "Viral Christianity" is how Joe puts it. "You don't even know you're infected until it's too late," he says, smiling. And for those who might be concerned; fear not, the disease is completely benign—it simply internalizes The Golden Rule in our lives. Joe is gloriously infected with Golden Rule Syndrome and that's why we work together on a handshake basis, something this repentant lawyer never expected to do.

And finally, dear reader, thank you. As I wrote this book, I thought of you so often that by now I think of us as good friends. The vote of confidence you cast in taking the time to read these stories is the greatest reward a writer can receive. And if Jeshua seems like the kind of person you'd like to meet someday; the kind of person who will put his arms around you and tell you that he loves you; the kind of person whose example you will try harder to follow, then it is my great pleasure to share him with you because you are the reason he revealed himself through these stories.

Kenny Kemp
August 2002
San Diego, California